Gardening
in New Zealand
month by month

Gardening in New Zealand month by month

Dennis Greville

Hydrangea macrophylla 'Mme Truffaut'

Echinops ritro

For the equally delightful Lily Sofia

Photographs
Front cover: Moorpark apricots
Front cover inset photos from left: Bourbon rose, *Rosa* 'Souvenir de la Malmaison', Paeony, *Paeonia* 'Dutch Gem', Mini Cos lettuce, Little Gem
Back cover inset photos from top: Hyacinth, Hyacinthoides 'Blue Ensign', Pricking out seedlings, Red onion *Allium cepa*,
Evergreen box *Buxus sempervirens*
Page 1: Marigold, *Calendula officinalis* Touch of Bronze Series
Page 2: Beetroot, *Beta vulgaris*

Contents

Introduction 6

Spring 8
September 10 • October 22 • November 34

Summer 48
December 50 • January 62 • February 74

Autumn 86
March 88 • April 102 • May 112

Winter 122
June 124 • July 136 • August 148

Glossary 158

Treatment of pests 160

Treatment of fungal diseases 162

Water needs of vegetables 164

Matching plants and propagation methods 166

Specialist nurseries and other useful addresses 167

List of feature tips 171

Index 172

Introduction

Gardeners are a unique group of individuals who trust enough in the abundance and power of life to believe that for every seed they sow and every plant they nurture the world will become a better place and growth will spring new and refreshed from the earth.

The gardener's capacity to trust in the rebirth of the garden, especially after the depths of winter, and to repeat the sowing and growing process year after year, with all its successes and failures, seems to me to be the very essence of what gardening is all about — an affirmation of life and renewal. The many gardeners I have known over the years are people who also express these positive sentiments in their everyday life. In the main they are a generous group who demonstrate a willingness to share their plants and their garden with a gentleness that is something very precious in today's busy and often hostile world.

Some gardeners also have an additional gift of knowing almost instinctively just when to plant what in order to get the best results. This special sensitivity comes from a close observation of the world around us, a luxury that few of us have time for as we rush from work to home and back to work again, leaving us with little energy to cultivate the soil and far too few quiet moments in which to contemplate the pleasures of the garden.

Our busy, time-constrained lives have pushed us towards the notion that we must leave the growing of fruit, vegetables and flowers to those who have the space and 'do it best'. Commercial growers are driven by the realities

LEFT: *Rhododendron* 'Trewithen Orange'

of a very competitive market where 'best' generally means 'cheapest', and so the use of chemical sprays has increased to produce crops as quickly and cheaply as possible. Thankfully in many areas there has been a steady increase of growers using organic methods.

Creating a healthy environment in our own gardens without resorting to powerful chemicals is surprisingly easy to achieve. The first, most basic way of doing this is to improve the soil. Healthy soil should be dark, rich and loose and drain easily. Most soils can be improved organically by digging in well-made compost, animal manure, leaf mould, sphagnum moss, tree bark or untreated wood ashes.

Secondly, the regular use of organic fertilisers reduces our reliance on chemicals. Fish manure or emulsion, chicken manure, dried blood, blood and bone, and even chopped seaweed are all excellent crop boosters. The benefits of organic fertilisers gradually accumulate in a garden so that after several years your soil will be improved to a point where you will need less fertiliser annually. Your crops will be healthier, more productive and tastier, while flowers, trees and shrubs will have richer colour and will also survive disease and drought more easily.

Judicious companion planting is another way of minimising our reliance on chemicals. Many plants, it has been discovered, release excretions into the soil through their leaves and roots; other plants find these excretions toxic while some thrive in such an environment. An awareness of 'good' and 'bad' companions will also reduce your reliance on chemicals. Plants growing together in the microclimate of the average garden interact with one another in many other ways as well. For instance, a tall-growing species gives shade, thus protecting shade-loving plants while at the same time suppressing other low-growing, sun-loving plants. And so sound gardening knowledge and sensitivity to the needs of plants will give you better flowering, heavier crops and a more beautiful garden.

Despite the best gardening practices, pests and diseases can still infiltrate the garden. Simple organic methods of prevention and control will maintain a healthy garden environment. Strong, healthy plants are less susceptible to pests and diseases — and to achieve this means watering and feeding your crops and flowers regularly. Homemade liquid fertilisers can be used to boost growth without the need to resort to costly chemicals, and, if you can, make your own pesticides from household products.

The long tradition of friendship among gardeners is well known and plants continue to be swapped and shared as they have been for hundreds of years. The cottage garden tradition grew from working people rescuing cast-off plants from the refuse heaps of the wealthy. These ancestors 'in spirit' were responsible for saving some of the plants that link us with the history of plant collecting. The love of plants and a spirit of generosity marks out the true gardener from those more concerned with passing fashion and instant display.

All gardeners know that both the flower and the vegetable garden can be places of usefulness, comfort, beauty, refinement and communion with our common humanity. Sir Francis Bacon neatly penned the following lines sometime about 1625:

> God Almighty first planted a Garden; and, indeed, it is the purest of human pleasures; it is the greatest refreshment to the spirits of man; without which buildings and palaces are but gross handy-works: and a man shall ever see, that, when ages grow to civility and elegancy, men come to build stately, sooner than to garden finely; as if gardening were the greater perfection.

Dennis Greville, February 2005

SPRING

Spring is officially here at last. It is an exciting time as the garden gets ready for its major growing period. This is often thought of as the beginning of the gardener's year throughout the country. All the preparation of the previous months will start to pay off as the combination of warmer days and longer sunlight hours begins to have a discernible effect on plant growth.

In many gardens the need for frost protection can be reassessed cautiously and some of the tender annuals and perennials that have been growing indoors waiting for the better weather can be placed in their outdoor positions. Even now, however, seed sowing in the open garden needs to be embarked on with considerable circumspection. Some spring weather is quite unpredictable. A late frost at this time of the year can cause considerable harm to fruit trees and ornamentals. This damage may be so great as to blight the affected plants for an entire season or even longer.

Spring is the season of major planting and also a time to deal with general garden renovations that were not undertaken or completed during autumn. Clumps of perennials such as phlox, shasta daisies and the late autumn-flowering aconite can still be dug, divided and shifted to their new homes. Hydrangeas in colder climates should be pruned promptly or they will soon burst into spring growth, only to be burnt by late frosts. The building up of vegetable beds and garden borders with compost and any mulching material that comes to hand should continue in order to create the conditions required for good gardening.

Spring flowers are favourites for many of us, and even if your heart doesn't leap at the sight of a thousand daffodils, there can be few of us who fail to admire a simple pot brimming with violas or a tree of *Magnolia campbellii*, *Magnolia* 'Heaven Scent', or the New Zealand-bred *Magnolia* 'Iolanthe' in full bloom. A patch of chionodoxa (glory-of-the-snow) or a hebe such as the beautiful 'Wiri Spears' or a native clematis in flower high in the crown of a tree all mark the arrival of spring. It is the return of so many garden plants we once thought lost forever that gives spring that special miraculous quality. Plants that were lost or forgotten are suddenly redis- covered — although it would be foolish to think for a moment that this can happen without the guiding hand of the gardener.

Even in spring, the process of clearing excess foliage from where something might just reappear is essential. If it isn't done, some precious plants will be lost to the jungle. Remembering just where it all is requires either constant tending throughout the year or the keeping of careful records and layout plans — but, then, what gardener has either the time or inclination to sit and write about daily doings when they could be spending the same time actually doing them?

As winter passes into August the return of spring is a wonderful thing. The dark, bleak days really do seem to be passing, even though fre- quently this turns out to be illusory. Suddenly we become aware of the reawakening of plants in our own gardens and elsewhere, many already flowering and making it quite clear that, as far as the seasons are concerned, life goes on. In what is officially the last month of winter, August heralds the return to longer daylight hours, balmy evenings in some warmer northern areas and the first real sign of spring — the smell of freshly mown grass.

LEFT: *Magnolia* 'Heaven Scent'
ABOVE: *Viola* Touch of Pink Series
BELOW: *Hebe* 'Wiri Spears'

September

Temperature and climate

Temperatures begin to rise in September, though it would be naive not to expect the occasional cold snap, especially in the southern regions. Both air and soil temperatures rise slowly, drawing daffodils, galanthus, tulips and other spring flowers up from the earth in early to late September. The return of birds to the garden also marks the beginning of the warmer weather. Feeding them regularly through winter helps them survive the cold weather. Many gardens will be suffering from wet, soggy conditions that will persist until November, making seed sowing difficult unless seed trays are used.

LEFT: *Narcissus* 'Geranium' with the yellow-flowered *Narcissus* 'Camellia'
BELOW FROM LEFT: *Narcissus* 'Valdrome'; *Tulipa* 'Queen of Sheba'; *Galanthus elwesii*

Food and water

Most garden plants will benefit from a light dressing of fine compost, general-purpose fertiliser, chicken manure or liquid fertiliser as they begin to grow. The amount and type of fertiliser you choose to use will depend on what is available and what best suits your local conditions. A wet, cold, heavy soil will not benefit much from the application of a powerful nitrogenous fertiliser such as fowl manure at this time of the year. It is likely to rot on the soil surface or develop a green mossy coating without reaching the roots of the plants you wish to cultivate.

Drainage is vitally important to enable plants to grow healthily, especially at this time of the year. If you don't have good drainage, one option is to implement a programme of feeding by spraying the foliage with a good liquid fertiliser, thus providing nutrients the plant may not be able to access from the cold, wet ground. Raised beds are another solution to drainage problems, but may require some planning and landscaping work.

As soon as the soil temperature rises and the soil begins to dry out you can begin to spread the heavier and more concentrated fertilisers onto the ground. Bulbs and shrubs can also be given small amounts of fertiliser at this time. Bulbs should be fed after flowering to encourage growth and the development of flowering spikes for the next season. *Buddleja davidii*, *Cornus alba*, fuchsias, hydrangeas and other plants that have been recently pruned will greatly benefit from a dressing of fertiliser at this time of year (apply 50 g or a good handful per square metre). This will strengthen new growth and improve flowering in the coming season.

It is easy, at a time of the year when water seems to be everywhere, to forget that in some areas of the garden some plants may slowly be expiring from lack of water. Under a hungry and overhanging hedge, plants can become dry. Attention to the individual water needs of your garden plants is important at this time of vigorous growth. Pot plants are also easy to overlook in these busy spring days. As many of them reawaken to new growth, their need for water and fertiliser increases.

> ### HOW FERTILISERS WORK
>
> GENERAL FERTILISERS
> General fertilisers contain three elements — nitrogen (N), phosphorus (P) and potassium or potash (K).
>
> Nitrogen is important to leaf and stem growth; without it many plants will not grow properly. Most natural fertilisers contain some nitrogen but sulphate of ammonia contains the highest concentration. This is a powerful growth stimulant but should be used carefully as it acidifies the soil and will readily burn plant tissue.
>
> Phosphates stimulate root development, fruitfulness and fruit-ripening. They also help lawn grasses and other plants to withstand the effects of drought.
>
> Potash is important in the formation of all starch and sugar crops such as potatoes and tomatoes and it also helps many plants resist diseases.
>
> LIME
> Lime reduces the acidity of the soil and is a most useful compound, releasing the plant foods locked within the soil. It helps plants access food while improving the general texture of a soil.

Pests and diseases

As the temperature rises and the gardening year begins in earnest, pests slowly emerge and begin their annual assault afresh. Snails and slugs should be removed by all means possible, but it is preferable not to use highly toxic snail bait in the vegetable garden. More conservative methods are recommended, such as attracting slugs and snails with dishes of beer in which they drown, or removing them by hand and dropping them into a bucket of salty water.

Though often welcome in the garden, birds enjoy nothing better than fresh young seedlings, especially lettuce, broad beans and peas. A simple cloche made from chicken wire, pegged into the ground and closed at the ends is the most effective solution to this problem.

In many spring gardens wind can be an ongoing problem, lowering temperatures and preventing seedlings from prospering. A simple screen made of hessian or nylon wind cloth tacked onto a frame and erected in the face of the wind will provide the protection your spring plants need.

Disease prevention is easier than trying to cure the problem once the plant is weakened. Maintaining good garden hygiene can help to remove many sources of infection. Clearing away garden debris that accumulates throughout the year will prevent some diseases from building up. Waste can be composted or burnt to remove any possible source of infection. Pots, seed trays and stakes used during one season should be sterilised with a little household bleach diluted in water to prevent diseases being carried over into the following season.

Crop rotation is another good garden practice. Don't grow the same crops in the same place year after year, otherwise diseases will build up in the soil. Rotating root crops with leaf crops is not only good hygiene but also maximises the use of nutrients available to plants from the soil.

Healthy plants have a higher resistance to disease than unhealthy ones. If you feed your plants well and water them when they need it, they will resist most diseases. However, if you overfeed and overwater, they will be weaker and more prone to disease. It is important to get the balance right. Many new varieties of plants, such as rust-resistant hollyhocks, are bred to withstand disease. If you know that your soil or conditions have a predisposition to particular diseases, choose only disease-resistant varieties.

The flower garden

The rate of new growth becomes increasingly rapid during September, and gardeners are kept busy sowing and planting to ensure continuous displays in the months ahead.

Sowing

The range of flowers that can be sown this month is the widest of the whole year (see the list on page 15). It will take at least six to eight weeks for seeds planted now to

ABOVE: Simple frost protection for seedlings is provided by a plastic soft drink bottle with the base removed.

TASKS FOR SEPTEMBER
- Prune and shape ornamental shrubs before any vigorous spring growth.
- Plant out new lawns as soon as the soil warms.
- Sow seeds in seed trays or directly in the soil.
- Constantly protect young seedlings from snails and slugs.
- Spray seedlings with copper to protect them from fungal diseases. A liquid fertiliser added to this mix will greatly advance plant establishment.
- Propagate cuttings in sharp sand and put in a warm, shady place to grow.
- Divide herbaceous perennials.
- Repot cymbidium orchids after flowering, if they are bursting out of their pots. Feed flowering orchids as the flower buds develop.
- Raise vegetable seeds in trays for planting out later, or plant directly into the soil.
- Plant herb seeds and cuttings now, in time for the summer table.

develop into young plants, which takes us into the months of October and November, so seeds need to be sown without delay.

In warm northern parts of the country you can begin sowing seeds directly in the flower garden. In the colder southern areas only a limited range of seeds can be planted directly into the soil. It is always better to sow seed thinly and in a seed tray or under a cloche, unless your soil is warm, well drained and friable. Sowing in seed trays and planting out later is the best way to avoid frost damage and to speed up seed germination in cold soils. However, a simple miniature greenhouse can be made out of a plastic soft drink bottle with the bottom removed, giving seedlings a head start when the weather is still very cold.

Damping off diseases can kill many seedlings, so for better results sow seeds in a mix of sieved pumice and sand and stand the tray in water for ten minutes (rather than watering it from above). When pricking out seedlings for transplanting, remember to hold seedlings by their leaves, not by their stems, as this can cause them to die back.

Raising climbers from seed is rewarding. If you plant seeds of the cup and saucer vine (*Cobaea scandens*), the snail vine (*Vigna caracalla*), black-eyed Susan (*Thunbergia alata*), or the semi-climber *Plumbago auriculata* syn. *capensis* now, they will quickly grow to fill the summer garden.

Propagation and division

Cuttings of carnations, chrysanthemums, dahlias and fuchsias taken now will strike well if planted in clean sharp sand and kept out of the direct sun. Slips of carnations taken with a heel, stripped of most leaves and split at the base will grow easily. A grain of barley put into the split is said to hasten root formation.

Herbaceous perennials can continue to be divided up before they are too advanced in growth. Violets should be dug up and replanted every year. To achieve the best flowering, plant them in sets that contain three crowns each.

TIPS FOR PLANTING ROSES

- Bare-rooted plants (above right) should not be allowed to dry out at any stage before they are planted, as this will cause considerable delay to their development.
- Dig a large hole into which the roots can be spread.
- Add well-rotted manure and compost to the soil before planting to help the rose establish. Bone dust or blood and bone added to the soil will also help young plants.
- Form a mound or cone of soil in the centre of the hole and spread the roots over and around this (below right).
- If the roots are damaged or very uneven, cut them back with sharp secateurs and then gently cover them with soil, firming it as you go.
- Standard or large shrub roses should have any necessary supporting stakes added now in order to avoid future disturbance to roots, which might be caused by inserting a stake when the plant is growing.
- Although roses favour a clay-based loam, they really do best in a mix of compost, peat, blood and bone or bone meal. A planting hole should be dug large enough to take the root of each plant without cramping it. Water the soil well before planting.
- When planting roses near a wall don't heap up the soil, but rather create a shallow, dish-like depression at the base of the new rose to hold moisture when watering. Wall-trained roses can miss out on rain and suffer from drought and drought-induced diseases such as powdery mildew, which are difficult to contain once they take hold.

Planting

When planting out well-hardened plants and seedlings it is important to give them a good start by ensuring that the soil you are planting them into is light, friable and fertile. A liquid fertiliser applied to the root ball at the time of planting will ensure that the new plants grow rapidly.

A word of caution for paeony fanciers — paeonies (including the tree, herbaceous and new intersectional types) planted in spring don't grow as well as those planted in March and April. It is better to buy these plants from specialist growers (see Appendix, page 167) in autumn rather than from garden centres now.

The climbing lily (gloriosa) can be planted as soon as frosts have gone. This native of tropical Africa and India does well in a pot, climbing several metres by means of tendrils at the end of its leaves. The red lily-like flowers are flushed with yellow at the edge of the wavy petals.

The planting of roses should proceed without delay. Many shrub roses will be coming into bud and any disturbance is best done before the plant begins to send out soft new growth.

Bulbs, corms and tubers

Planting of many flowering bulbs, rhizomes and tuberous begonias will result in a colourful summer and late summer flowering. It is fun to try unusual bulbs; many are hardy enough to grow in most areas of the country without the need for winter protection. Arisaema (Jack-in-the-pulpit) are hardy plants and many will flower in late December if they are planted now. *Arisaema candidissimum* is the hardiest and makes a beautiful garden plant. Galtonia (summer hyacinth) should be purchased as a large bulb if you want it to flower in the first year; it grows best in a sandy soil. The white-

FLOWERS TO PLANT NOW

SOW THESE SEEDS

Ageratum	Gypsophila
Alyssum	Hollyhock
Antirrhinum	Honesty
Aster	Impatiens
Calendula	Larkspur
Candytuft	Lobelia
Canterbury bells	Lupin
Carnation	Marigold
Catananche	Mignonette
Clarkia	Nasturtium
Cobaea scandens	Petunia
(cup-and-saucer vine)	*Plumbago capensis*
Cornflower	Sunflower
Cosmos	Sweet pea
Delphinium	Thunbergia (black-eyed Susan)
Dianthus	*Vigna caracalla* (snail vine)
Eschscholzia	Viola
Geranium	Wallflower
Godetia	Zinnia

PLANT THESE SEEDLINGS

Alyssum
Bassia scoparia syn.
   Kochia scoparia
Calendula
Candytuft
Cleome
Cornflower
Gloriosa
Gypsophila
Marigold
Penstemon
Polyanthus
Scabious
Verbena

PLANT THESE BULBS, CORMS AND TUBERS

Arisaema
Begonia (tuberous)
Crinum
Dahlia
Dierama
Eucharis
Galtonia
Gloriosa (climbing lily)
Haemanthus
Hemerocallis
Hymenocallis
Sandersonia
Schizostylis
Tigridia
Tropaeolum peregrinum,
  T. tricolorum, *T. tuberosum*
  (climbing)

---

flowered *Galtonia candicans* is more hardy than many of its relatives and will cope quite well with heavy frosts. Hemerocallis (day lily) are available in many different forms and colours and will survive considerable degrees of frost. They are a delight in the summer garden with their cheery flowers and attractive foliage. *Schizostylis coccinea* (crimson flag) and *Tigridia pavonia* (tiger flower) also have spectacular flowers.

Plant care

Ornamental shrubs can be lightly pruned and shaped before their main spring growth. In very cold areas roses can be pruned as late as September, thus preventing any late frost from destroying the newly emerging buds and flowers. One advantage of late pruning is that it is possible to see and choose the best buds to cut back to.

Buddleja davidii and *Buddleja salvifolia* will benefit from a hard pruning now to invigorate them for summer flowering. *Cornus alba* and any other ornamentals grown mainly for their winter-coloured stems can also be hard-pruned to ensure fresh new stems for the coming season. Ceanothus and tropical hibiscus pruned now will produce fresh new growth for the summer; ceanothus should be trimmed after flowering. Many clematis hybrids can be cut to about a metre from the ground and will quickly regrow for a flowering in late spring and summer. Exceptions are the evergreen *Clematis armandii* and several others, such as *Clematis cirrhosa*, which begins flowering in late winter and continues until late spring throughout most of the country. Fuchsias can be hard-pruned now, as can hydrangeas, and any cuttings struck easily.

Lawns

Start mowing the lawn as soon as it begins to grow again in the early spring. Continue to mow weekly, but avoid mowing if the lawn is frosty or very wet, as this will damage the lawn and break down the edges of the garden border.

In gardens where spring bulbs are planted in the lawn, wait at least six weeks after the flowers have finished before mowing to give the bulbs time to replenish their supplies for the next season. Feeding the lawn and the bulbs will benefit both and ensure that the grasses growing near the bulbs will be ready to take over when the bulb leaves die back. If the grass surrounding the bulbs looks shabby, rake it and clear away debris and any dead bulb leaves. Tying the dying bulb leaves is one way to tidy them, but this looks artificial and doesn't do the plants much good either.

The edible garden

This is a very busy month in which many kinds of vegetable seed can be sown but only if you have a friable, well-drained soil. In cold, heavy soils it is still best to plant seedlings of hardy vegetables.

Sowing

Many vegetables, such as beetroot, broad beans, broccoli, carrots, celery, kumara and spinach, can be sown in warmer areas of the country. (See list on page 18.) In cooler southern parts sowing is best done under the protection of cloches. Once the soil has warmed to approximately 7°C, leeks can be planted, as can the first crop of peas. In very cold southern areas it is best to hold off sowing until October. Cabbage and cauliflower can be sown now in a free-draining soil. Tender seeds, such as aubergine, capsicum, cucumber, melon, tomato and zucchini, are best sown under glass. Getting them started early is the secret to a successful crop. (See page 153 for tips on sowing.)

Many herbs sown now will grow readily from seed. Coriander and chervil will grow quickly to provide the essential ingredients for many delicious meals. Dill seeds sown directly will germinate and provide garnish for the summer table. Herbs such as tarragon, thyme and marjoram can be split up and replanted in fresh soil in new parts of the garden.

A considerable advantage can be gained in growing time by sowing under a wire cloche covered in plastic. Pegging a large sheet of clear plastic onto the seedbed some weeks before sowing will warm the soil and provide better growing conditions. Seed can then be sown and the plastic replaced until germination occurs. Supporting the plastic above the seedlings with several sticks 'tepee style' will provide ventilation, some protection and room for growth. It should then be removed, as fungal diseases can form in enclosed conditions because of the high humidity.

Planting

In warm and protected gardens the first potatoes can be planted. Use good quality seed potatoes to be sure of a good return. Potatoes require plenty of compost in the base of the bed, and a good handful of blood and bone per square metre will aid the development of the crop. Several possible methods can be used to grow potatoes, including trenching, mulching with straw, or growing under black polythene, or 'planting' in a tyre or large black plastic bag.

Many other vegetables such as cabbage, spinach and silver beet can be planted as soon as soils have drained and warmed. Cabbage plants, cauliflower, lettuce and onions planted out now will develop quickly. Globe artichokes planted in a sunny well-drained position will often return year after year without replanting, as will asparagus if the bed is well prepared and looked after.

BELOW: Broad beans ready for sowing.

GROWING POTATOES

- Potatoes are not frost hardy, rather they are considered half hardy and need to be planted so that as the tubers sprout the foliage is not burnt by late frosts. Covering sprouting potatoes with frost cloth and earthing them up (building up soil around them) regularly will help to guard against frost damage.

- Potatoes grow best in a peaty, acid soil in a sunny, well-drained position, or in sandy soil if plenty of well rotted compost and manure have been mixed in before planting. A specific potato fertiliser is available but blood and bone or a balanced fertiliser will also get good results.

- Certified seed potatoes are available throughout the country. Tubers should be 50–60 g in weight and well sprouted. If they are not well sprouted, cover them with a dry loose material, like newspaper strips, woodchips, hay or straw, and place them in a dark place until each sprout is at least 4–5 cm long. This process is commonly referred to as 'chitting'. Seed potatoes that have been well chitted and have plenty of strong shoots will be ready for the table long before those that are planted with few well-developed shoots.

- Plant tubers 5 cm deep and 25–30 cm apart, in rows 50–60 cm apart. If you are short of tubers, large seed potatoes can be cut into pieces. Although this practice isn't recommended as the cut surface can often rot, old-time gardeners used to dust the cut surfaces with flowers of sulphur to prevent the spread of disease while at the same time making their seed potato stock go further. Potatoes can also be grown from seed, although this process takes longer to produce a viable crop.

- When the potatoes are 20 cm high above the ground 'earth up' around the plants, covering some of the shoots and lower leaves. Continue this process at two-weekly intervals until the plants begin to flower. Potatoes that are planted in a confined space such as a tyre or pot are more easily earthed up. Those that have been planted under black polythene do not need earthing up.

- Once your crop flowers, the foliage will begin to die back and the potatoes can be dug and eaten, usually 16–20 weeks after planting, depending on the variety. Dig only those plants that you require. In loose soils it is even possible to scratch out the few that you need, leaving the rest of the plant to continue growing.

- Potatoes for storage should only be dug when the stalks and foliage have dried off completely. Destroy any diseased tubers and examine the good ones regularly, rubbing off any developing shoots. Cover harvested potatoes to prevent them greening.

- Potatoes can be grown under black polythene. Be sure to use a thick gauge black polythene and prepare the soil as you would for normal trench-planted potatoes. Use polythene strips 1 metre wide and anchor each down at the sides by covering with soil. Cut a cross-shaped slit every 40 cm and, using a trowel, plant a potato in each slit. As the plants grow, the crop begins to form on the surface of the soil under the plastic. Do not let holes or gaps appear in the plastic, as any light getting to your crop will ruin it. When flowering is over, the plastic can be rolled back and the crop gathered easily.

- Potatoes can also be grown successfully in a tyre or large plastic bag filled with good quality garden mix, however they grow best in the open ground where they have access to moisture, sunlight and air.

ABOVE: Planting punnet-grown red cabbage.

Fruit

Destructive mould diseases can be prevented by following a regular spraying programme on a fortnightly basis. Peach and apple trees sprayed with a suitable fungicide now will not develop brown rot or black spot later in the season.

These diseases are well worth spraying against, as a severe attack can destroy an entire crop. Pip crops will benefit from an application of a copper-based spray. Pear trees should be sprayed at bud burst with the same fungicide that you use for apple trees.

Raspberries and gooseberries will benefit from a spraying of a copper fungicide when the buds begin to burst. Berry and vine crops should also be sprayed with a systemic fungicide to prevent grey mould and mildew when the fruits begin to form.

Disease prevention is easier than trying to cure the problem when the plant is already weakened. Garden hygiene can help to remove many sources of infection. Clearing away any garden debris that accumulates throughout the year will prevent diseases building up.

> **VEGETABLES TO PLANT NOW**
>
> | SOW THESE SEEDS | PLANT THESE SEEDLINGS |
> |---|---|
> | Artichoke (globe) | |
> | Aubergine (eggplant)* | Artichoke (globe) |
> | Beetroot | Asparagus |
> | Broad beans* | Cabbage |
> | Broccoli* | Capsicum* |
> | Cabbage | Cauliflower |
> | Capsicum* | Leek |
> | Carrot* | Lettuce |
> | Cauliflower | Onion |
> | Celery* | Silver beet |
> | Cucumber* | |
> | Kumara* | |
> | Leek | **PLANT THESE TUBERS** |
> | Lettuce | Potato* |
> | Melon* | |
> | Onion | |
> | Parsnip | |
> | Pea | |
> | Silver beet | |
> | Spinach* | |
> | Squash* | |
> | Tomato* | |
> | Zucchini* | *Only practicable in warm areas |

September features

Native clematis

The sacred flower puawananga (*Clematis paniculata*) was, according to Maori legend, the first-born child of the stars Rehua (Antares) and Puanga (one of the Orion cluster) and is said to be charged with the duty of signalling the return of spring with its blossom. This was the time for serious gardening to begin in the old Maori calendar. This beautiful climber lights up the bush with its sprays of pure white flowers with fine yellow-and-mauve stamens.

Hybrid clematis have been bred from this plant and are now available throughout the county. Introduced hybrid clematis tend to die back in the spring. These plants should be cut to within a metre of the ground so that they can regenerate.

BELOW FROM LEFT: Native clematis, *Clematis paniculata*; flowering currant, *Ribes sanguineum* 'King Edward VII'; kowhai, *Sophora tetraptera*

Flowering currant

You may decide that there is a place for a shrub with one short-lived but spectacular flowering. The flowering currant *Ribes sanguineum* is just such a plant. It does best in gardens where there are hard winter frosts. If you can't find it in garden shops, it is easily grown from cuttings taken at the end of the flowering season, in late September or October. The flowers are highly scented — not unlike blackcurrant jam — and the raspberry redness of the flowers is a stunning sight with the sun shining through them.

Kowhai

The kowhai deserves a place in almost every New Zealand garden, providing the same mass of golden spring blossom as the ubiquitous laburnum and cohabiting with exotics and natives alike. *Sophora microphylla*, the small-leafed kowhai, grows happily from North Cape to the deep south. It flourishes in full sun, in semi-shade, in the snow or by the sea, as well as flowering profusely in the spring. Individual trees have flowers that vary in colour from golden yellow to a pale green-yellow. Like the native clematis, the flowering of the kowhai was, to the early Maori, a sign that the days were becoming warmer and that it was now time to plant the first crops of kumara. The golden kowhai *Sophora tetraptera* is one of the few native trees to completely lose its leaves in the winter. This makes its flowering all the more spectacular, appearing as it does on bare branches in the spring.

Paeony

Paeonia lutea and *P. suffruticosa* are tree paeonies. They are shrubby plants, rather than true trees, and produce some of the most showy flowers in the gardening year. They are deciduous during the colder months of the year but are very hardy — although young, tender spring growth can be damaged by frosts in the late spring. Most of these choice plants are long-lived and will flourish in any well-drained, fertile soil in semi-shade. Both the herbaceous and tree paeonies dislike being crowded by other plants and can develop botrytis in such condi-

BELOW: The Japanese flowering quince, *Chaenomeles* 'Flame'
RIGHT: The miniature herbaceous paeony, *Paeonia* 'Dutch Gem'
FAR RIGHT: Beauty bush, *Kolkwitzia amabilis*

tions. *Paeonia lutea* can grow as tall as 1.5 metres under good conditions. The flowers are somewhat sparse but of a pure golden yellow. The variety *P. l.* var. *ludlowii* is a very similar but stronger-growing plant, reaching 2.5 metres. *Paeonia delavayi* is another tree type that has dark wine-red flowers. These plants all have handsome divided leaves that make them worth growing for this feature alone. Hybrids of the tree types include the spectacular *Paeonia* 'Yachiye Tsubaki' and New Zealand raised varieties such as *P.* 'Timaru'. For sheer spectacle in the flowering world it is hard to go past *Paeonia suffruticosa*, or moutan (Mandarin), growing to some 2.5 metres. These plants produce deeply divided leaves and flowers with silky petals; the flowers can be either single or double and range in size from 15 cm to 30 cm wide.

Paeonies should be planted in March or April so that they become established for the spring flowering season. While it is possible to grow these plants in the warmer northern areas of New Zealand they need cold winters and summers without humid conditions.

Beauty bush

Kolkwitzia amabilis (beauty bush) is a splendid sight in the spring garden, delighting many who meet it for the first time. Although happier growing in the more southern areas of the country, it will grow in most places if it is given a well-drained but moist soil in sun or semi-shade. Free-flowering with a graceful arching habit, this dense, twiggy bush bears clusters of long, pale-pink flowers with a yellow throat. It prefers a limey soil, and associates well with many delicately coloured spring flowers such as digitalis, lupins and roses.

Berberis

Berberis was once extensively used in Victorian gardens. It has fallen prey to the caprices of garden fashion but large and showy plants can still be seen in old, established gardens throughout southern regions of the country. Some, such as *Berberis darwinii*, have become invasive pests and are prevented from sale, propagation and distribution within New Zealand. A specimen such as *Berberis thunbergii* 'Rose Glow' or *B.* 'Atropurpurea', however, is not at all noxious and can make an excellent and showy hedge if trimmed regularly. In the spring a well-clipped hedge of these plants will burst into growth, lighting the garden with their rosy colours.

Japanese flowering quince

Chaenomeles, the Japanese flowering quince, flowers spectacularly in the spring. They are sparse growers at the best of times, but are excellent for espalier work against a wall or along wires. *Chaenomeles × superba* varieties are generally more compact in their growing habits and are therefore more suitable for the general garden border. These shrubs come in a wide range of colours and are hardy under most garden conditions, tolerating dry, cold and windy locations. In the autumn, yellow and green japonica apples form on the branches, providing winter interest in the garden. Chaenomeles train well and make excellent plants for growing in pots.

October

Temperature and climate

October weather marks the high point of the spring flowering season throughout the country. As the soil begins to warm, plants produce a rush of flowers, made all the more exciting by the relative absence of blooms in the garden only a few weeks earlier. Many roses are in full flower, as are camellias, magnolias, rhododendrons and other spring-flowering ornamentals. Fruit and blossom trees are also in full flower, with some varieties such as the free-flowering *Prunus* 'Awanui' and the old favourite *Malus floribunda* creating quite a spectacle in the garden.

LEFT: *Malus floribunda*
BELOW: *Prunus* 'Awanui'

Some areas continue to receive a lot of spring rain into October, making it difficult to sow in the open garden. This month marks the end of frosts in most parts of the country and many tender annuals and bulbs can be planted out as the days lengthen and grow warmer. Gladiolus bulbs should be planted out at fortnightly intervals until Christmas to ensure a long succession of blooming.

of strong fertilisers at this time will burn the roots and damage the plants. Serious feeding is best carried out when the weather warms and the plants are established.

Seedlings under glass and indoor pot plants need to be watered regularly during October as they can easily dry out and die. Roses will require special care during this busy flowering time. Regular moisture is essential for the development of strong, healthy buds.

Pests and diseases

Pests multiply in the garden as the temperature rises. Whitefly, mealy bug, caterpillars and codling moth will

Food and water

Foliar feeding with liquid fertiliser will greatly help to establish young plants in the garden. However, this is no substitute for good, fertilised, well-drained soil, as foliar sprays are quickly washed through the soil and their effect is brief when compared with a barrowful of compost. Pot plants and seedlings in pots and trays benefit from foliar sprays more than garden plants because the nutrients are not so readily lost to heavy spring rains. When planting out seedlings a weak solution of liquid fertiliser will help the roots to re-establish. The application

increase rapidly if left unchecked. Aphids infest the flowering buds of roses and other ornamentals and can be removed with soapy water or washed off with the hose, or use a general insecticide if neither of these homely remedies works. Bronze beetle will demolish whole flower heads if unchecked but can be effectively controlled by spraying with Target. Slugs and snails can wreak havoc at this time of year catching up on lost eating time and need to be removed by hand or killed with bait. A planting of delphiniums can be demolished in a single night if they are not protected by bait or a vigilant

DEALING WITH SLUGS AND SNAILS

- Snails and slugs are persistent pests in the garden for most of the year. Leave out saucers of beer for them to drown in, or remove them by hand.
- You're most likely to catch them at work if you patrol the garden at night, armed with a torch and a bucket of salty water into which to drop them.
- Commercial snail bait should be used with caution; keep it out of the reach of young children and animals and wear gloves when sprinkling pellets.
- Care should be taken when using highly toxic pellets on food that is to be eaten.
- Quash is a relatively safe product to use in the garden.

gardener. It is equally important to counter slug and snail damage in the vegetable garden.

White butterfly and aphids will attack cabbages and cauliflowers at this time of the year; Nature's Way natural derris dust is a safe and effective means of controlling these destructive pests. Cutworms can also do a lot of damage to young seedlings. These pests must be attacked with highly toxic sprays if the garden is to be rid of them. If you don't like the idea of spraying, try enticing birds into your garden with breadcrumbs or a suet-based bird pudding made with nuts and seeds. Birds will quickly and naturally remove many garden pests.

Signs of porina caterpillars may begin to show in your lawn. Quick action with Diazinon pellets will solve the problem.

The flower garden

Hardy annuals such as candytuft, poppy, cornflower and scabious can be sown now and many other seedlings planted out into the garden. In heavy wet soils the planting of dahlia tubers should be resisted until the soil has warmed.

Sowing

Seeds of most annuals can now be sown either in the open ground or in seed trays for later transplanting. Perennials can also be sown and should be planted out quickly as they will soon be in flower. The seeds of flowers such as ageratum, aster, carnation, coreopsis and Livingstone daisy (*Dorotheanthus bellidiformis*) must have the best of seasonal conditions if they are to germinate. (See the list of seeds to sow on page 26.)

BELOW: Livingstone daisy, *Dorotheanthus bellidiformis*

Propagation and division

Valuable cuttings can be struck from recent prunings of ornamental plants that have finished flowering (see page 93). Cuttings from azaleas, fuchsias and hydrangeas will also strike well if taken now. Division of chrysanthemums, delphiniums, gerberas and violets will give you stock to give to friends, or to replenish any areas of the garden left bare by ornamentals that have finished flowering. Dahlias and chrysanthemums will also strike from cuttings.

Planting

Warm day temperatures, moist conditions and gentle sun guarantee that most seedlings planted now will flourish. Once the soil is prepared, many ornamental plants and the seedlings grown in the last part of winter can be bedded out for late spring and early summer flowering. Watch out for slug and snail damage.

This is the last month that sunflowers (*Helianthus annuus*) can be planted if they are to have enough time to develop fully. New dwarf sunflowers such as 'Symphony Mixed' are splendid for garden beds and borders. These plants will grow to 70 cm and produce colours ranging from yellow, through gold, cream, bronze, mahogany and red, and combinations of all of these. Other low-growing varieties include the sturdy compact pom-pom type 'Teddy Bear', 'Sunspot', 'Music Box', and 'Munchkin' with bright yellow flowers and green centres. Medium-height types include the

TASKS FOR OCTOBER
- Dig soil to aerate it and add compost.
- Continue to take cuttings of fuchsias, dahlias and chrysanthemums.
- Sow French marigolds for planting out later.
- Plant tuberous plants such as begonias and gloxinias in pots.
- Plant gladiolus bulbs at fortnightly intervals until Christmas.
- Pinch back the growing tips of chrysanthemums to encourage more flowering heads.
- Mow lawns regularly, at least once a fortnight.
- Check constantly for snails and slugs.
- Dust cabbages and cauliflowers with derris to kill caterpillars.
- Sow lettuce and radish every few weeks.
- Plant main crop potatoes.
- Spray apple and pear trees after blossom-fall to protect bees.

ABOVE: Taking fuchsia cuttings.
BELOW: Sunflower, *Helianthus annuus*

FLOWERS TO PLANT NOW

SOW THESE SEEDS

Agapanthus	Delphinium
Ageratum	French marigold
Agrostemma (corncockle)	Geranium
Alstroemeria	Godetia
Alyssum	Hemerocallis
Amaranthus	Hollyhock
Antirrhinum	Larkspur
Aquilegia	Livingstone daisy
Aster	Nasturtium
Astilbe	Papaver (poppy)
Begonia	Petunia
Calendula	Phlox
Candytuft	Salvia
Canna	Scabious
Carnation	Snapdragon
Cleome	Stachys (lamb's ears)
Coreopsis	Stokesia
Cornflower	Sunflower
Cosmos	Verbena
Dahlia	Zinnia

PLANT THESE SEEDLINGS

Agrostemma (corncockle)
Carnation
Catananche
Cosmos
Dianthus
Echinops ritro
Erigeron
Eryngium (sea holly)
Geum
Larkspur
Limonium (statice)
Lupin
Moluccella (bells of Ireland)
Nigella
Petunia
Sweet pea
Verbascum
Viola
Wallflower

PLANT THESE BULBS, CORMS AND TUBERS

Amaryllis
Begonia
Callas
Canna
Dahlia
Gladiolus
Gloxinia
Nerine
Zephyranthes

'Floristana' branching variety with reddish-bronze petals with yellow tips, 'Jade' with yellowish-green flowers, 'Sunny', 'Sonja' and the rich orange 'Soraya' with dark centres. Tall sunflowers such as the classic 'Skyscraper' and the field helianthus will grow to 3.6 metres and 'Crimson Queen' and the deep chocolate-red 'Moulin Rouge' to 2 metres.

Bulbs, corms and tubers

Amaryllis (belladonna) bulbs planted now will flower in the late summer and early autumn. Amaryllis prefer a subtropical or near frost-free environment. Winter temperatures of −12°C can be tolerated if the bulbs are planted 15 cm deep and mulched.

Gladiolus bulbs should be planted at fortnightly intervals from now until Christmas to provide a succession of summer blooms. Zephyranthes are also a member of the amaryllis family and come in white, pink and yellow. They prefer cool, frost-free, subtropical gardens, but in cold climates they can be grown in pots and taken indoors if temperatures fall below freezing. They make excellent pot plants if planted in a peaty mix and kept moist at all times. In subtropical areas they should be kept moist even when the leaves have died down.

Begonias, callas and nerines can continue to be planted and will flower in the late summer and early autumn. Begonia tubers and other bulbs planted in August and September should be given a little liquid food. Give newly planted bulbs a little bone dust or dried blood at the time of planting.

Plant care

Ornamental plants such as cytisus (broom), deutzia, philadelphus, viburnum and weigela should be pruned hard after flowering, cutting back to within 10 cm of the old wood. From these pruned shrubs some valuable cuttings could be struck. Any dead wood should be cut out and burnt. Roses will need to be regularly deadheaded during this season to encourage further flowering and keep them at their best.

ABOVE: A light trimming of evergreen box, *Buxus sempervirens*.

Hedges

October is an ideal time to trim the hedge. The first flush of spring growth will be covering the hedge as well as paths in some gardens. Evergreen hedges such as box (*Buxus sempervirens*), holly (*Ilex aquifolium*), laurel, olearia, pittosporum, privet and yew should be close-pruned now. Do not cut back beyond the natural green into the structure unless you are renovating a tired, old hedge.

Large-leafed types such as laurel and pittosporum should be cut with secateurs or very carefully with hedge clippers rather than an electric trimmer, which will leave unsightly ragged leaves. This is quite time-consuming but the end result is worth it.

Feeding the hedge with a general all-purpose fertiliser will produce healthy growth. (See pages 142–43 for further information on hedges.)

Lawns

The spring lawn requires regular mowing. As the temperatures rise the lawn will begin to grow more rapidly. If the lawn is mowed twice a week the clippings can be left on the lawn at this time of year to feed back into the soil. Very wet areas may still need some help to drain. Push a fork or spade deep into the lawn to enter the sub-soil, thus enabling some of the surface water to drain away. If worm casts on the lawn worry you, sweep them away with a light broom, or collect them for giving to pot plants as a bonus food. Control moss in lawns by raking thoroughly and taking great care to collect and dispose of every small piece of moss to prevent it from spreading. Sow grass seed on any bald patches that are left from the winter.

Late October is the best time to feed your lawn with a suitable nitrogenous fertiliser to strengthen it before the hot, dry weather. If necessary apply a weed-killer to the lawn one or two weeks after feeding. Weed and feed products for the lawn are available; just put them on the end of the hose and spray.

MAKING A TOPIARY

With lots of patience and regular care, growing topiary plants is easy. Rosemary (the upright, not the weeping form) makes an excellent topiary plant as it is decorative and hardy, is easy to grow from cuttings and tolerates drought. Follow these hints to begin your topiary:

- Select strong, straight tips 12–14 cm long from a large healthy plant. Plant in a mix of equal parts peat and sand. Place in a warm, moist position out of the direct sun until the cuttings have rooted (six to eight weeks).
- Plant rooted cuttings in separate pots. Stake and tie them well. Remove any small side growths, thus forcing the development of a single stem. At this stage the tiny topiaries can be placed in full sun.
- Keep pinching back any side growth until the plant reaches the desired height. Then pinch out the growing tip and allow branchlets to form before also pinching them back to achieve the desired shape. Growing within a wire or metal framework can speed the formation of the shape.
- Make sure the ties do not cut into the trunk as it grows. Loosen and retie to prevent damage. Turn the pots every few weeks to ensure even growth and continue to pinch back new branchlets to maintain the shape. Water only when the soil is dry. Feed with a liquid fertiliser such as Nitrosol, or a slow-release fertiliser such as Osmocote.

The edible garden

In warm, sheltered areas it is possible to plant French beans, sweet corn and a few outdoor tomatoes. Plant out cabbage and cauliflower seedlings as well as seedlings of silver beet that have been raised in seed trays.

Sowing

Now that all danger of frost is past and the soil is warming, many vegetable seeds can be sown directly in the soil. A wide variety of vegetables can be sown from seed. (See list on page 32.) If your garden is small, it is a good

ALTERNATIVES TO A LAWN

While grass makes a neat, green carpet in most of our gardens there are alternative and scented solutions to lawn, which in some cases don't even need mowing. Lawn substitutes include chamomile (*Anthemis nobilis*), mercury bay weed (*Dichondra* 'Silver Falls'), marjoram, oregano, mini mondo grass (*Ophiopogon japonicus* 'Minor'), black mondo (*Ophiopogon planiscapus* 'Nigrescens'), the native cotula, marjoram, oregano, woolly thyme, *Acaena purpurea*, *Scleranthus biflorus*, *Sedum mexicana* and the Corsican mint *Mentha requenii*. All of these, while slowly growing to form a good lawn, require a lot of work to keep them looking neat.

Thyme (above) is a good ground cover, but needs regular trimming to keep it dense. Thyme does well in conditions of full sun and good drainage. It is able to withstand severe drought conditions. Many different colours, leaf variants and scented varieties can be used for a thyme lawn. Perhaps a mix of types could be used to create a tapestry effect.

Mondo grass (ophiopogon or turf lily) is a moderately hardy evergreen and will grow in sun or shade. It takes a while to establish a lawn with these grasses but a form like the black *Ophiopogon planiscapus* 'Nigrescens' can make an exciting addition to your garden. Some of the more rampant grasses can become invasive in the garden and should be used carefully.

If you don't mind rampant spreaders try *Cotula squalida*, which will happily establish in shady areas of the garden and then set out to colonise the rest of the garden. Most of these substitute grasses tolerate only light foot traffic; regular traffic will kill them. In areas of heavy traffic these plants are effective at the edge of a path, or in patches between stepping stones.

BELOW FROM LEFT: Winter hardy Cos Romaine lettuce, Rossimo; mini Cos lettuce, Little Gem; nasturtium, *Tropaeolum majus*

idea to make a list of the vegetables that you need and plant only them. It makes little sense to grow a lot of beetroot if you and your family don't like them!

In warm, well-drained northern soils it is just possible to plant kumara. Planting on ridges or hillocks of soil improves drainage and can also add to soil warmth. Raised kumara, however, need careful watering, especially in the summer as they are inclined to dry out.

yellow on the inside. The flavour is sweet and spicy. Regular moisture is again essential for the development of top quality, tasty produce. Sowing carrot seed is best done by mixing it with dry sand and planting directly into beds prepared with well-rotted compost. Manure that is too fresh will produce forked roots.

The range of lettuces available today is astonishing. The tastiest varieties tend to be Butter head types such as Mignonette, Buttercrunch, Speckles, Tom Thumb and Perella Red. Many of these types do not heart but produce highly decorative, luscious leaves in a range of colours and forms such as Ruby, with deep red,

Shelter from strong winds is also important when you are establishing kumara. Watch for any signs of blight on potatoes; spray with Cuprox or a similar product.

Carrots are favourites on the table; many varieties are available for every type of soil, from sand to clay. Chantenay varieties produce the sweetest and juiciest roots. Early Short Horn is an ideal type, with a short broad root. Newer varieties such as Minicor, Mini sweet and Touchon are heavy yielding, sweet and juicy. The 1000-year-old heirloom variety 'Purple Dragon' produces reddish-purple roots that are bright

finely curled leaves, Red Sails, with frilled green and burgundy leaves, Oak Leaf types, Lollo Rossa, Lollo Bionda with leaves of pinky red and green, and Red Salad Bowl, with bronze-red leaves of a delicious flavour. Types such as Tom Thumb and the winter hardy Cos Romaine types such as Cimmaron, Little Gem, Freckles, Rossimo and Paris White Cos are most suitable for the smaller garden. It is useful to scarify (refrigerate) your lettuce seed for a couple of days before sowing; this will ensure better germination. The secret of producing sweet and juicy lettuces is to grow them quickly.

A highly nitrogenous fertiliser such as dried blood, poultry manure or blood and bone will ensure rapid growth. Lettuces need regular moisture to prevent them from becoming bitter and tough. Plant seeds at regular fortnightly intervals as it is always better to have half a dozen ready, some coming on and some just beginning.

Most herb seeds can be sown now. Caraway, chervil, coriander, dill and parsley are best if sown directly and later thinned to leave only the stronger plants. Basil seeds should be planted in a warm place under cover until large enough to plant out. They like warm or hot humid weather without extreme temperature changes.

Tropaeolum majus (nasturtium or Indian cress) is a twining annual plant. The peppery leaves are delicious added to salads, as are the colourful flowers. Nasturtiums are easily raised from seed and will tolerate poor, dry soil.

Planting

Most seedlings can be transplanted into the garden now that the weather is warmer, and the longer daylight hours mean that seedlings make rapid growth. The choice of seedlings that can be planted at this time of year is very wide. (See the list on page 32.)

Planting some vegetables in a muddy puddle of soil and water greatly helps their establishment. A little weak liquid fertiliser at planting time also helps plants to cope with the shock of transplanting. Soaking punnet-grown seedlings overnight before planting can loosen tangled, compacted roots and prevent damage from occurring at this critical time.

Mulching the garden will help to conserve moisture as the soil begins to dry out during the hotter months of the year.

Most gardeners will want to plant at least a few tomato plants. All tomatoes are highly sensitive to cold weather and fungal diseases, yet given a warm, well-drained soil, a little compost and dried blood or potash they will flourish. Young tomato plants should be starved until the first set of fruit has formed, then fed regularly with fertilisers high in nitrogen, such as blood and bone, dried blood, decayed poultry manure or a compost made from seaweed. Laterals should be removed to produce single-stem plants with a maximum of fruiting trusses. These laterals can be planted and will quickly produce strong plants. Sawdust mixed with compost and applied around the roots will conserve moisture and prevent blossom end rot. Heavy mulching encourages tomatoes to produce aerial roots and will increase the crop yield. A regular watering programme is essential.

To ensure that the tomatoes (and other vegetables) you plant are delicious, choose only the most delectable varieties and if necessary grow your own from seed. The prize for the best-flavoured tomato ever has to go to the fat, ridged, ugly and irregular Rouge de Marmande and the delicious, large and meaty Brandywine Pink. Other types such as Grosse Lisse, Gardeners Delight, Beefsteak, Tommy Toe, Sweet 100, Green Zebra and Red Cloud are all tangy, delicious and bear heavy crops if treated well. Microtom F1 is a true miniature and has been specially bred for growing in hanging baskets and containers.

Sweet corn is another garden favourite planted at this time of year. It needs heavy feeding to do well. Any highly nitrogenous fertiliser such as fowl manure, cow manure or blood and bone will help produce heavy crops. A consistently moist soil is also necessary to produce fat, juicy cobs. Mulching with seaweed, straw, newspaper, old carpet, grass clippings or sawdust is essential to the development of a good corn crop. Like tomatoes, corn also produces aerial roots. If these can be fed (by mulching heavily) the crop yield will be greater.

Many new and super-sweet forms are available with names like Florida Supersweet F1 and Honey Sweet, although older forms such as Supergold, Golden Cross Bantam and the American heirloom variety Country Gentleman, introduced in 1891, are also good, reliable and well-flavoured varieties.

All vegetables including beans, broccoli, cabbage, cauliflower, celery, cucumber and squash benefit from regular watering and feeding. This helps them to develop the best and most delicious crops. If you choose your seed types carefully and fulfil simple growing requirements, you can have vegetables of a perfect ripeness, quality and distinctiveness of flavour you quite simply could not buy.

Herbs such as sage, oregano and rosemary will form denser, healthier bushes if they are trimmed regularly. The clippings can be either used as cuttings added to salads or dried for later use in the kitchen. Many herbs can now be planted, including basil, coriander, dill, marjoram, parsley, rosemary, tarragon and thyme.

Fruit

Apple, citrus, feijoa, fig, peach, pear, plum, persimmon and quince trees can still be planted for late summer and early autumn fruiting. Good drainage is essential for the well-being of any young fruit tree. Shelter from cold winds is also important if a tree is to flourish.

Spraying for codling moth is essential if pip crops are to be successful. The larvae of these destructive

LEFT: Punnet-grown seedlings, such as the cabbage shown here, should be soaked overnight.
BELOW: Perennial herbs such as oregano benefit from a light trimming.

VEGETABLES TO PLANT NOW	
SOW THESE SEEDS	PLANT THESE SEEDLINGS
Aubergine	
Basil	Artichoke
Bean (dwarf and runner)	Aubergine (with cover)
Broccoli	Bean* (French and runner)
Cabbage	
Caraway	Broccoli
Capsicum	Carrot
Carrot	Cauliflower
Cauliflower	Cabbage
Celery	Cucumber
Chervil	Kumara*
Coriander	Leek
Cucumber	Lettuce
Dill	Onion
Leek	Parsnip
Lettuce	Pea
Marrow*	Potato*
Melon*	Pumpkin
Nasturtium	Spinach
Parsley	Silver beet
Parsnip	Sweet corn
Pea	Tomato*
Pumpkin*	Zucchini
Radish	
Silver beet	
Spinach	
Sweet corn	
Tomato*	
Zucchini	*Only practicable in warm areas

pests overwinter under the bark of the tree or on the ground under leaves. As spring blossom begins so does the life cycle of the moth. It will quickly lay its eggs and in less than nine days they will hatch and begin working their way into the centre of the developing fruit. After some months they begin the journey out, destroying the fruit in the process. An insecticide such as Garden Master will limit the damage that this pest can cause. Spray after petal fall to minimise the impact of the toxic spray on bees, as they will no longer be interested once the pollen has gone. The programme of spraying started in September should be continued to prevent brown rot, black spot or leaf curl from ruining the season's crop. A copper spray will combat most fungal diseases.

Grape and passionfruit vines can be planted now, and all bush and cane fruits should be planted and pruned for their main growing season. Any dead wood from the previous season's crop should be cut out and burnt. Strawberries should be mulched to prevent the new fruit from being ruined by the soil.

October features

Hibiscus

Alyogne hugellii (syn. *Hibiscus hugellii*) is a plant found in the warmer parts of Australia. It grows happily in warm parts of New Zealand and fine plants exist in areas as far south as Hawke's Bay. These tall shrubs, which grow to 2.5 metres, have downy, divided leaves and come in a range of colours that includes blue, mauve, white, yellow and pink. A warm, sunny, well-drained situation suits these plants best. Even in the south, given suitable conditions in such microclimates as Sumner or Diamond Harbour, they will survive a winter and begin flowering once the soil has warmed in the spring. When buying these plants it is best to do so when they are in flower, as colours can vary considerably if you buy seed-grown plants.

Magnolias

At this time of the year the spectacular magnolias light up the spring garden. These ancient trees are said to date back some 120 million years, making them some of the oldest flowering plants known. Some are small and would easily be accommodated in the city garden, growing no more than 1.8 to 3 metres, while others will grow as large as 12 by 8 metres. They can be pruned severely if they become too large and will regenerate quickly.

Container-grown plants are a better buy, as they will have a more developed root stock when it comes to planting out. Magnolias resent root disturbance and must be handled carefully because of this. If the roots are cut or damaged by clumsy or careless handling, this will markedly impede the tree's development. It is worth

BELOW FROM LEFT: Hibiscus, *Alyogne hugellii* (syn. *Hibiscus hugellii*); *Magnolia stellata*; *Magnolia campbellii*

paying a little more for advanced trees, because varieties such as *Magnolia campbellii* can take more than ten years to flower if you buy a small, young plant. Even then, it will take several years to build up the flowering framework that you would wish for.

Magnolias require a sheltered position in good soil. A heavy clay soil, wet soil, or a sandy soil does not suit these trees. A deep, moist, well-drained soil, on the other hand, is all that they require to grow quickly. They resent wind, which is all too common during the spring months. Wind can not only slow the tree's growth but also damage the leaves and flowers.

When planting your tree dig a large hole and mix in several layers of peat. Carefully remove the bag or sacking from your tree and gently lower it into the hole that you have made. Do not loosen the roots. Press soil around the roots, and water well.

There are many magnolias to choose from, including New Zealand-bred varieties such as 'Iolanthe' and 'Vulcan' which would please even the most discerning gardener. *Magnolia campbellii* is the largest and arguably most spectacular of its family. At over 12 metres, the sheer splendour of its spring display makes it a must for the large garden. For the city or small garden a shrub such as *Magnolia stellata* is more suitable. It grows little more than 2.5 metres tall and has a neat, rounded shape. The pure white flowers are produced in abundance during early to mid-spring. The form *Magnolia stellata* 'Rosea' has pink starry buds that fade to white. *Magnolia delavayi* and *Magnolia grandiflora* (Southern bay or bull bay) suit the warmer parts of

New Zealand. This latter is a large-growing tree reaching 15 by 12 metres in twenty-five years. The large leaves are glossy, dark green, 20 cm long, pointed at both ends and felted with a rusty brown down beneath. The flowers, which can grow as large as 25 cm across, are creamy white and highly scented. From early summer until autumn the warm, heady perfume can fill a sheltered garden. In tropical and subtropical climates it can be almost continually in flower. Tolerant of lime but preferring an acid soil and a semi-woodland setting, this is an ideal tree for the large garden.

November

Temperature and climate

The chance of frosts, even in the coldest parts of the country, has almost passed and in areas throughout New Zealand the planting and sowing of a wide range of vegetables and ornamentals is possible. Rainy weather and wind are common in many areas during this last part of spring but the longer daylight hours and warmer temperatures promote rapid growth. By early November daylight saving gives keen gardeners an extra hour in the evening for gardening. Constant growth at this time of year means that there is always work to do in the garden.

LEFT: *Crinum moorei*
BELOW FROM LEFT: *Callistemon citrinus* 'Splendens'; *Bracteantha bracteata*

Food and water

Summer-flowering perennials and shrubs will respond to a feed of a general garden fertiliser. Gardenias fed with a liquid fish food will respond with greener leaves and will set larger and more fragrant flowers. Foliar feeding should continue with all flowering annuals and vegetables. Spring shrubs should be fed after flowering flowering next spring. Generous watering is not essential to the development of all plants (see page 164). However, lack of water during critical growing periods will limit the quality and quantity of flowers and crops.

Now is a good time to start a mulching programme. Mulching trees, shrubs, vegetables and ornamentals is essential if growth is to be encouraged and a successful crop enjoyed. When you apply a mulch, the soil should always be well soaked first. Putting a mulch on already dry soil can actually prevent moisture from reaching the plants' roots. If you have only a little mulching material, concentrate it around those plants that are most vulnerable

and given a good soaking to wash the fertiliser in. Rhododendrons should be dead-headed after flowering during November and mulched with compost. Overfeeding these plants can encourage leaf growth at the expense of flowers. Azaleas and rhododendrons with yellowing leaves or chlorosis have too much lime in the soil; a dressing of sulphate of ammonia mixed with an equal quantity of iron sulphate will rectify the problem.

As the weather gets hotter so the need for moisture in the garden becomes greater. Spring-flowering bulbs require water after they have flowered to ensure a good to drought rather than spreading it thinly to little effect. The regular use of a push hoe to remove weeds will also help to conserve moisture.

Recently transplanted vegetables and ornamentals should have the highest priority for water during dry periods. Newly sown seed requires consistently moist soil. It is good practice to fill open seed drills with water several hours before sowing. Lettuce and radish given regular supplies of water will grow quickly, resulting in sweet rather than bitter crops. Regular watering will help fruit develop on citrus and set on other fruit trees.

> **THE BENEFITS OF MULCHING**
>
> Mulching will conserve soil moisture, keep roots cool and prevent weeds from growing. Organic mulches will also improve the quality of the soil.
>
> **WHAT TYPE OF MULCH?**
>
> A huge variety of material can be used for mulching — old carpet, plastic sheeting, sawdust, straw, peat, grass clippings, well-rotted compost or manure, large stones, shingle. The materials need not be expensive.
>
> It is best to check whether the mulching material has been treated with preservatives or herbicides as these could do serious damage to plants and should be avoided. If using black polythene sheeting, lay soak-hoses underneath as the plastic is an impermeable barrier to water. Plastic mulches are particularly suitable for where you want to keep crops such as strawberries clean and dry. In the shrub and herbaceous borders a plastic mulch will enhance growth during the early years.
>
> **BEFORE APPLYING THE MULCH**
> - Always soak the soil well or wait until just after heavy rain. Mulching dry soil can prevent moisture from reaching the plants' roots.
> - Remove perennial weeds as mulching with weeds still present in the soil could make the situation worse.
> - Fertilise heavily with a nitrogenous fertiliser such as blood and bone.
>
> **APPLYING THE MULCH**
>
> If you are using an organic mulch, it should be at least 15 cm deep and cover the area of the plant's root run for maximum effect. It is advisable to check for snails, slugs and slaters. Other serious pests can be carried in carelessly made compost and need to be guarded against.
>
> When placing a mulch near the base of a tree or plant, leave a 5-cm space to prevent contact and possible stem rot.

Pests and diseases

In the flower garden earwigs begin their assault in earnest. Trap them in upturned flowerpots stuffed with straw or hollow tubes of bamboo and then dispose of them by burning or drowning. Roses need regular spraying during November to prevent fungal diseases, aphids and bronze beetle from destroying the flowers. Spraying with a general-purpose fungicide/insecticide will cure most problems. Bronze beetle may need heavier treatment and a spray, such as Target, may be called for.

Pot plants and ornamentals inside the house, on sheltered verandahs or in glasshouses may be attacked by whitefly and thrips which can be eliminated by a systemic fungicide/insecticide or simply washed off the infected plants with a jet of water from the garden hose.

Fruit pests and diseases are on the increase in the garden during November. You should continue to combat codling moth by spraying at least until the end of this month. A good spraying at blossom fall and about three weeks later will remove most of the pests. Black spot and other fungal diseases on apples and pears can be remedied by spraying with a suitable fungicide. Keriberries, loganberries and raspberries should be sprayed with a general insecticide about a fortnight after flowering, again as the tiny fruit begin to turn pink and then finally several weeks later. Gooseberry crops can be devastated by mildew, which covers the skin with an unsightly cloudy-looking blemish. Fruits look unpalatable but can be eaten as they are or peeled. This disease is hard to stop and a systemic fungicide must be used. Invicta, a mildew-free variety of gooseberry, is now generally available. Careful note should be taken of any withholding period after spraying in which the fruit should not be eaten. Any badly diseased plants should be dug out and burnt.

The flower garden

Violets will benefit greatly from dividing and replanting especially if they have been in the same part of the garden for several years. In warm gardens the first gladioli can also be planted out and summer flowering annuals and perennials can be dropped into the space vacated by faded spring plants.

Sowing

Direct sowing of many annuals is now possible throughout the country. (See the list on page 38.) Seeds are generally better sown in trays, watered, fed and grown on until they are strong enough to be planted out into the garden. A folded piece of paper is a useful tool that gives more control when sowing into seed trays.

Ageratum, alyssum, candytuft, chrysanthemum, clarkia, cornflower and cosmos can be sown directly. Aster, helichrysum, marigold, mignonette, nasturtium, phlox, sunflower and zinnia will, if sown now, fill the late summer garden with colour. Delphinium, forget-me-not (in cold gardens), geum, larkspur, lupin, Oriental poppy, pansy and wallflowers should be sown now for late autumn and winter flowering. Watch constantly for any signs of roaming slugs and snails.

> **TASKS FOR NOVEMBER**
> - Mow the lawns regularly but raise the blades a little as the weather becomes hotter.
> - Feed the grass to strengthen it for the coming dry season.
> - Dead-head rhododendrons once they have flowered.
> - Roses, indoor plants and pot plants need checking for pests and fungal diseases.
> - Watch for slug and snail damage.
> - Take chrysanthemum cuttings.
> - Divide snowdrops after flowering, for next season.
> - Hoe and hand-weed as often as possible. Weed control is essential in November.
> - Mulch to conserve as much water as possible. Water recently transplanted seedlings first.
> - Earth up potatoes to protect tubers from the light.
> - Spray fruit trees for fungal and destructive insect pests with an all-purpose spray.
> - Spray gooseberries for mildew with a suitable systemic fungicide.

BELOW: Folded paper is useful when sowing seed.

FLOWERS TO PLANT NOW

SOW THESE SEEDS		PLANT THESE SEEDLINGS	PLANT THESE BULBS, CORMS AND TUBERS
Ageratum	Godetia	Ageratum	Achimenes
Alyssum	Helichrysum	Alyssum	Agapanthus
Amaranthus	Larkspur	Amarathus	Allium
Aquilegia	Lupin	Aster	Amaryllis
Aster	Marigold	Bells of Ireland	Begonias
Bells of Ireland	Mignonette	Candytuft	Calostemma
Candytuft	Morning glory	Chrysanthemum	Cyclamen
Chrysanthemum	Nasturtium*	Cornflower	Dahlia
Clarkia	Pansy	Helichrysum	Gladiolus
Cornflower	Phlox	Mignonette	
Cosmos	Poppy (Oriental)	Marigold	
Delphinium	Sunflower*	Sunflower*	
Forget-me-not	Wallflower		
Geum	Zinnia		

*Better if sown in August and planted out after all frost danger has passed

Planting

Seedlings that were sown in September will now be ready for planting out. Chrysanthemum cuttings should be planted into a rich soil where they can develop. When planting out annuals, the soil should be dug and well-watered before transplanting begins. Having a watering can handy makes it easy to give each seedling a good splash of water once planted.

As the flower garden begins to dry, it makes sense to sow or plant ornamentals that enjoy such conditions. Many of the plants in the Compositae family are capabile of growing in the most arid and poorest of soils. The daisy-like flowers of *Bracteantha bracteata*, helichrysum and ozothamnus have papery, straw-like petals and are very long lasting if cut before fully open and hung upside down to dry.

The recently released strawflower *Helipterum* syn. *Rhodanthe* 'Paper Cascade' is a most adaptable plant. It is tolerant of frost, prefers some shade and thrives in dry, poor soil and with little care, it will happily grow in pots or hanging baskets. Helipterums will flower from early spring until late summer.

RIGHT: Taking chrysanthemum cuttings.

FAR RIGHT: Red silver beet, *Beta vulgaris* 'Charlotte'

Bulbs, corms and tubers

The soil should be dug and well-watered before planting out bulbs such as gladioli. *Crinum moorei* is an elegant plant for the shady summer garden. The leaves are strap-like and grow out from the neck of the bulb. The

pale pink and in some cases dark pink flowers are ideal for picking. In cultivation this family prefers shelter, shade and a deep, rich, well-drained soil. The plant will tolerate sun but the leaves tend to become burnt and marked in such conditions. The bulbs should be shallowly planted in spring. *Crinum* is ideal for planting at the back of the border or in containers. If winters are very cold the bulbs can either be lifted and dried or the pots taken indoors. Propagation is either from seed or offsets and by division.

Lawns

In late spring lawns require regular mowing but by now you should have lifted the mower blades up a notch or two. Lawns that are cut too close will burn and be hard to re-establish before the autumn. The ideal height for the first main cuts of the spring lawn should be 2.5 cm. The next two or three cuts should be about 2 cm and thereafter 1.5 cm for the rest of the lawn's growing season.

Lawn clippings should not be allowed to lie on the surface in large clumps after cutting. This will damage the lawn and also cause brown patches and increase the risk of fungal diseases. Either mow with a catcher or rake the lawn after mowing.

Weeds in the lawn can also be poisoned now before they have a chance to develop and seed. If you don't want to use chemical sprays, you will have to dig the weeds out by hand; commercial weed-extractors may make this arduous task a little easier.

This is the last chance before summer to sow grass in any bald patches. Feeding the lawn in the late spring is another good way to ensure that it stays healthy throughout the drier weather. Even if it does go brown it will quickly regenerate once water is applied.

The edible garden

Some parts of the far south of the country may still experience a late frost and it is a good idea to use frost cloth not only to raise soil temperature but also to protect crops from sudden cold snaps.

Sowing

In all but the coldest southern regions beans, beets, broccoli, Brussels sprouts, cabbage, carrots, lettuce, parsnips, peas, potatoes, radishes, silver beet, tomatoes and turnips can be either sown or planted. Colourful forms of silver beet such as Charlotte have bright scarlet mid ribs and maroon-and-green leaves. These plants are delicious, nutritious and can also be used to great effect in the flower or vegetable garden. Kumara can be planted on well-drained north-facing slopes. In these conditions they will grow quickly and establish their tubers before the summer sun starts to dry the ground.

Aubergine, cucumber, melons, peppers and pumpkins are susceptible to small changes in temperature and should only be planted where warm conditions are certain. If you are worried about cold weather, sow your seeds in a seed tray and keep it safe in a warm location. Try raising tender plants in a glasshouse.

Planting

The thinning of vegetable seedlings is important if good crops are to be had. The removal of weed growth is also important now or tiny plants will be choked and starved of water. Cauliflower, celery, lettuce and radish will benefit from as much water as you can give them. Summer salad vegetables should be planted out regularly every few weeks to ensure a constant supply.

Fruit

Apple thinning can be started now as soon as the natural thinning process has finished. Thinning will ensure better quality and tastier fruit. Trimming large, leafy and non-productive branches out of the tree will allow sun into the centre, ensuring a better and tastier crop. Fruit on nectarine, peach and pear trees should also be thinned to a number that the tree can reasonably be expected to carry and develop. Plum trees are

---

VEGETABLES TO PLANT NOW

SOW THESE SEEDS	PLANT THESE SEEDLINGS
Aubergine	
Bean	Aubergine
Broccoli	Broccoli
Cabbage	Cabbage
Capsicum	Cauliflower
Carrot	Kale
Cauliflower	Kumara
Celery	Leek
Chicory	Lettuce
Cucumber	Pepper
Kale	Potato
Leek	Red beet
Lettuce	Silver beet
Melon	Tomato
Parsnip	
Pea	
Pumpkin	
Radish	
Red beet	
Silver beet	
Sweet corn	
Tomato	
Zucchini	

LEFT: Ripening strawberries, *Fragaria ananassa*

also best thinned if a quality crop is wanted. A mulch applied at the base of young trees will help them develop. Mulching older trees will ensure a better fruit set. Remove old canes from the earlier-fruiting types of raspberry.

Strawberries will be in full flush in northern areas. Water is needed if the fruit is to be tasty and plump. Birds will begin to attack strawberries and fruiting trees. Protection with nets, bird-scarers and plastic hum lines are some of the ways that this damage can be prevented. Take care that weeds do not grow up around strawberry crops or around young trees and rob what little water there may be in some soils.

November features

Rhododendrons

Rhododendrons are ideal if your garden has an acid soil and light shade. Many rhododendrons require some shelter in cold winters and shade in the summer. However, many of the hardy hybrids will cope well in full sun and exposed conditions. Rhododendrons are tough plants, have few diseases and few pests will attack them.

Colours, forms and sizes vary greatly, as does their flowering period. Some types flower from August to September, others in September and November, with some flowering into December and January. Some rhododendrons will grow to over 10 metres while others range down in size to 1 metre. Some, including the New Zealand-raised hybrid *Rhododendron* 'September Snow' with heavily scented white flowers and *R.* 'Charisma', a deep rose-pink bud that opens to a rose pink, flower from August to September; and others, such as the spectacular pink, English-raised *R.* 'Charlotte de Rothschild', the New Zealand-bred *R.* 'Floral Dance' (with white-flushed rose-pink flowers with a blotch of yellow) and *R.* 'Barbara Jury' (a dusky yellow with flush of pink) flower on into December and January.

RECOMMENDED RHODODENDRONS

RHODODENDRON	HEIGHT	FEATURES
TALL HYBRIDS FOR BEGINNERS		
Rhododendron 'Anna Rose Whitney'	2–3 metres	Pink flowers with light brown spotting on the upper lobes. A vigorous plant.
Rhododendron 'Fragrantissimum'	1.2–1.5 metres	White flowers flushed rose. An intensely fragrant flower. The plant responds well to cutting.
Rhododendron 'Unique'	1.2 metres	Pink flower buds open to cream-coloured flowers. Very free flowering plant with attractive foliage.
SMALL HYBRIDS FOR BEGINNERS		
Rhododendron 'Blue Diamond'	1.2 metres	Rich violet-blue flowers. Upright growth.
Rhododendron 'Dora Amateis'	1 metre	White flowers spotted with green. Dwarf spreading compact growth. Good foliage.
Rhododendron 'Trewithen Orange'	90 cm	Pendant-shaped flowers of a clear orange. Attractive bluish foliage.
DWARF HYBRID TYPES (UNDER 1 METRE)		
Rhododendron 'Ginny Gee'	45 cm	White flowers with a light pink flush, 2.5 cm wide. Small leaves often turn red in winter.
Rhododendron 'Pink Drift'	50 cm	Prolific, pinkish plum-coloured flowers. Bronze-coloured foliage.
Rhododendron 'Ptarmigan'	30 cm	White flowers. Plant forms a spreading mound.
SPECIES RHODODENDRON		
Rhododendron campylogynum	45 cm, with a spread of 45 cm	Produces small trusses of wide and bell-shaped white, salmon pink, red, purple or almost black flowers in late spring.
Rhododendron wardii	8 metres in ideal conditions	Flowers are a soft, clear yellow with a crimson blotch. *Rhododendron wardii*, *R. w.* 'Ludlow' and *R. w.* 'Sheriff' require shelter in cold winter conditions.
Rhododendron williamsianum	1.5 metres	Bears bell-shaped flowers of rose pink.
Rhododendron yakushimanum	1.5–2.5 metres	Native to Yakushima Island, Japan. Flowers are deep pink in the bud, opening pale pink or white. Often grown for its foliage, which is leathery with a heavy fawn indumentum ('down').

FROM LEFT CLOCKWISE: *Rhododendron* 'Charlotte de Rothschild'; *Rhododendron* 'Fragrantissimum'; *Rhododendron falconeri*

Most rhododendrons lack a thick, spreading root system. The entire root ball is made up of fine roots and for this reason they require careful planting. They grow best in cool climate areas and thrive with regular mulching. The surface roots, however, must be able to breathe and applying a heavy layer of mulch is usually counter-productive. A thin, even layer will enable the mainly surface roots to spread and keep cool in summer.

Good drainage is essential, as the fine roots of all rhododendrons will soon rot if they remain waterlogged for any length of time. Soil should be well broken up before planting as the fine roots cannot penetrate compacted soils or hard, rocky ground. Rhododendrons require an acidic soil with plenty of well rotted compost added when planting to retain moisture.

In wet areas with an alkaline soil, create raised beds with a base of fine shingle and then add a heavy layer of compost mixed with topsoil before planting. Special rhododendron mixes are available.

Most rhododendrons prefer dappled shade or some protection from sun and strong winds. They require little maintenance apart from the occasional removal of dead wood and dead-heading after flowering.

Modern shrub rose, *Rosa* 'Wife of Bath'

Rosa rugosa

Hybrid musk rose, *Rosa* 'Autumn Delight'

Wild or species rose, *Rosa moyesii* 'Geranium'

Roses

Roses flower in profusion and are often highly scented. There is one for almost every purpose. Roses can be divided into the following groups:

Modern shrub roses
These include the floribundas, the polyanthas and the English or David Austin roses such as *Rosa* 'Wife of Bath'. Produced mainly over the last 150 years for their fragrance and vigour, many are continual flowering, highly coloured and disease-resistant.

Rugosa roses
These are all hybrids of the wild Japanese *Rosa rugosa*. These are all tough roses able to cope with extremes of cold, dry, salt spray and motorway pollution. A rugosa such as *Rosa rugosa* 'Roseraie de l'Hay' or *R. r.* 'Scabrosa' is highly perfumed and has hips in the autumn.

Hybrid musk roses
These are highly scented, have healthy foliage and will, unlike many old roses, give a second flowering in the autumn. *Rosa* 'Cornelia', *R.* 'Felicia' and *R.* 'Prosperity' are all fine examples of this family of roses.

Wild or species roses
These occur naturally throughout the world. They flower for a short season, but many have leaves of unusual colour, such as *R. rubrifolia* with its blue-grey foliage. Some have spectacular hips, such as *R.* 'Fimbriata' and *R. moyesii* 'Geranium'. The leaves of *R. virginiana* turn scarlet, orange and yellow in the autumn. Some members of this group have fern-like foliage while others have spectacular glowing thorns.

Gallica roses
These are perhaps the first of the cultivated roses. *Rosa gallica officinalis*, or the Apothecary's rose, is ancient, as is *Rosa* 'Rosa mundi'. Gallicas are not tall-growing and suit the smaller garden, although they can sucker and spread.

Damask roses
These are spreading bushes, with some growing to over 2 metres. They require good soil to do well. The

Rosa gallica versicolor

Damask rose, *Rosa* 'Rose de Rescht'

Alba rose, *Rosa* 'Jeanne d'Arc'

Centifolia rose, *Rosa* 'Gruss en Aachen'

beautiful green-eyed, white, highly scented *Rosa* 'Madame Hardy' and *R.* 'Ispahan' (pink and highly scented) are excellent roses for the bigger garden. The beautiful rich red, highly scented, compact *R.* 'Rose de Rescht' is well worth a place in any garden.

Alba roses

These are beautiful, mainly pink roses with lead-grey leaves. Growing to about 2 metres, they are healthy plants. *Rosa × alba* 'Königin von Dänemark' is a beauty.

Centifolia roses

As their name implies, these are many-petalled, globular and highly scented. The soft pink *Rosa × centifolia* 'Fantin Latour', named after the great impressionist painter of flowers, is an excellent example of this family. This rose will grow to about 2 metres in height.

Moss roses

These are characterised by soft, sticky glands that project from the bud. These glands look like moss and give rise to the name. Moss roses are highly scented even when still in the bud. *Rosa × centifolia* 'Muscosa' and *R. × c.* 'Chapeau de Napoléon' are good examples.

China roses

These came originally from China and introduced many characteristics into the previously mentioned old roses that have given us modern garden roses. These roses have fine, sparse leaves and delicately scented flowers. *Rosa* 'Parsons Pink' (China Blush) is a good example.

Bourbon roses

These are thought to be a naturally occurring cross between a China and a Damask rose growing on the French island, Île de Bourbon. These roses are highly scented and bear large flowers; *Rosa* 'Mme Isaac Pereire' is an excellent example of a Bourbon rose.

Hybrid Tea roses

Very popular in the late nineteenth century, with many beautiful and hardy varieties developed. They grow well in tubs and pots and many require little pruning. 'Archduke Joseph' is said to be the first of the tea roses.

Moss rose, *Rosa* 'Shaillers White Moss'

China rose, *Rosa* 'Comtesse du Cayla'

Bourbon rose, *Rosa* 'Souvenir de la Malmaison'

Hybrid Tea rose, *Rosa* 'Mrs Oakley Fisher'

SUMMER

LEFT: *Papaver orientale* 'Lady Bird'
ABOVE: *Arctotis* Hybrid cultivar
BELOW: *Gaillardia* 'Mahogany'

In the southern hemisphere, summer for most of us is both the season of Christmas and of the long vacation. The word evokes images of traditional festivities and leisure activities, many of them enjoyed out of doors. It is a time when, if we have worked at our gardens well during the rest of the year, we can take a well-deserved rest from our gardening labours and enjoy some of the fruits of our toil.

Elements of the summer garden that can give a great deal of pleasure include the perfumes of flowering plants, the activities of bees and the colours of our favourite blooms. We can relax in a thoughtfully placed shady spot, dawdle along a warm, aromatic path lined with flowering herbs, pick or dig fruit and vegetables we planted months ago and enjoy at last the results of our efforts. We may be thumbing through advertisements for garden furniture, or dropping hints for Christmas presents along these lines to family members. Outdoor living at this time of year can, for some, be the glorious culmination of a whole year's planning and hard work.

Summer is also a time when we need to be aware both of abundant growth, which will require us to trim back any rampaging plants, and of a diminution of rain, which means we have to ensure that our gardens do not suffer from lack of water. If we plan to take holidays at this time of year, we need to be sure that we have provided our gardens with ongoing care in our absence. As spring plants die back or are lifted until the following year, gaps emerge in the flowerbeds that can easily be filled with flowering or leafy plants in attractive garden pots. Towards the end of summer we can be faced with the major task of cleaning up, unless we approach the job piecemeal and do a little tidying and clearing throughout the summer season.

December

Temperature and climate

Although December is officially the first of the summer months, in some areas the soil may have already begun to dry out. However, usually by December the weather is much more settled and less capricious than the ravages and extremes of spring.

Food and water

To be confident of a healthy garden, we need to provide food to guarantee vigorous trees, shrubs, flowers, vegetables and even the humble lawn. Liquid fertiliser sprayed on leaves, roots and fruit will produce quick results. (See page 150 for fertiliser recipes.)

LEFT: *Freesia leitchlinii*
BELOW FROM LEFT: *Lavandula stoechas* 'Pippa Alba'; *Plumbago auriculata* syn. *capensis* 'Alba'; *Gaillardia grandiflora* 'Kobold'

Well-rotted animal manure can be of great benefit when applied directly to the root zone of flowering annuals and perennials and to summer crops. Compost is another excellent food for the garden. A well-made compost consisting of garden refuse, fruit and vegetable scraps and grass clippings will quickly rot if it is kept

to be taken when siting the water outlets to ensure the water reaches the plants that need it.

Sprinklers and soak-hoses are still the best means of watering a large garden. They are reasonably cheap to buy, effective, economical and infinitely flexible to use. A sprinkler used with a timer is a good means of conserving precious water, as is watering in the cool of the evening or early morning to minimise loss through evaporation. Automatic watering systems have their place, but in many instances a regular walk around the garden with the hose in hand is the best way to get to know just what plant needs what and when.

warm and moist. A handful of superphosphate sprinkled on top of the heap each time new waste is added will ensure that the smell does not become offensive. Seaweed is a most useful addition to the compost heap.

Early December is a key time to sort out how to deal with water shortages in the garden throughout the rest of the season, and to overhaul your watering systems. Replace worn-out hoses; purchase hose reels to prevent hoses tangling and developing leaks; and consider investing in an automated watering system. These can be a great boon to a busy gardener, but care needs

While watering is essential, it need not be the only, or even the main, means of protecting plants from lack of water. Once they are stressed in this way plants are susceptible to wilt and fungal disease and will fail to thrive. Use mulch around plants to conserve the water that you put into the soil, to suppress weed growth and to help keep plant roots cool. (See page 36.) Applying a heavy layer of mulch now will also help keep the soil warmer in the coming winter and prevent it from freezing, thus ensuring less crop and plant damage, and enabling better spring growth.

DROUGHT-RESISTANT PLANTS

Probably the most effective weapon against summer drought is to acknowledge the condition and follow nature's lead. The best and simplest solution is to have plenty of plants that can be relied upon to survive without much water.

TREES AND SHRUBS

Acacia
Bottlebrush
Broom
Callistemon
Chaste tree (*Vitex agnus-castus*)
Dodonaea (akeake)
Dogwood
Elder
Eleagnus
Eucalyptus
Feijoa
Frangipani
Gardenia
Grevillea
Jacaranda
Kolkwitzia
Kowhai
Laurel
Lavatera
Lavender
Japonica
Magnolia
Mallow
Manuka
Melia
Nerium (oleander)
Ngaio
Ninebark
Oak
Olive
Plumbago
Rhus
Rose
Rosemary
Tamarisk
Tecoma
Wattles

PERENNIALS

Arctotis
Argemone
Artemesia
Bergamot
Cardoon
Carnation
Digitalis (foxglove)
Echium
Euphorbia
Flax
Gaillardia grandiflora
Glacium
Hesperis
Honesty
Honeysuckle
Iberis
Iceplant
Iris
Jack-in-the-pulpit
Jasminum
Kalanchoe
Kniphofia
Oriental poppy
Pandorea
Penstemon
Romneya
Salvia
Scabiosa
Strelitzia
Ugni molinae and *U. montana*
Ursinia
Verbascum
Xeronema (Poor Knights lily)
Zea
Zinnia
Zygocactis

BULBS, CORMS AND TUBERS

Agapanthus
Belladonna
Freesia
Gladiolus
Nerine
Watsonia
Zephyranthes

CLIMBERS

Campsis radicans
Hedera (ivy)
Ipomoea (morning glory)
Kennedia nigricans and *K. rubicunda*
Pea (varieties)
Thunbergia (varieties)
Wisteria

HERBS

Dittany
Oregano
Sage (both edible and ornamental)
Thyme
Valerian

Pests and diseases

Pests begin their invasions in earnest in December, encouraged by the warmer weather and abundant foliage. Whitefly appear in legions during December, sucking the sap of ornamentals, tomatoes and other vegetables. They can do considerable damage and should be treated quickly by using either a Safers spray or similar organic product, soapy water, or Nature's Way natural derris dust. Edible crops are best treated with organic sprays as they will not harm bees, which are essential to the pollination process.

Aphids, thrips and mites also suck the sap from a whole range of ornamentals and vegetables. Leaves will begin to show silver, white and brown speckled patches before they fall off and deplete the plant. A pyrethrum-based spray will effectively remove most of these pests.

Red spider mite is a destructive pest during the drier months. It sucks the leaves of ornamentals as well as vegetables until the leaf changes colour and seems to be covered on the underside with a coat of red dust. This pest can stunt and kill plants; a powerful miticide such as Super Shield is necessary to stop it.

> **TASKS FOR DECEMBER**
> - Remove all spent flower heads from flowering plants, especially sweet peas, to encourage extra flowering.
> - Cut back or pinch out chrysanthemums to increase autumn flowering.
> - Plant dahlia tubers.
> - Lift tulips, daffodils and hyacinths, clean them and store in a cool, airy place.
> - Mulch as much of the garden as possible to conserve moisture.
> - Provide regular moisture and shade for young seedlings.
> - Mulch all vegetables with compost, grass clippings, sawdust, and the like to conserve moisture.
> - Water in the evening or early morning. One good watering once a week is better than a little each day.
> - Water with a hand-held hose rather than a sprinkler. This will help to conserve our summer water supply.

BELOW: Use a spray hose to water vegetables and ornamentals.

Scale is another warm-weather pest that deforms and debilitates plants. It is difficult to cure. Use systemic insecticide with the addition of a little Conqueror Oil.

Caterpillars are another problem in the summer garden. Try sprinkling them with kitchen flour or spraying with an insecticide such as Mavrik, Target or Orthene. Snails and slugs are more active in cool, wet weather but can also cause considerable damage now.

The porina moth is active until December, by which time it will have laid many eggs, each programmed to become a destructive lawn-devouring grub. Diazinon prills (grains) are an effective deterrent, but they are also toxic to animals and humans and should be used with great care. A safer organic spray such as Thuricide is also effective in stopping this pest.

Red thread is a fungal growth that produces a mat of red-and-brown threads that quickly invade the lawn. Spraying with a systemic fungicide is useful in the control of this pest.

Many fungal diseases, such as black spot and mildew on roses, are prominent at this time of year. Spray with a fungicide, and burn infected material.

The flower garden

Summer tasks such as mowing and watering are important, and they will be much easier to do if you have planned well during the cold, wet winter months, and used easy-care plants, leaving you time to enjoy the garden over the festive season.

Sowing
Many seeds sown at this time will, if they are kept well watered, grow quickly. In areas not subject to early frosts, aster, Canterbury bells, cineraria, cosmos, foxglove, hollyhock, Iceland poppy, larkspur, polyanthus, sweet William and zinnia can still be sown for late autumn flowering.

Propagation and division
Cuttings taken from dahlias and chrysanthemums will develop rapidly if they are given applications of liquid fertiliser. Cistus, cuphea, daphne, fuchsia, hydrangea, lavender and poinsettia cuttings taken now will grow.

Planting
In most regions plantings can be made of ageratum, amaranthus, aster, balsam, celosia, cleome, cosmos, dianthus, marigold, petunia, phlox, rudbeckia, salvia and zinnia. New lavender hybrids, such as *Lavandula* 'Innocence', will flower all summer if planted in a warm, sunny position.

Bulbs, corms and tubers
Some bulbs need to be planted during early summer. Some are frost-tender while others are either summer-growers or summer dormant. Amaryllis (belladonna or naked lady) is a South African native that prefers a frost-free climate. It flowers in late summer and autumn. Soft pink, rose, mauve or white, it is highly scented and makes an excellent cut flower.

Caladiums (elephant ears), prized for their tropical foliage, are suitable for planting now. South African bulbs, such as polyxena, corymbosa, schizostylis, dierama, and the bright red anomatheca can also be planted.

December is an excellent time for planting dahlia tubers, especially in areas where the soil is poorly

FLOWERS TO PLANT NOW

SOW THESE SEEDS

Ageratum	Hollyhock
Alyssum	Gypsophila
Amaranthus	Honesty (lunaria)
Aquilegia	Larkspur
Aster	Lupin
Bellis perennis	Marigold
Calendula	Mignonette
Candytuft	Nasturtium
Carnation	Petunia
Cineraria	Polyanthus
Coleus	Poppy (Iceland)
Cornflower	Snapdragon
Cosmos	Sweet pea
Dahlia	Sweet William
Delphinium	Viola
Dianthus	Wallflower
Foxglove	Zinnia

PLANT THESE SEEDLINGS

- Ageratum
- Aster
- Balsam
- Celosia
- Cleome
- Cosmos
- Dianthus
- Gypsophila
- Marigold
- Petunia
- Phlox
- Polyanthus
- Rudbeckia
- Salpiglossis
- Salvia
- Scabiosa
- Snapdragon
- Statice
- Zinnia

PLANT THESE BULBS, RHIZOMES AND TUBERS

Achimenes	Freesia
Amaryllis	Fritillaria
(belladonna lilies)	Lycoris
Anemone	Nerine
Anomatheca	Polyxena
Caladium	Oxalis
Colchicum	Schizostylis
Corymbosa	Snowdrops
Crocus	Sternbergia
Dahlia	
Dierama	
Cyclamen	

LEFT: *Lavandula* 'Innocence'
BELOW: *Dahlia* 'Maltby Shirley'

drained and the spring subject to late frosts. They are a versatile and underrated flower. *Dahlia* 'Maltby Shirley', bred in New Zealand by Cunnard in 1989, is a splendid cut flower and striking in the garden border.

Anemones planted in late December will produce a winter flowering. Freesias planted now, either as seed or as corms, will develop into flowering plants by spring. Bulbs of autumn-flowering colchicums, crocuses, cyclamen and sternbergia planted in early December will wake into rapid growth. Colchicums have large crocus-like flowers without any leaves from March to May. *Colchicum autumnale* will produce approximately a dozen flowers per corm. *Sternbergia lutea* or autumn daffodil looks like a golden yellow crocus. To grow well it needs a sunny, sheltered well-drained spot.

Plant care

Unless we begin in early summer the tasks of restraining rampant growth, such chores as shaping trees, and trimming back shrubs, perennials and annuals will become a never-ending and unwinnable battle during

DEAD-HEADING AND CUTTING BACK AFTER FLOWERING

Dead-head regularly	Cut back to ground level after main flowering
Ageratum	
Alyssum	
Antirrhinum	*Aconitum napellus*
Argenome	*Campanula persicifolia*
Calendula	Coreopsis
Centaurea	Delphinium
Cosmos	Echinacea (cone flower)
Dahlia	Geranium
Digitalis (foxglove)	Geum
Erigeron	Lupin
Eschscholzia (California poppy)	Nemesia
	Oriental poppy
Helichrysum	Pansy
Iberis	
Phlox	
Scabiosa	
Sweet pea	
Verbena	
Viola	

January and February. A little careful trimming back and dead-heading of spring-flowering plants such as sweet pea will encourage them to continue producing blooms into the early summer. They are generous plants — the more you pick, the more they flower. The frost-hardy *Dianthus chinensis* (Chinese Pink) hybrids such as 'Strawberry Parfait' will flower all summer long if they are fed, watered and regularly dead-headed. Foxgloves will continue to flower if they are cut back.

Many other flowering plants will only give a second flush of flowers if they are cut to the ground immediately after flowering. These include delphiniums, geraniums, lupin and oriental poppies.

Sometimes a continuous vibrant mass of flowers day after day in brilliant summer sunlight can become irritating and we may yearn for the simpler, quieter greens of foliage. Trimming flowers off some prolific blooming plants, such as Shirley poppies and Dame's rocket (hesperis), calms the overall effect.

Hedges

Trimming the hedge in early December is a good way to make the most of the summer growth. Careful and regular pruning will soon produce a dense, strong hedge. Any hedge will respond to an occasional feeding, either foliar spray or fertiliser, and its colour and general appearance will be greatly enhanced.

Lawns

To keep a lawn in top condition during December it must be cut at least once a week. Raise the cutting blades of the mower to reduce stress on the summer lawn. Regular mowing will produce a dense, firm surface, and will also rid the lawn of large weeds and daisies that can threaten and overwhelm finer grasses. Dig out broad-leafed weeds by hand if necessary. A good soaking three times a week will keep lawns green. A nitrogenous fertiliser can be used to boost colour and density throughout the year. Lawns should be fed with urea at least once over summer. This fertiliser is cheap but must be spread on a rainy evening and also watered in well, otherwise the lawn will be damaged by unsightly burns.

The edible garden

Although vegetable gardening is one of the most demanding types of gardening, it is also one of the most rewarding. Fresh vegetables straight from the garden have a quality that you can't buy, and give immense satisfaction.

Sowing

Another crop of either dwarf or runner beans can be sown in northern areas. As December is the beginning of the dry season, any fine seed is best sown in trays where moisture can be more easily controlled.

Planting

In warm northern areas it is still possible to plant beetroot, broccoli, capsicum, carrots, celery, fennel, lettuce, marrows, melon, parsnip, peas, pumpkin, silver beet, sweet corn, tomatoes, turnip and even zucchini. Sweet corn, kumara, beans and sweet peppers may be better planted in the middle of the month in the south and then only in sheltered warm microclimates. In southern gardens many crops needing a long maturing time and hotter weather are not suitable for planting now. Beets (red and silver), carrots, cauliflower, celery, lettuces, parsnips, radishes, spring onions and swedes can be planted out now.

Harvesting

The beetroot, cabbage, carrot, lettuce, peas, radish, onions, silver beet and spinach that you planted in late August, September and early October will now be starting to crop. Early potatoes such as the cold-hardy black potato or urenika and strawberries planted in late winter will be ready now. For many long-maturing vegetables such as aubergines, beans, capsicum, and tomatoes this will be the only cropping time in southern gardens. Garlic,

VEGETABLES TO PLANT NOW

SOW THESE SEEDS

Artichoke (globe)	Marrow
Aubergine (eggplant)*	Melon*
Beetroot	Onion
Broad beans*	Parsnip
Broccoli*	Pea
Cabbage	Pumpkin
Capsicum*	Silver beet
Carrot*	Spinach*
Cauliflower	Squash*
Celery*	Swede
Cucumber*	Sweet corn*
Fennel	Tomato*
Kumara*	Turnip
Leek	Zucchini*
Lettuce	

PLANT THESE SEEDLINGS

Artichoke (globe)	Lettuce
Cabbage	Onion
Capsicum*	Silver beet
Cauliflower	Spring onion
Leek	

*Only practicable in warm areas

LEFT: *Dianthus chinensis* 'Strawberry Parfait'
BELOW: Red onion, *Allium cepa*

traditionally planted at mid-winter (22 June), can now be harvested and those asparagus so carefully composted and manured in autumn will, in colder districts, still be cropping in December. Onions planted in the autumn should be lifted as soon as their tops fall over. Storing of onions and garlic is best carried out in a cool, shady, dry place. They can be plaited into strings, stored in old stockings or laid out on wire racks to dry.

Fruit

Many fruit trees will have set heavy crops of fruit by this time. December is the month of the earliest stone fruit and berries. Blueberries, boysenberries, cherries, peaches, plums and raspberries are just beginning their season. Cherries are in full flush during December and January and apricots continue bearing well into February. It is better to hand-thin fruit to ensure that only the best of the crop is left to develop.

BELOW: Urenika, Maori potato
RIGHT: Ripe cherries of *Prunus avium* 'Sonnet'
FAR RIGHT: Moorpark apricots

Apple trees should be sprayed in December with Carbaryl for codling moth if crops are to mature satisfactorily. The moths will just be starting to lay their eggs on the fruit, so acting now is essential to protect the coming crop. Plum, pear and quince trees will need to be protected from pear slug. This pest is small, slimy and black and in a very short space of time it can easily defoliate an entire tree. A spraying of Target will help remove this pest. If you prefer an organic approach, a spray of derris or pyrethrum can be used instead. As derris is toxic to earthworms some care is needed when applying it. Plum and peach trees are often affected in the summer by curly leaf (bladder plum). The crop as well as the leaves can be severely affected. Unfortunately, once the symptoms are visible it is too late to spray. The same applies to brown rot, which affects stone fruit at this time of the year.

Lemon and other citrus trees may need spraying for wax scale. This pest looks like small, scaly, brown lumps on the plant, which can be removed by hand or with a small brush. Where infestations are very heavy, Conqueror Oil applied at summer strength will effectively remove this pest. A little Target added to this

spray will effectively kill smaller scale. Feeding and watering of citrus will help a good set of fruit. A general citrus fertiliser should be applied either now in colder areas or in the autumn and spring in warmer parts. A mixture of three parts blood and bone to one part dried blood applied at a rate of one kilo per year of the tree's growth will produce excellent results. A layer of compost applied at the tree base (but not touching the trunk) will help conserve moisture.

Grapevines should be stopped in their growth by pinching out the excess growth beyond a point where the fruit has set. The training of grapevines is important to prevent tangling and where there is an excess of set bunches of fruit, they should be thinned. The final grape crop will be much improved by this treatment.

Gooseberries need to be sprayed with a fungicide or the crop will be destroyed.

Botrytis or mildew is another destructive fungal disease that will destroy grape and berry crops. Guardall is a good spray for the prevention of botrytis. These sprays, if applied early, will cure the problem. There is a fourteen-day withholding period for these sprays, during which time the crop should not be eaten. For organic gardeners, sulphur in a powdered form can be placed in an old stocking and shaken over the affected parts. A mild vinegar and water spray can also be effective in slowing this disease. Spray Fix is sometimes added to the spray mix to make it adhere. A little milk added to sprays will also help them stick and withstand light showers.

Spraying should be done either in the early morning or at night. Spraying in the heat of the day will burn the plants. When using systemic sprays note that for vegetable and fruit crops there is a withholding period in which they should not be eaten.

December features

Pohutukawa

The pohutukawa (*Metrosideros excelsa*), once familiarly referred to as the New Zealand Christmas tree, is sensational in flower; spectacular enough to supplant the holly from its position as a symbol of regeneration and rebirth and having the added advantage in this hemisphere of perfect timing. It flowers at just the right

LEFT: Pohutukawa, Metrosideros excelsa
BELOW FROM LEFT: Elderberries Sambucus nigra; Alstroemeria pulchella

time. Given space and a warm climate these crimson, vermilion or cream-green treasures make grand garden trees. The golden pohutukawa (*Metrosideros fulgens aurata*) is a most gentle shade of green-yellow, an ideal garden specimen. The southern rata (*Metrosideros umbellata*) provides an excellent alternative for those in the deep south of New Zealand.

Perhaps the most unusual one maintains that if you stand under an elder on a mid-summer evening, you will see the king of the fairies and all his retinue pass by.

The golden-leafed and the cut-leafed elder are both very desirable plants for the garden. Although prone to sunburn, if planted in a shady corner of the garden they will flourish and bring light to a dark corner. The common elder *Sambucus nigra* produces flowers that can be made into champagne, cordial or even wine. Elderberry wine is an excellent pick-me-up during the winter months and the berries also make a tasty and colourful jam.

Elder

The first flowers of the elder (sambucus) appear in October and continue until late January. The elder is a useful and very decorative plant — the rich green sturdy leaves ably support flat discs of pure white flowers. Some elders need a cool climate yet others, particularly the ornamental varieties, prefer frost-free growing conditions. At mid-summer this plant creates a cool atmosphere in the garden.

Many legends and tales of magic surround the elder. They are said to protect the home from misfortune.

Alstroemeria

Although a South American native, *Alstroemeria pulchella* was once known as the New Zealand Christmas flower. These adaptable plants flourish if they are given reasonably well-drained soil in a shady position where they can spread freely. They make very good cut flowers and new hybrids have become popular garden plants. The flowers of *A. pulchella* are dark red, tipped with green and spotted with brown, and bloom in time for Christmas. It needs to be grown in an area where it can spread freely without crowding out other plants.

January

Temperature and climate

By this time in most regions, it has become very hot and dry. As the month of January progresses, southern parts of the country will begin to experience a drop in the evening temperature. Northern areas of the country will be experiencing dry, settled weather — still warm enough to allow a final planting of some of the more tender crops as well as those needing a long maturing period.

Food and water

Feeding plants gives an important boost to growth in January. Dry conditions will slow growth down unless

LEFT: Globe artichoke, *Cynara scolymus*
FROM LEFT: Sage, *Salvia officinalis* and basil *Ocimum basilicum*

adequate moisture and food are provided. Any growth during this month will provide plants with the bulk and stamina to survive the winter. Using organic fertilisers appeals to many of us, yet, although they make us feel that we are doing our bit for the environment, there is not much evidence to suggest that they are any more effective in reducing nitrates in the environment, are better at growing tastier fruit, help plants resist disease clippings, vegetable scraps, tea leaves, shredded waste, in fact anything of an organic nature can be safely added to the compost heap. Seaweed is a most useful addition to the compost heap and greatly aids the growth of tomatoes and the vegetable garden generally. Collect this material together in a shady hidden part of the garden until you have a large heap several metres square. Hiring a mulcher can quickly reduce the collected material to a fine size. These small pieces will rot more quickly. Animal manure (pig, cow, horse or chicken) added to the compost combines with the plant matter to make an ideal soil conditioner.

or are better for plants, than processed chemical fertiliser. A garden compost made with the addition of well-rotted animal or poultry manure is one remedy for soil that is not producing as much or as well as you require. An application of artificial fertiliser can be used to give a quick boost to dull soil. The committed organic gardener can then proceed by slowly adding the compost while cutting down on artificial fertiliser with no loss of yield.

Compost making is easy and many different methods exist. Spent plants from any season, grass and hedge

All compost heaps require warm, moist conditions to speed the breakdown of organic matter. They also require good air circulation so that the breakdown of plant material can occur in the absence of anaerobic micro-organisms that will cause putrefaction, rather than decomposition, to occur when no air is present. Aeration is achieved by turning the compost periodically with a pitchfork. Artificial activators which speed the growth of the micro-organisms that make the compost are also available.

If a heap is well made, temperatures of 70°C can

easily be reached. These temperatures will kill most weed seeds and other unwelcome guests in the mixture. A compost heap 2 metres wide by 2 metres high will produce a reasonable amount of compost. If all the ingredients of the heap are chopped into approximately 4-cm bits and mixed thoroughly together and then placed in 20-cm layers divided by a thin layer of garden soil, a dusting of lime, a little urea, superphosphate or blood and bone, decomposition will be rapid.

A well-made heap should be stacked firmly but not compressed heavily for best results. A simple method for making small amounts of compost is to place your chosen material in a black plastic bag, slightly moisten it and then place all this inside a clear plastic bag tied at the top. Left in the full heat of the summer sun excellent weed-free compost will quickly result in about three weeks. High temperatures are reached using this method, killing weed seeds and fungus spores.

In biodynamic composting a set of six herbs is used to control the fermentation of composts and manures.

Stinging nettle (*Urtica dioica*), dandelion, oak bark and leaves, yarrow (*Achillea millefolium*), chamomile and valerian are all excellent compost makers and soil conditioners and can be added to the heap either as a liquid or as foliage.

Commercially available compost bins — usually large, green or black upright plastic containers open to the soil below and with a lid on top — can be used, as can the boarded twin-box system which used to be a feature of nearly every Kiwi back yard.

By January, water is an ongoing need in nearly all gardens. By now you should already have decided on your mode of operation (watering can, hose, soak-hose, or automated system), and all you will need to do is carry out this chore regularly and check to ensure that individual plants are receiving what they require; remember the danger of treating all plants alike. Some vegetables require a lot of water to produce a satisfactory crop, while others require very little (see page 164). Others require water only at specific times.

Bamboo requires a lot of water now during its growing period, as do many tropical and lush-growing plants such as dahlias, ferns, hostas and many others. Do not forget that lawns and hedges also enjoy their

BELOW: *Salvia argentea*
BELOW RIGHT: Parsnip, *Pastinaca sativa*

share of this life-giving liquid. A soak-hose around the foot of a hedge is a simple answer to hedge care and moveable sprinklers will look after the lawn.

Watering should ideally be carried out either (or both) in the early morning or late evening, when temperatures are generally cooler and when the vegetation is not being subjected to the fierce heat of the sun. If you water during the middle of the day, a great deal of the water will evaporate before ever reaching the roots of the plant you are tending.

Your daily or twice-daily perambulations of the property are ideal for checking on the continuing health of the plants; small changes in growth, early signs of disease and readiness for harvest or pruning can be observed. Some plants have a clear preference for water in the early morning rather than in the evening, as they then have the warmth of the day ahead, rather than the chill of the night, to assimilate the water. Fuchsias, however, prefer a soak in the evening and enjoy water on their leaves. Many felted plants, such as *Salvia argentea*, resent any water on their foliage; their thick hairy leaves quickly become saturated and will rot if they get too much water. Basil, on the other hand, enjoys being watered in the full heat of the summer sun. And unlike marrows and pumpkins, basil enjoys having its leaves sprinkled with copious quantities of water. For many plants, however, drops of water on their leaves in the summer sun act as magnifying lenses that concentrate the heat and cause burnt, brown patches.

If you are away from the garden for any length of time during the holiday season, you will need to make arrangements to have the garden watered. This may be something a neighbouring child will be happy to do in return for a small reward. Potted plants inside and out are particularly vulnerable at this time of year because they cannot send their roots down in search of deep-lying water supplies in the soil and consequently have no ability of their own to survive the dry season. It may be possible to leave them with a friend to plant-sit for you while you are away on holiday. Alternatively, place them in the bath on a thick layer of wet newspaper, or stand them on bricks in a bath filled with several inches of water.

At times when there are water shortages and rationing is in force, we need to think of ways to prevent

TASKS FOR JANUARY

- Keep lawns and pot plants well watered. A healthy lawn will resist the invasion of weeds that may occur when lawns are weakened by drought.
- Spray roses at regular intervals to control black spot, powdery mildew and insect pests.
- Spent flower heads should be cut back regularly to encourage new growth and extra flowering.
- Feed the garden to encourage growth.
- Continue mulching the soil with any suitable material; even newspaper will work effectively.
- Water with a handheld hose to conserve what in many areas is a dwindling resource.
- Spray pip and stone fruit for fungal diseases, caterpillars and codling moth.
- Treat porina damage on lawns with Diazinon.
- Protect small seedlings from slug and snail damage.
- Use Nature's Way natural derris dust to prevent caterpillar damage.

BELOW: Hoeing will ensure water is easily absorbed into the soil, and also conserves moisture by suppressing thirsty weeds.

> **TIPS FOR WATERING**
> - Thoroughly wet the whole root depth of the soil. If necessary check by digging a hole three hours after watering to assess soil moisture.
> - Apply water to the base of the stem; do not water the rest of the soil.
> - When watering crops just water a narrow strip along the stems.
> - Space plants more widely than usual if drought conditions look likely, so that each plant can be administered to individually without plants robbing water from one another.
> - Shelter crops from drying winds by using shrubs or wind cloth.
> - Refer to the table on page 164 for watering requirements of specific vegetables. Some vegetables require little water to bear well, whereas others require plenty of water when the fruit begins to swell. Still others like to be 'puddled in' at planting and will then grow with little extra water.

plants drying out. Mulch (see page 36 for tips on mulching) can be a most effective aid; a mulch put down in November or December could be added to now for extra protection. The recycling of household water from baths and washing, although a chore, can mean the difference between survival and demise for many plants. If you spray this soapy water on foliage, it has the additional benefit of controlling aphids and adding extra nutrients to the soil.

Hoeing is another conservation technique that can be used to make the most of any moisture applied to the soil, as loose, friable soil will absorb moisture more readily than a hard surface. Regular hoeing will also help suppress weed growth that can steal moisture from more desirable garden plants.

Pests and diseases

Along with the seasonal abundance in the vegetable garden goes a parallel increase in activity within the animal kingdom — larger numbers of hungry garden pests will now rampage through our plants, unless we have some means of controlling them. Leaf rollers, mealy bugs and spittle bugs are just some of the many insect pests that are out to devour the garden.

Ridding the garden of pests or learning to tolerate them is a matter of personal philosophy. You may take the position that if your garden is abundant and well cared for, you can spare a few morsels for the odd bug or bird, and use some organic sprays that stop short of killing any bugs, particularly if you are mindful of the beneficial effects of such insects as bees. Or you may throw caution completely to the wind and opt for the most lethal spray you can find, safe in the knowledge that it will do the job. However, even Nature's Way natural derris dust, though organic, can cause skin

BELOW FROM TOP: Leaf roller on a bergenia leaf; mealy bugs at the base of a flax plant; spittle bugs.

rashes and should be used only with gloves and in still conditions. The active ingredient in derris dust is rotenone, a natural compound found in a number of tropical and subtropical plants.

The flower garden

Many flowering bulbs add interest to the summer garden. Dahlias, though a little sniffed at by some gardeners, are deservedly popular. They are available in a huge range of colours and types, are easy to grow, are good for picking and flower profusely.

> **MAKING YOUR OWN GARDEN SPRAYS**
> **GARLIC SPRAY**
> Making your own garlic spray is easy and if it is used regularly it is most effective. Weekly sprayings will bring speedy results.
>
> YOU WILL NEED:
> 2 whole heads garlic (about 10 cloves each)
> 1 teaspoon kerosene
> 1 litre water
> 1 tablespoon grated pure soap or Lux soap flakes
>
> TO PREPARE THE SPRAY:
> Crush the garlic with the kerosene. Boil the water with the soap flakes until they are dissolved. Cool, then add the garlic and kerosene mixture. Strain and store in a sealed jar or bottle.
>
> To use, dilute one part mixture to one part water. Add a little Conqueror Oil at summer strength or milk to help the spray stick on the foliage.
>
> **RHUBARB SPRAY**
> Substitute the garlic with the boiled liquid from 12 rhubarb leaves. Add 1 litre of water and follow the same method. Rhubarb leaves are highly toxic; the high oxalic acid content of these leaves makes them unpalatable to insect pests.

Roses should be watched for attacks of mildew and black spot. Potash can help to combat black spot but it pays to spray at the first sign of the disease and also to remove any fallen leaves from the soil, as they will contaminate the plant. Now is also a good time to take cuttings from carnations.

Sowing

Seeds of dahlias sown now will grow quickly, forming small tubers for next season's flowering. Many seeds (such as stocks, wallflowers and Iceland poppies) if they are sown now will germinate and grow rapidly so that they become established before winter, and are ready for an early burst in spring. (See list on page 69.)

Planting

January is a good time to start planting into pots for winter colour. Ivy, pansies, polyanthus, sweet William and violas planted now will look most effective come late winter or early spring. Now is a good time to prepare some home-grown plant gifts for friends. It is possible to organise surprise plant gifts for almost any season. Polyanthus, for example, if planted now and given a little ongoing care, will have evolved into a glamorous potted garden by mid-August.

Bulbs, corms and tubers

Some plants have an incredibly accurate internal clock. The tropical *Hymenocallis littoralis* (the spider or Queen Emma lily) has this facility. It flowers each year almost to the day. It requires high summer temperatures and some humidity to do well. The first flower opens with a star shape and within two hours it has become long and spider-like, the petals lengthening almost as you watch them.

Other bulbs that should be flowering now include hippeastrums, arisaemas, alliums, alstroemeria, tigridias, crinums, standard gladioli such as *Gladiolus* 'Lowland Queen', dahlias, galtonia and lilies. *Tigridia pavonia* (jockey's cap) is a brightly coloured Mexican native that blooms in summer. Tigridias are tropical plants preferring a warm, frost-free climate. In frosty areas, the bulbs should be lifted and stored during winter or the plants grown in a greenhouse. They need ample watering and a sunny, well-drained position.

January is the time to check any stored bulbs for pest infestation, disease or mould. A light dusting of Nature's Way natural derris dust, flowers of sulphur or an insecticide/fungicide powder will help limit the spread of these diseases.

Water planted bulbs well and then mulch heavily. All spring-flowering bulbs will have become dormant by now. Those that have become crowded should be lifted, cleaned and the best bulbs selected for replanting in soil that has been fertilised with a bulb food or a little bone dust. When buying bulbs inspect them carefully. Avoid buying bulbs that are under-sized or shrivelled, or show

BELOW FROM LEFT: *Gladiolus* 'Lowland Queen'; *Tigridia pavonia*; *Nerium oleander*

In colder areas, it is time to plant bulbs. Agapanthus, belladonna, clivia, crinum, iris rhizomes, lachenalia, nerine, sternbergia and watsonia will develop quickly in December. Agapanthus prefer a subtropical or tropical climate (and indeed thrive to the point of being a pest in the north). Most of the plants mentioned above will do best in a warm climate, with the exception of the iris, which will rapidly form strong clumps in colder areas.

signs of damage, have soft or wet patches indicating fungal disease, or are bruised from rough handling. A guideline when buying bulbs could be to choose the best varieties for your situation rather than buying on impulse and then trying to find somewhere to plant them. Buy bulbs as soon as they are in the shops and only buy those that are firm and resilient, not rock-hard or soft, and avoid buying those bulbs that have already begun to grow. An exception to these rules are lilium bulbs that have roots on the dormant bulb, and crocuses and tulips that often have small shoots.

Picking

Picking flowers and taking them inside to enjoy is one of the great joys of gardening. During January many flowering plants are in bloom and flowers are readily available for picking either as gifts or for the house. Good planning will ensure a balance between plants bearing flowers suitable for picking, while still providing blooms best left in the garden; but not all flowers make good picked blooms for the vase.

Picking flowers in the cool of the evening and standing them up to their necks in a bucket of water

FLOWERS TO PLANT NOW

SOW THESE SEEDS	PLANT THESE SEEDLINGS	PLANT THESE BULBS, CORMS AND TUBERS	
Ageratum	Aster	Agapanthus	Lachenalia
Alyssum	Celosia	Belladonna	Leucojum (snowflake)
Cineraria*	Cosmos*	Clivia	Lycoris*
Cyclamen	Gazania*	Crinum	Narcissus
Dahlia	Gerbera	Colchicum	(plant now in cold
Linaria	Ivy	Crocus (autumn-flowering)	climates, later in warm
Lupin	Nasturtium*	Cyclamen	climates)
Mignonette	Petunia*	Eranthis (winter aconite)	Nerine
Nasturtium*	Phlox	Erythronium	Oxalis*
Nicotiana*	Rudbeckia	Freesia	Sternbergia
Opium poppy	Salpiglossis	Fritillaria	Watsonia*
Pansy	Sunflower*	Galanthus	
Poppy, Iceland	Viscaria	Gladiolus	
Primula	Zinnia*	Habranthus*	
Stock		Ipheion	
Sweet pea		Iris	
Viola			
Wallflower	*Only practicable in warm areas		

overnight will ensure that they last when placed in vases inside. If flowers wilt after being picked the vase can be filled with scalding water and the flowers placed in it. The results of this apparently sadistic action are remarkable. Flower stems can also be crushed to prolong flowering display.

Alstroemeria, artemesia, asters, buddleja, chrysanthemum, cleome and cornflower are some of the many plants flowering now. Hydrangeas such as the pure white *Hydrangea macrophylla* 'Madame Emile Mouillère' (bred by Mouillère in 1909) or the pale pink *H. m.* 'Mrs Kumiko' with huge round heads of creamy pink flowers in summer and autumn kniphofia (red-hot pokers), lavender, oleander, phlox, rudbeckia, shasta daisies and sunflowers are ideal flowers for picking. Scented blooms such as gardenia, jasmine, lemon, liliums and orange can either be brought inside in pots for short periods, picked, or planted near a window or door where the perfumes can drift into the house. *Onopordum acanthium* (Scotch thistle) is a very prickly plant but its silver leaves make it a most decorative plant in the garden or it can be picked and placed in a vase.

BELOW: Scotch thistle, *Onopordum acanthium*

Plant care

This is a month when rampant growth and flowering in the garden must be kept in check. Plants left to run riot will soon become tangled brown heaps. To avoid this happening constant nipping-back of the bits that are going to seed will extend the life and flowering period of your plants. All early-flowering annuals will be past their best. They should be removed and the ground prepared with compost for the next plantings. But do go easy with the hoe and secateurs when tidying up. It is easy to cut through that precious clematis vine or hoe in those pansies self-seeded from last year's plants.

Lawns

Continue mowing grass weekly or more often when it is growing rapidly. Trim edges to keep the lawn looking good. If red thread appears (pale brown patches of grass with red needles on grass leaves), apply a nitrogenous fertiliser such as aluminium sulphate, applied at 15 g per square metre. This fertiliser can burn if not watered in well. Adding fertiliser will make the grass grow more, so you will need to mow it more often. A healthy lawn will survive dry periods, although it may look a bit brown. But if you prefer a green, perfect lawn during the summer months, you will need to mow least twice a week and water at least three times a week.

The edible garden

Now is the time to think ahead and prepare for the autumn and winter garden. Keep moisture up to all seeds and plants and if necessary cover with frost cloth to prevent burning and excessive moisture evaporation. Mulching the soil also helps to limit moisture evaporation.

Sowing

Sowing of beans, cucumber, marrow and melons is still possible in the warmer areas of the country. Many crops requiring a long maturing time should not now be sown except in the most sheltered and warm areas. It is now time to sow those vegetables that will quickly establish themselves before the onset of winter; cabbage and cauliflower sown now will be ready to transplant in eight weeks. Some varieties are better suited to warmer areas, while others, such as Savoy, are best suited to areas with cold winters. White butterfly caterpillar and other insect pests need to be guarded against. Brussels sprouts can still be sown and will flourish in areas that experience winter frosts. Lettuce seed can be sown for an autumn salad vegetable. A succession of sowings of autumn and winter vegetables will ensure a regular supply.

Planting

A wide variety of vegetables can be planted out now. If they are kept well watered and fed, seedlings will grow rapidly and yield an extra crop before autumn. Beetroot, broccoli, Brussels sprouts, carrots, cauliflower, cucumber, leeks and lettuce planted now will all benefit from the warm weather and grow rapidly.

Bay, lavender, lemon verbena, rosemary and sage can all be grown from 5–7 cm cuttings taken from semi-hardwood. Germander, horehound, lemon balm, marjoram, orris root, salad burnet, sorrel, tansy, violets and yarrow will grow rapidly from division and now is the time to do it.

VEGETABLES TO PLANT NOW

SOW THESE SEEDS	PLANT THESE SEEDLINGS
Bean*	
Beetroot	Beetroot
Broccoli	Broccoli
Brussels sprout	Brussels sprout
Cabbage	Cabbage
Cauliflower	Carrot
Celery*	Cauliflower
Cucumber*	Celery*
Leek	Cucumber
Lettuce	Leek
Marrow*	Lettuce
Melon*	Parsnip
Parsnip	Radish
Radish	Silver beet
Silver beet	
Swede	
Turnip	*Only practicable in warm areas

COMPANION PLANTING

Many plants have developed the ability to repel predatory insects intent on eating them and some have developed this special ability to a high degree. A mixture of these beneficial plants in the garden can give some degree of pest control. Some plants enjoy the company of others and will grow considerably better if they are planted together.

PLANTS THAT ARE HAPPIEST GROWING TOGETHER

Asparagus	Basil, parsley, tomatoes
Beans (climbing)	Cabbage, carrots, radishes, sweet corn
Beans (dwarf)	Beetroot, cucumber, potatoes, strawberries
Beetroot	Beans (dwarf), cabbage, lettuce, onions, silver beet
Broad beans	Sweet corn
Broccoli	Mint, rosemary
Cabbage	Beans (climbing), beetroot, mint, onions, peas, potatoes, radishes, sweet corn
Carrots	Beans (climbing), chives, leeks, lettuce, onions, peas, radishes, sweet corn, tomatoes
Celery	Cucumber, tomatoes
Cucumber	Beans (dwarf), celery, lettuce, potatoes, sweet corn
Leeks	Carrots
Lettuce	Beetroot, carrots, cucumber, onions, radishes, strawberries
Melons	Sweet corn
Onions	Beetroot, cabbage, carrots, lettuce, potatoes, silver beet
Peas	Cabbage, carrots, mint, radishes, turnip
Potatoes	Beans (dwarf), cabbage, cucumber, onions, sweet corn
Pumpkin	Sweet corn
Radishes	Beans (climbing), cabbage, carrots, lettuce, peas, sweet corn
Silver beet	Beetroot, onions
Spinach	Strawberries
Strawberries	Beans (dwarf), borage, lettuce, spinach
Sweet corn	Beans (climbing), broad beans, cabbage, carrots, cucumber, melons, potatoes, pumpkin, radishes
Tomatoes	Asparagus, basil, carrots, celery, chives, parsley
Turnip	Peas

PLANTS THAT PROTECT OTHERS FROM INSECT PESTS
- **Chives will keep nearby plants free from aphids**
- **Nasturtium keeps away aphids and whitefly**
- **Onions, parsley and rosemary will all keep away carrot rust fly**
- **Peppermint and sage will both deter white butterfly**
- **Pyrethrum daisies will keep spider mites and aphids at bay**
- **Rhubarb will protect surrounding plants from spider mite and whitefly**
- **Mints keep ants and aphids away**
- **Marigolds keep nematodes away from crops. They also keep the vegetable garden free from many insects**
- **Borage attracts bees into the garden and is an ideal companion plant to strawberries**

RIGHT: Black mulberry, *Morus nigra*

BELOW: Using colour theory to good effect: the bright orange *Eschscholzia californica* contrasts with the strong blue wall.

FAR RIGHT: The grey leaves of *Cynara cardunculus* are a useful foil for brighter colour.

Harvesting

By January we should be getting regular supplies of food from our vegetable gardens. In most regions, tomatoes will be ripening rapidly. Aubergines, French and runner beans, beetroot, capsicum, carrots, celery, cucumber, gherkins, melons, sweet corn and zucchini planted in October will be bearing heavy crops. Salad plants will be maturing rapidly and need to be replanted systematically in order to ensure a constant supply. Lettuce, radish and other quick-maturing salad crops planted at two-weekly intervals will provide a continuous supply. It is better to sow just ten or twelve seeds each time at two-weekly intervals rather than sowing all of them at once.

Fruit

Stone fruit trees in January will be covered in rapidly ripening fruit. Pip and stone fruit may need spraying with Saprol to control brown rot and black spot. Peach and nectarine trees can be pruned as soon as all the fruit is picked. Many fruit trees tend to bear well only once every two years, but summer pruning can help to break this cycle by forcing the tree to form fruiting spurs and turning the energy of the tree to the production of fruit rather than leaf buds. The process of summer pruning ensures heavier fruiting in the coming year.

Citrus trees need to be sprayed with a copper-based spray to prevent fungus from deforming and limiting the crop. Mulberry trees will be beginning to bear heavily. The fruit of this tree, once highly prized by the Romans, makes delicious pies, fruit salads and, if juiced, a sweet, delicious drink. A simple way to pick fruit such as mulberries is to place a fine net under the tree. Ripe mulberries are easily shaken from the tree. This procedure can be used to gather other soft fruit such as guavas, or nuts such as walnut and almond.

January features

Colour is a serious consideration in the garden. We all know the primary colours are red, blue and yellow and that the opposites or complementaries are green, orange and purple. Red flowers grown with a mixture of blue will create a visual impression of purple. This is particularly so if the colours being mixed are of the same or similar intensity. Yellow and red flowers will create the impression of orange, and yellow and blue mixes will create the impression of green. Opposites placed together create a visual clashing which intensifies the effect of each. Red will attempt to overpower a green if it shows the slightest deference in intensity; blue can affect orange; and violet reacts similarly with gold-yellow. Outstanding original solutions to problems of design may be found by consciously using such colour combinations in the garden. For example, other garden features, such as a painted wall, can be used to contrast with planting schemes.

An understanding of the relationships between colours and the way they work together is a useful tool in the gardener's bag of tricks. Gertrude Jekyll (1843–1932) was an enormously influential English garden designer who developed the so-called 'rules of colour'. These orginated in the theories of the French chemist Michel Eugène Chevreul (1786–1889), whose well-known colour circle or wheel is made up of the primary and secondary colours together with any number of tones between these, arranged in the order of the colours of the rainbow. Gertrude Jekyll believed that no colour stands alone, and it can only have real value if it is thought of in relation to the colours beside it.

The colours on the warm side of the circle (orange, red and yellow) attract, exhilarate and yet disturb the eye, while those in the cool side are calmer, restful and passive. Harmony is achieved when the relationship between colours on the wheel is close. Colours adjacent to each other on the circle give emotional harmony, as they are based either on the warm or cool side of the spectrum.

There can also be harmony between the opposite colours of the circle if they are balanced in intensity. This idea of a 'family' of colours has about it a sense of calm and rational order and to Jekyll, this was the way the garden and the world should be.

February

Temperature and climate

Early autumn approaches, and February sees the continuation of hot, dry, settled weather. However, regional differences will become more noticeable now, with cooler temperatures night and morning in more southern districts and even a danger of early frosts in vulnerable areas. Daylight hours have noticeably begun to draw in and in some areas there are hints of the autumn weather to come. Nationally, temperatures are still generally in the low twenties with areas in Hawke's Bay, Nelson and Central Otago reaching into the high twenties.

LEFT: *Chrysanthemum* syn. *Dendranthema* × *grandiflorum* 'Shamrock'
BELOW FROM LEFT: *Petunia* 'Blue Ensign'; *Zinnia elegans*; *Aster* × *frikartii*

Food and water

Apply fertiliser weekly to help the development of flowers and give a boost to vegetables such as pumpkins, melons and zucchini that are still growing towards their full size and ripeness. Fertilise seedlings with a liquid food, either homemade, or one of the commercial brands such as Phostrogen. Annuals such as petunia, to feeding. Well-rotted animal manure makes an ideal food and mulch. Chicken manure is a quick-acting fertiliser and all plants except acid lovers such as azaleas, camellias, daphne, rhododendrons and native plants respond quickly to this food. It is particularly useful for producing lush-leafed crops in the vegetable garden. All fertilising done now will ensure that plants have the energy to survive the winter and be ready to produce a fine autumn and spring flowering.

With the prolonged dry season, water continues to be an ongoing requirement for most of the garden. (See mulching techniques on page 36.) Dry plants are much

phlox, sunflowers, zinnias and other summer flowers will give an excellent show if they receive enough water as well as a little liquid food. Roses will respond to a good feeding at this time with a burst of flower lasting well into the autumn. In the late summer azaleas, camellias and rhododendrons should be fed monthly with a suitable plant food. You can use small quantities of acidic plant food or blood and bone, which should be well watered in. Azaleas respond well to both foliar and root feeding with liquid fertiliser. Summer-flowering hibiscus, mallow and oleander will also respond quickly

more susceptible to diseases such as mildew, rust and black spot, so it is important not to relax the watering routine in this often arid month. If water has to be rationed, the priority should go to the more recently planted and to the more shallow-rooted plants such as annual bedding plants, perennials and vegetables.

If a tree or shrub wilts at its growing tip there is an urgent need for extra water. Chrysanthemums such as the early spray type *Chrysanthemum* 'Red Wendy' and the fantasy types such as *C.* 'Shamrock' need plenty of water and side feeding with compost if the flowers are to

ABOVE: *Chrysanthemum* syn. *Dendranthema* × *grandiflorum* 'Red Wendy'

develop to their full potential. Dahlias also need a continual supply of water for good flower development and asters such as *Aster* × *frikartii* will flower until the first frosts if it is watered and fed regularly.

Pot plants need to be checked regularly. They rapidly dry out and will quickly succumb under such conditions. Regular watering, at least three times a week, is essential for the survival of your pot plants. Once again, vigilance pays off.

However, by this time there are other plants that should be allowed to dry out and die back. Irises, lewisias and many of the alpine plants do not like a lot of water during this period. Overwatering can be fatal for many plants, causing them to rot.

Pests and diseases

During this month the hot, dry weather puts plants and trees under great stress and they become susceptible to a wide range of diseases and pests. Vegetables, particularly tomatoes and sweet corn, are susceptible to fruit worm, which can cause a great deal of damage. Systemic sprays will certainly control this menace. However, these sprays are toxic to all living things, including humans. A withholding period is suggested with many systemic sprays, but even this may deter the more cautious from using them. A safer but more labour-intensive way of dealing with fruit worm is to remove them by hand from the plants at night when they come out to feed.

Hedges and trees shelter many pests and diseases that can easily spread to the garden. Although it may seem a radical undertaking to spray an entire hedge, it is often well worth cleaning out what may have become reservoirs of these diseases and pests. If the hedge is then prudently fed and cared for it will develop the strength to resist most future attacks.

However, spraying ornamentals and crops on a regular basis with systemic sprays is not desirable as this prevents a natural balance from becoming established in the garden. A programme of regular spraying may be necessary at first in a new or neglected garden, but after a season it should be possible to spray less frequently.

Indoor plants often suffer from scale, aphids and mealy bug especially during the warm summer months. Scale is difficult to remove. An oil-based spray, or a careful cleaning with a little vinegar and water on a rag or old toothbrush, should check the rapid spread of this unsightly and destructive pest. Aphids and mealy bugs can be hosed off with a sharp jet of water, washed off with soapy water or sprayed with a suitable insecticide.

Young seedlings need protection from slugs and snails, white butterfly caterpillars and thrips. Nature's Way natural derris dust is an organic pesticide derived from natural plant extracts. It controls chewing and sucking insect pests, including caterpillars and leaf hoppers, and it is also helpful in the control of aphids. Fungal diseases are also most prevalent during this season when plants are likely to suffer stress from lack of water and are being subjected daily to what can sometimes be quite extreme temperature changes. The same diseases abound in February as in the preceding month. Powdery mildew will continue to disfigure cucumbers, pumpkins, zucchini and marrows but by the end of the month it is not worth worrying about. The remaining crop will mature anyway.

The flower garden

Fuchsias are yet to return to general popularity yet they deserve to be more widely used than they are at present. Free flowering with beautiful pendulous flowers in a huge variety of colours, they are not only useful in the garden border but are also suitable for growing in pots and hanging baskets.

Sowing

Seed can very often be sown directly into the places where you want the plants to grow. However, in these dry summer days it may be wiser to sow into seed trays as the emerging seedlings can be nurtured more easily, protected from the burning rays of the sun, defended against slugs and snails and watered when they need it.

When sowing seed in a tray, scatter thinly and cover with a fine layer of soil. Water well after sowing, cover the tray with a sheet of newspaper topped with a sheet of glass and leave the seedlings to germinate. As soon as the tiny plants break the surface they can be given a weak solution of liquid food and gradually introduced to the light.

The highly scented alyssum can be sown directly into cracks in paths or planted in pots. Aquilegia or granny's bonnets (columbine) grow readily from seed. Selecting seed from the best-formed plants and flower types is a good way of keeping these flowers from becoming muddled in form and muddied in colour. They easily cross-pollinate but some also seem to stay true to form. Plant aquilegia in seed trays and you will have many small plants to set out in the spring.

> **TASKS FOR FEBRUARY**
> - Heel cuttings can be taken from many plants.
> - Cut and hang flowers for dry winter arrangements.
> - Tall plants such as artemesia, delphinium, lilies and sunflowers will require staking.
> - Protect tiny seedlings from the sun.
> - Water newly planted seeds and seedlings; germination and plant development will slow if they are allowed to dry out.
> - Protect seedlings with snail and slug killer, or place seed trays well above soil level.
> - Dust cabbages and cauliflowers with Nature's Way natural derris dust to prevent an invasion of white butterfly and caterpillars.

Calendula (English or pot marigold) is undeservedly unpopular and many new forms of this adaptable, tough and easy-to-grow plant exist. The Touch of Gold and Touch of Bronze series of calendula are well worth trying. See the list on page 79 for other seeds to sow, many of which can be sown directly into the soil. The coming autumn seems to signal to many plants that time is running out and nature's seed production factory is working overtime to ensure the survival of each species for the following season.

BELOW FROM LEFT: Sow seed thinly and cover with a fine layer of soil; gently water with a watering can; cover with a sheet of paper, then glass, until the seedlings germinate.

LEFT: Seedlings of marigold, *Calendula officinalis*.
BELOW: Taking heel cuttings of barberry, *Berberis thunbergii*.

Propagation and division

Heel or half-ripe cuttings can be taken from many plants and shrubs including abutilon (lantern tree), azalea, camellia, carnation, daphne, fuchsia, geranium, hebe (koromiko), lavender, karo, rhododendron and viburnum. Carefully tear a young, semi-developed shoot (including the 'heel') from older growth, dip in hormone rooting powder, a little willow water or honey, and plant in a pot in gritty soil. Enclose the cuttings and pot in a clear plastic bag until growth begins.

Planting

Planting out during this time of the year when the sun is at its hottest needs to be done with care to avoid damage to small, vulnerable plants. This task should not be carried out in the heat of the day. Water is essential at

FLOWERS TO PLANT NOW

SOW THESE SEEDS

Ageratum	Pansy
Alyssum	Polyanthus
Antirrhinum	Ranunculus*
(snapdragon)	Scabious
Aquilegia	Shirley poppy
Campanula	Stock
Candytuft	Sweet William
Carnation	Sweet pea
Cineraria*	Verbena
Cosmos*	Viola
Cornflower	Wallflower
Cyclamen	
Delphinium	
Dianthus	
Foxglove	
Gypsophila	
Hollyhock	
Honesty	
Iceland poppy	
Larkspur	
Lupin	
Marigold*	
Mignonette	
Nigella	

PLANT THESE SEEDLINGS

Aquilegia
Aster
Carnation
Cineraria*
Cornflower
Cosmos*
Dianthus
Dimorphotheca*
(African daisy)
Foxglove
Gerbera*
Hollyhock
Iceland poppy
Linaria
Lupin
Marigold*
Pansy
Primula
Statice
Stock
Sweet pea
Sweet William
Verbena
Viola
Wallflower

PLANT THESE BULBS, CORMS AND TUBERS

Agapanthus
Anemone
Babiana
Clivia*
Convallaria (lily of the valley)
Crocus
Daffodil
Dutch iris
Eranthis (winter aconite)
Erythronium
Fritillaria
Gladiolus
Habranthus
Hippeastrum
Hyacinth
Ixia
Lachenalia
Leucojum (snowdrop)
Lycoris
Nerine
Ranunculus
Sparaxis
Sprekelia
Sternbergia
Triteleia
Veltheimia

*Only practicable in warm areas

planting time. As you dig each hole, fill it with water and then 'puddle in' the young plants firmly into place. This process ensures that precious water resources are put to the best and most productive use. Alyssum sown as seed in mid-December is at the right stage to be planted out in the garden now, but can also be planted in pots. It has a powerful perfume in the summer garden.

Bulbs, corms and tubers

Anemone and ranunculus are best planted now so that they can develop a strong root system before winter. Ranunculus prefer warmer conditions than many bulbs and may be best planted in a sheltered, moist soil.

Plant care

Perennials that have flowered should be cut back and fed with compost to build stronger plants for the coming year and the ground prepared for the planting of spring flowering bulbs.

Lawns

If you are using seed to repair worn or thin areas in the lawn do it now or in early autumn when the soil may be more moist but not yet cold. The soil should be lightly forked before any bare patches are reseeded. Spray any emerging weeds before they seed with a weed specific spray. Thatch can be a problem in fine lawns; a layer of fibrous material forms between the green leaves and the soil. This problem is greatest in fine, dense lawns. Thatch usually makes grass roots vulnerable to drought, but it can also act like a sponge, keeping the soil saturated and encouraging disease. Regular raking, at least once a month, can help break up this layer and allow better circulation of air and water. Top-dressing the lawn with coarse sand, or a sand and soil mix, will break down the fibre. Brown patch or fusarium disease is most prevalent in warm, moist weather in late summer and early autumn and can be prevented by the use of a fungicide. Specially prepared lawn sand and moss killers containing dichlorophen will also control this disease.

The edible garden

As autumn advances the emphasis is now on growing cooler season vegetables and storing a little of the season's harvest for use in the winter. Harvest mature vegetables and store only the healthiest specimens.

Sowing

Regional variations in temperature will begin to show by the end of this month, with the south becoming considerably colder than the northern regions. In warmer districts it is still possible to get in a last crop of dwarf beans but in colder southern areas little remains to be

---

SAVING SEED

Now is the time to begin saving seed. Seed saved from precious annuals and vegetable crops will give you a thrifty and independent start to next year's garden.

WHAT SEED TO SAVE
- Steer clear of hybrid plants, as many will not come true to type from seed.
- Seed from variegated plants usually produces green offspring.
- Some plants such as perennials are better propagated from root division.

KNOWING WHEN THE SEED IS RIPE
When seeds are ripe, the seed heads usually turn brown or black, dry out and start to split. The exceptions to this are the seeds of delphinium, hellebores and larkspur, which ripen and split before they turn brown. Some seeds, such as those of hepaticas, are green even when ripe. Watch for when the first seeds start to fall and you will know when they are ready to collect.

HOW TO COLLECT SEED
Cut seed heads with sharp secateurs and place them upside down in a dry container. Many will spill out in a few days and can be labelled and stored carefully when they are thoroughly dry.

Paper bags are excellent for collecting seeds in. The bags can be hung up in an airy, shady place for at least a week for the seeds to dry. Never use plastic bags or sealed plastic containers, as this will encourage fungal infections if the seeds are the slightest bit wet.

STORING SEED
Make sure the seed is clean of any leaves or bits of seed capsule, as these can introduce diseases when new seedlings are grown. Put the seeds or seed heads in a sieve and shake over a large piece of white paper. Remove any insect pests and debris. Pour the clean seed into labelled envelopes and store in a sealable container. To keep the seed dry, place a teaspoon of silica gel (cobalt chloride, available from the chemist) in a cloth bag inside the container.

sown or planted other than cabbage for the winter and spring, cauliflower for the spring and lettuce for the winter. Seedlings of broccoli, cabbage, cauliflower, celery, lettuce and silver beet will develop more rapidly than if seed-sown now. Winter radishes can grow into large roots, but even when they are large they can be grated and used in salads. Sown now, they will be ready for use in the middle of winter. (See list opposite for vegetables to sow.)

Chervil and parsley sown now will soon establish and provide foliage for winter picking.

Planting

By planting salad vegetables now, or even in March, you can continue to provide salad greens for the table throughout winter. Land cress is easy to grow and has a peppery, hot flavour and is a good substitute for watercress. It is a hardy, fast-growing plant and prefers a damp, shady site. Spring onions planted now will be ready for the winter and spring tables, but may need some protection in severe winter weather.

Winter purslane (*Portulaca oleracea*, miners' lettuce or claytonia) is a very hardy plant that can either be left to mature or used as a cut-and-come-again crop. Chicory (*Chichorium intybus*) has been bred into a whole range of leaf forms and colours, some looking more like Buttercrunch lettuces. It gains in flavour as the weather becomes colder and when blanched is a delicious winter vegetable, either cooked or used in salads. Endive is similar to chicory, being slightly bitter and also in need of blanching. Curly-leafed endive is very decorative in salads.

You can have herbs for the winter if you prepare now. Most herbs die down for the winter, but there are ways to extend their season. Cloches can be used to protect plants from the damage of frosts. In mild areas, chives, parsley and mint will crop all year if they are grown under cloches. Cloches can also be useful for covering hardy evergreen herbs like thyme and sage, and protecting them from the worst of the winter weather.

Evergreen herbs such as bay, lavender, rosemary and sage, although frost hardy, can be easily killed by cold winds, wet soils and sudden frosts. These plants can be potted up and wintered over in a frost-free place, or taken inside and placed on a window ledge. Many perennial herbs can also be harvested regularly throughout winter from pots. If plants are divided up now and placed in a warm airy place, such as a kitchen window ledge, they will be available for use during the colder months. Hardy plants such as sage, parsley and thyme are ideal.

VEGETABLES TO PLANT NOW

SOW THESE SEEDS	PLANT THESE SEEDLINGS
Bean, dwarf*	
Beetroot	Broccoli*
Brussels sprout	Cabbage*
Carrot*	Carrot*
Leek	Cauliflower*
Lettuce*	Celery*
Parsnip*	Chicory
Radish*	Endive
Spinach*	Lettuce*
Spring onion	Parsnip*
Swede*	Purslane
Turnip	Radish*
	Silver beet
	Spinach*
	Swede*

*Only practicable in warm areas

MAKING THE MOST OF YOUR HERBS

Freezing herbs is one way of having them handy for use during the winter. Whole sprigs can be frozen and transferred to freezer bags. Herbs can also be chopped and frozen in small tubs or ice cube trays for use as required.

Drying herbs is easy. Choose a dry day to collect herbs, handling them as little as possible. Herbs dry best in a dark, warm, airy place between 20°C and 40°C. The airing cupboard would be a suitable place. Most herbs take about a week to dry. Once they are dry they are easily stored in airtight containers until needed.

LEFT: Zucchini, *Cucurbita pepo*
BELOW: Harvested pumpkins, *Cucurbita pepo* 'Queensland Blue'

Harvesting

Heavy crops of beans, capsicum, lettuce, tomatoes, sweet corn and zucchini can almost be an embarrassment at this time of the year. Tomatoes are best picked as they turn colour and placed on a warm (not sunny) window sill to ripen. This ensures good sugar development and also protects the fruit against fungal disease.

Pumpkins can be lifted and stored as can kumi kumi, melons and winter squash. Pumpkins should be picked when the skin is dry and hard. Take care not to damage the skin as fungi can enter and cause the fruit to rot. Leave a small length of stem when cutting pumpkins to prevent fungi entering the fruit. Melons are usually ripe when the stalks begin to turn brown.

Herbs can be harvested now when they are at their best. The first frosts will quickly kill the more tender herbs and diminish the flavour of some.

Fruit

February is the best time to carry out major pruning jobs on stone fruit trees. Trees such as plum, peach and apricot should have any dead wood and any tangled, diseased or unsightly growth removed. All diseased wood should be destroyed. As soon as the crops are picked many trees will begin to produce lush, strong growth. This new growth rarely fruits well and is best cut out now. Pruning either in early or late summer helps fruiting spurs to form, which will bear crops during the next fruiting season. If there is too much leaf growth now, next year's fruit will be shaded and consequently small, less sweet and lacking in colour. The tree will also make weaker growths and therefore weaker buds for next year's fruiting. Shoots intended to form fruiting spurs should be cut back so that only five or six leaves remain.

Trees can be trained at this time using a system of nicking and notching to alter growth patterns and give you the shape of tree that you want. Nicking involves taking out a small wedge-shaped piece of bark just below a shoot or bud. This bud will slow down and stop growing. Notching involves the opposite; that is, taking a wedge-shaped piece of bark from just above a shoot or bud. This process directs more sap and energy into the bud, which develops more strongly.

CLOCKWISE FROM TOP: Pears ready for harvesting; the red raspberry, *Rubus idaeus;* Damson plums

This method of checking exuberant growth with judicious pruning and directing sap with nicking and notching will produce better-sized fruit with better colour for the next season. Following these practices now will also help to considerably reduce the tasks of winter pruning.

Many fruit ripen this month and can either be used now, stored over the winter, or frozen, either raw or cooked. Pick all fruit before it falls to avoid bruising. Don't pick apples when they are rock hard, as they will not ripen but wither slowly. When fruit is ready for harvesting it will usually come away easily from the tree. Pears are best when they are not tree-ripened, but they also can be picked too soon. Pick them when they separate easily from the fruiting stem, and store in a cool, dry place to ripen.

Damson plums will begin to fall early in the month. A somewhat neglected fruit, they make excellent jam and even better damson gin.

Late summer-fruiting raspberries will by now be developing a crop. Those earlier-fruiting types will also carry a small crop of fruit if old tired canes were removed in late November.

February features

Fragrance in the garden

Fragrance should be a major consideration when you are choosing plants for the garden. The exotic fragrances wafting from the subtle oils of many flowers can be used to create a mood in the garden — just to delight the gardener, or to set the scene for garden parties and romantic evenings, making for truly memorable, intimate occasions.

Some of the most celebrated flowers of all time, such as the rose and dianthus (*Dianthus carophyllus*),

BELOW FROM LEFT: Pineapple-scented sage, *Salvia elegans*; chocolate cosmos, *Cosmos atrosanguineus*; sweet pea, *Lathyrus odoratus* 'Cupanii'; bergamot, *Monarda didyma*; *Lilium* 'Casablanca'; *Dianthus* 'Royal Velvet'

Pineapple-scented sage

This hardy bushy shrub (*Salvia elegans*) will grow to 1.8 x 1 metre. The light green deciduous foliage has a distinctive pineapple scent and flavour. The leaves and flowers are delicious and can be added to salads, desserts, drinks and teas for both colour and flavour. Plant in full sun in a light soil and give plenty of water in

have been used for everything from flavouring beer, wine, jams and other foods to making pot-pourri and medicines. An especially strongly scented honeysuckle, a clump of pineapple sage or groups of flowering liliums can smell good enough to eat. There is even an iris that smells of beer! Spectacular and deliciously scented, many of the following plants can be planted where you pass by, sit and entertain, or at entrances either in the garden bed in pots or window boxes to introduce those rosy, mint, lemony, spicy, delicious and supremely satisfying scents into the garden.

the summer. When the foliage dies back in late autumn cut plants to the ground and propagate by dividing the dense root system.

Chocolate cosmos

Chocolate cosmos (*Cosmos atrosanguineus*) grows to 60 cm in height, with a spread of 30 cm. Clump-forming and frost-tender, it dies back at the onset of cold weather. This cosmos should be treated like the dahlia and the tubers lifted and stored in a dry frost-free place until the following spring. On warm days the dark reddish-brown flowers have a distinctly appealing chocolate scent with hints of caramel. It is a chocoholic's delight. Propagate by dividing the tubers in autumn or spring.

Sweet pea

Lathyrus odoratus 'Cupanii' is an old-fashioned sweet pea, bred hundreds of years ago in Sicily. It is highly fragrant, almost overwhelmingly so. A mass of them in the garden can scent a large area with a heady, spicy sweet scent. Frost-hardy, they are easy to grow in a fertile, well-drained soil in full sun. Young seedlings need protection from slugs and snails and training up twigs to get them started. Regularly pick blooms for indoor use or dead head to keep plants flowering. Sow in late autumn in warm areas or in spring where winters are cold.

Bergamot

Both the leaves and the flowers of bergamot (*Monarda didyma*) are spicy and highly aromatic. They are not only very decorative garden plants but have also been used to flavour teas (Earl Grey and English afternoon tea) and for making pot-pourris. Plain tea can be delightfully flavoured by the addition of a few bergamot leaves or flowers. As with most highly fragrant flowers, bees are strongly attracted to them. Plant in full sun or part shade in a fertile, moist, well-drained soil. Increase stock by dividing up established plants in the late autumn when they have died back after the first frosts.

Lily

The sweet and heady spicy perfume of the hybrid lily (*Lilium* 'Casablanca') is intense. It grows up to 1.8 metres and can produce up to 20 pure white trumpet-shaped flowers on a single stem. Plant bulbs shallowly in a well-drained, sandy, alkaline soil in full sun or part shade. A pot or two of these beautiful bulbs at the entrance to the house or garden are a real delight in the late summer.

Dianthus

Dianthus 'Royal Velvet' has a musk scent with a touch of clove. Like *D. carophyllus*, the wild clove pink, it is a delightful garden plant for dry sunny areas. Frost-hardy, this plant likes regular dead-heading and flowers freely from spring until autumn. Take cuttings in late summer or early autumn. Sow seed in autumn or early spring.

AUTUMN

Autumn is a time in which the seasonal variations throughout the country begin to become much more clearly marked. The weather is still dry, but it is clearly time to prepare for winter. As the year slowly winds down, our mood may either sink into sadness at its passing or be exhilarated by the unique seasonal variations that autumn has to offer.

Traditionally the time of harvest, autumn can bring with it a sense of fulfilment and deep satisfaction at a year well run and a harvest all in, with the added pleasure of colours not seen at any other time of the year. Weeds run amok, butterflies and bees are stocking up for winter, yellow and red admirals are busy gathering nectar.

In the south fuchsias should now be at their best, while in the north they will have been in top form for some time. Abutilons will be in full flower, and the Japanese anemone (*Anemone hupehensis*) has beautiful leaves for most of the year and pure white or pink flowers in the autumn.

Autumn foliage is a feature of these months. The English maple or *Acer campestre* and the white mulberry (*Morus alba*) are both quick-growing trees and both turn a golden yellow in the autumn garden. The brilliant autumn colouring of full moon maple *Acer japonicum* 'Aconitifolium', claret ash (*Fraxinus oxycarpa* 'Raywood'), crab apples such as *Malus tschonoskii* or *Malus ioensis* 'Plena' can turn a street or home garden into a blaze of orange, red and purple. Many of these trees bear highly coloured fruits and a plant like the malus hybrid *M.* 'Golden Hornet', *M.* 'Red Jade' or *M.* 'Jack Humm' will carry its fruits right through winter, not dropping them until the spring if the birds leave them alone. New lawns can be sown where there is sufficient moisture.

Bringing in the harvest, bottling, preserving, drying and pickling were once common home activities at this time of the year. For most of us it just seems too much trouble and many of us no longer feel we have the time. However, there is great pleasure to be had during the winter from opening a jar of homegrown, home-bottled tomato soup or preserved plums — and they also taste better. Garden produce preserved in jars and bottles also makes ideal gifts for friends. Attractively bottled and presented they provide an opportunity for generosity.

Colour is a special feature of the autumn garden. This is particularly noticeable in the colder and more southern areas of the country. A dry summer followed by cool autumn evenings will produce a blaze of leaf colour in deciduous trees, shrubs and some ornamentals. Walking about and observing the clear seasonal changes, reflected in the changing colour of the leaves as autumn begins, can be a source of great pleasure. Collecting chestnuts or walnuts and taking them inside to dry can also be a source of great satisfaction at this time of year.

Autumn-flowering bulbs such as colchicum and zephyranthes are delightful in the garden as are the fine, elegant flowers of the miniature cyclamen. *Cyclamen hederifolium* is a hardy plant, tolerant of the harshest of conditions. Colourful berry trees and shrubs also add a richness and diversity to the garden. These berries are soon stripped by hungry birds, but for a brief time they add another dimension to the season of mists and mellow fruitfulness.

LEFT: *Acer japonicum* 'Aconitifolium'

March

Temperature and climate

March marks the beginning of autumn throughout the country. Although dry, hot weather continues in many places, with warm, humid evenings in both the North and South Islands, slightly cooler mornings begin to be experienced in more southern regions. Day temperatures are generally in the low twenties throughout the country. The first ground mists and mushrooms will be in evidence in some areas and before long the first autumn foliage will begin to appear on deciduous trees such as the glowing European ash (*Fraxinus excelsior* 'Aurea'). Autumn temperatures are generally cooler in

LEFT: *Calendula* Touch of Red Series
BELOW FROM LEFT: *Fraxinus excelsior* 'Aurea'; *Chrysanthemum* syn. *Dendranthema* × *grandiflorum* 'Chenile'

the south, particularly at night, and differences between the islands become more marked.

Food and water

Mildew is a disease that starts in the dry months of summer and attacks with severity during early autumn. Ornamentals such as hydrangea, lupins, roses and sweet weather slows them down. Compost placed on the garden will be advantageous, as will liberal dressings of blood and bone or general-purpose fertiliser. Green fertilisers are an excellent method of boosting soil fertility. Chop any seed-free weeds or other greenery (with a rotary mower or mulcher if you have one) and add them to the garden. Lawn clippings also greatly improve the fertility of the soil and cost nothing if you have a lawn. Apply them under perennial plantings, shrubs and trees to provide enough insulation to ensure a cool root-run during the hotter months and a warm root-run during cooler months.

peas, and vegetables such as cabbages, cucumbers and pumpkins are severely affected by this disease, as are blackcurrants. Attacks of mildew are generally worse when plants are crowded together in sites protected from the wind and are short of water. The removal of affected foliage is a simple way of stalling this disease, but it must be done as soon as the first powdery signs are noticed. Watering stressed plants will also be beneficial, but must be carried out on a regular basis to have any lasting effect.

Feeding the March garden is one way of ensuring that plants grow as quickly as possible before the cooler

Garden beds should be forked over, weeds removed and a general fertiliser applied at a rate of two good handfuls per square metre and well worked in. Heavy soil will benefit from the addition of two handfuls of dolomite or lime per square metre. Use this with care as some plants, such as rhododendrons, do not thrive in alkaline conditions. Sandy and light soils improve markedly with the addition of humus in the form of compost. Any spent materials, from coffee grounds to mushroom compost and sawdust, will enrich the soil and vastly improve the coming seasons' crops.

MAKING THE MOST OF CLAY SOIL

- Improving clay soils is difficult if they are low lying and wet. It may be necessary to dig trenches and lay drains to dry some very wet clay soils or to raise the beds above the soil surface.
- Dig and break up clay soils in the spring when they are beginning to dry out. The time to do this is limited as these types of soils change quickly from very soft to hard in a matter of weeks.
- Clay soils are very well suited to some plants. Roses enjoy clay and will flourish, given a little food. Many bulbs such as bluebells, narcissi, snowdrops and snowflakes thrive in clay conditions. Many perennial plants are happy in clay including acanthus, astilbe, bergenia, hellebores, hemerocallis, hostas, paeonies, rudbeckia and shasta daisies.

Helleborus orientalis

Paeonia lactiflora 'Yachiye Tsubaki'

- Trees will eventually penetrate clay soils and flourish. Many shrubs will also grow in clay, including bamboo, berberis, cabbage tree, cherries, cornus, cotoneaster, flax, hebe, holly, hypericum, kauri, laurel, lilac, pyracantha, totara, viburnum and weigela.
- Vegetables such as broad beans, broccoli and cabbage do well in a clay soil, as do potatoes, which can help to break the soil up. Blackcurrants, figs, gooseberries, plums, and strawberries are all capable of growing and fruiting well in clay conditions.
- Clay soils are often cold and wet in the winter and spring. They can be warmed up and dried out by covering with large sheets of plastic or you can also plant under cloches.
- Once warmed up clay soils hold their heat longer than sandy ones.
- Digging clay soils in the winter is likely to do more harm than good.
- The best time to plant is in late winter or early spring, while the soil is moist, not wet or dry. In wet climates autumn planting is the best option.
- Adding compost, manures or commercial fertiliser on wet, cold clay soils will result in formation of toxic compounds that will only poison your plants. Add these as the soil warms in the spring.
- Clay loams are easier to break up than their more solid cousins, pure clay soils.
- Compost and regular additions of gypsum, sand, peat, lime or dolomite to the clay will quickly produce a good productive soil.
- During autumn and winter when the soil is wet and cold, avoid compacting it by walking on it. If necessary, put down planks to form paths.
- Raised gardens are another way of coping with heavy, wet soils. A raised bed can be created relatively easily by building up a frame of wood, railway sleepers, brick or stone. Adding compost and sand until the bed is full may take a little time but the result will be a garden of rich, friable soil that is easy to plant and care for raised above the troublesome, sticky clay.

Crop rotation is an old and tried method for growing successful vegetables. If crops are planted in the same beds year after year, diseases and pools of destructive pests can build up. Crop rotation is also a good way of saving on fertiliser. For example, plant root crops after cabbage, cauliflower, lettuce and other leaf crops, which are all heavy feeders. The practice of having a fallow bed each season may not suit the small city garden, but if there is room, the quality of crops can be considerably improved.

Any garden beds that are not going to be used in the winter can have green fertiliser crops planted in them. This procedure will not only improve the texture of the soil but also raise the humus level. Lucerne, blue lupin, mustard, oats and wheat have all been traditionally used as fertiliser crops. These plants are sown, grown and then dug in when they reach their flowering stage in the early spring.

Constant attention to the water needs of individual plants continues to be necessary in early autumn just as it was through the dry summer months. However, conserving moisture levels is equally important. Mulch applied as it becomes available will conserve moisture and protect and shelter roots during the coming winter season.

> **TASKS FOR MARCH**
> - Plant spring-flowering bulbs.
> - Lift summer-flowering bulbs as they die down. Allow to dry out, then store in paper bags in a cool, dry place until planting in late spring.
> - Guard ornamentals from caterpillars and earwigs by using Nature's Way natural derris dust, or remove by hand.
> - Young seedlings will need careful protection from pests such as earwigs, cutworms, slugs and snails.
> - Caterpillar infestation is high at this time of the year and they need to be checked on a regular basis. Removing them by hand is safer where edible crops are concerned.
> - Nature's Way derris dust is a reasonably safe material to use when infestation is severe.

LEFT: Mildew on hydrangea leaf.

Pests and diseases

The predominant enemies of the March garden are pests such as caterpillars, earwigs, aphids and fungal diseases such as brown rot. Caterpillars are easily removed and squashed underfoot or sprayed with a systemic insecticide. Aphids and earwigs can do considerable damage to dahlias and other flowers. Many of these pests can be removed by trapping them in small, dark receptacles (such as small pieces of hollow bamboo, tubes of newspaper or little boxes stuffed with dry straw) strewn about the garden. Check these traps daily and dispose of the contents; you will soon reduce the incidence of these pests in the garden. Nature's Way natural derris dust will also effectively eradicate these pests.

Looper caterpillars can devour plants with a great ferocity. Both ornamentals and vegetables alike come in for their share of devastation, which is sometimes so severe that plants may be totally defoliated and fail to regenerate. Nature's Way natural derris dust will help to check this problem, but in cases of heavy infestation you might have to resort to Target or Garden Master, or if you want a spray-free garden, remove them by hand, sprinkle with household flour, or use a thuricide.

Watch indoor plants for infestations of scale and other pests. Spray or remove them by hand before they become established. Scale insects are beginning on the next stage of their life cycle and are most vulnerable in their crawler stage as they drop on tiny strands of silk. This is when they can be easily eradicated by spraying away either with water or with an insecticide. Killing this pest now is easier than when they have developed their scaly, waxy shield. Scale left to develop can become a most difficult pest to remove.

Ornamentals, vegetables and fruit trees showing any signs of mildew or other fungal disease should be sprayed with Saprol immediately. Roses will need to be sprayed with Gild to control aphids and black spot. Camellias should be sprayed with Gild at two- to three-weekly intervals to control thrips. Slugs and snails still need to be watched for and, preferably literally, stamped out.

The flower garden

Flowering asters, nerines and chrysanthemums are useful plants in the autumn garden and will often go on flowering well into winter if they are sheltered from frost. Regular liquid feeding and dead-heading will not only keep plants looking good but also ensure a strong and prolific blooming.

The sasanqua family of camellias are excellent free-flowering shrubs and small trees for the autumn garden. They flower through autumn and into winter in mild to temperate areas. In areas subject to frost the flowers are often damaged and should be planted where they can receive some shelter from overhead trees. Many sasanquas can be clipped and make ideal hedging plants.

Sowing
Sow hardy annuals that you want to have flowering in the spring. Larkspurs, calendula, pansies, violas and stocks can be sown or planted out now. In areas where the winters are mild, plant out sweet peas for late winter and early spring flowering. In cold areas it is better to wait until spring or sow into seed trays for planting out when the weather and the soil has warmed. (See the list on page 97 for a selection of seeds to sow.)

ABOVE: *Nerine bowdenii*

Propagation and division
March is the best time of the year to propagate, whether by division, cutting or seed. The seeds you collected during summer and autumn can be sown now in places that are not subject to frost. In other regions it is best to wait until spring. The survival of plants that are not reliably hardy can be ensured if cuttings are taken now and wintered over in an area that is protected from frosts. Taking cuttings is an excellent way of raising cheap perennials and small flowering plants can be produced within a year. Many perennial plants such as geraniums, lavender, pelargoniums, penstemons, rosemary and verbena will strike readily if they are planted now.

Planting
Seedlings sown in January and February should be planted out before the soil becomes cold and slows down plant growth. Alyssum planted in seed trays can still be planted in paths, pots and hanging baskets. Larkspur seedlings will grow rapidly and become established before the cold weather hits. Polyanthus, primula

METHODS OF PROPAGATION

DIVISION

Division is an excellent and economical way of increasing your stock. Plants such as asters, liriope and phlox need to be divided every few years to keep them healthy and prevent them from swamping other plants. The best time to divide plants is when the clumps stop growing and become choked in the middle, but plants with thick, fibrous crowns, such as hemerocallis (day lily), are usually divided after flowering when the new shoots are developing. Use a fork to lift clumps for dividing. Small clumps should be washed free of soil; cut stems to about 10 cm, then pull or cut the clumps apart into separate pieces. Large clumps should have as much soil as possible shaken loose, then prise pieces apart with two forks. Cut the fleshy crowns of hostas or red-hot pokers with a knife and dust the cut surfaces with a fungicide such as flowers of sulphur. Plants with rhizomes, such as trillium and bergenia, should be cut away from any old woody rhizome and only the healthy pieces replanted.

STEM CUTTINGS

There are several types of stem cuttings. Greenwood (softwood or tip cuttings) are taken near the growing tip. Usually 6–10 cm long, they should be taken both beneath and above a node. (A node is the slightly enlarged portion of a stem where buds, leaves and branches originate.) These are usually taken in the spring or early summer and should be placed up to half their length in the soil. Semi-ripe cuttings are taken from early to late summer from semi-mature wood which is usually part of the current season's growth.

DIVIDING PERENNIALS

Hardwood cuttings are usually taken at the end of the growing season, or just before any new growth begins. Usually this wood is the previous year's growth.

Stem cuttings can be taken throughout the summer and early autumn. These cuttings are best if they are 5–10 cm in length and have non-flowering shoots. Remove the tips of stems with approximately two pairs of leaves attached; trim the cutting below a leaf joint and remove the bottom leaves. Plant in sharp, gritty soil or directly into the ground if your soil is well drained and reasonably warm. Cover with clear polythene and keep in the shade until the cuttings have rooted.

HEEL CUTTINGS

A heel cutting is created by pulling side-shoots away from the parent plant so that a strip of the parent stem comes away with the cutting. Trim cuttings and plant out as for stem cuttings.

ROOT CUTTINGS

Taking root cuttings is one method of propagating a number of otherwise difficult plants. Choose a healthy plant and lift it as it becomes dormant for the winter season. Cut back any top growth and, using a clean, sharp knife, cut off all the roots near the crown. Then cut these roots into 5 cm pieces about the thickness of a pencil, sprinkle with a fungicide and set out in planter trays in a sharp, gritty soil mix, where they will quickly form lateral roots and leaf growth.

ROOT CUTTINGS FROM *Anemone hupehensis*

and many other seedlings will develop rapidly if fed with a little dried blood.

Paeonies are best ordered from specialist growers and planted now. (See Appendix on page 167 for sources.)

Bulbs, corms and tubers

March and April are the months for planting most of the spring-flowering bulbs. Tulips, daffodils and hyacinths that were lifted in summer should be replanted now. Anemones and ranunculus share a common family and enjoy a climate with cool to cold, rainy or snowy winters, followed by hot, dry summers. *Anemone coronaria* is happy growing in full sun while *A. nemorosa* and the dark lavender-blue *A. blanda* 'Atrocaerulea' are happier in dappled sunlight or shade. The well-known garden flower *Ranunculus asiaticus* thrives in a well-drained soil, in cool, moist conditions. Plant the fleshy roots points down in full sun or part shade. Varieties such as the Bloomingdale hybrids have been bred for growing in pots

BELOW: *Anemone blanda* 'Atrocaerulea'
OPPOSITE CLOCKWISE FROM LEFT: Lily bulbs ready for planting; plant lily bulbs in sand if the soil is heavy; planting hyacinth bulbs; *Gladiolus* 'Circe'

PLANTING AND CARING FOR RHODODENDRONS

The best time to plant rhododendrons is in autumn or spring. Dig a large hole and fill it with good garden compost. (Avoid mushroom compost as it contains lime, which does not agree with many rhododendrons.) Tramp the compost down firmly, then make a smaller square hole for the plant. Position the plant, firm it in and top with a dressing of peat. In heavy, wet soils site the plant higher with the root ball projecting slightly above the soil level. In quick-draining soil place the roots slightly lower than the surface, creating a shallow area you can water into. Stake taller and more open-growing types.

Rhododendrons have a shallow, compact root system, making them vulnerable to prolonged dry conditions. When plants are young they require heavy mulching and regular watering. If hot or dry winds are a problem, erect a mesh screen of wind cloth or hessian until the plants are established.

Dead-heading and pruning keeps rhododendrons in good condition. Spent seed pods should be removed immediately after flowering. Long strappy branches cut back in late winter or early spring will respond with new vigorous, bushy growth. Liquid fertiliser applied at intervals during the growing season will further encourage growth.

Diseases are few, other than chlorosis, which will show as yellowing leaves that will later drop. Wind and water-logging will also cause leaves to yellow. Late frosts will often deform or even destroy the flowers. For this reason, early flowering varieties may need the protection of a wall or canopy plants. Black buds caused by fungal infection, or leaf damage caused by lace bugs, red spider mites or thrips, need to be controlled with an insecticide such as Maldison. Rhododendron wilt is caused by a fungus and it occurs mainly in subtropical areas with high rainfall. Plants grow slowly, are stunted and develop yellow leaves. This is a difficult disease to cure although good drainage will prevent the disease from occurring. Lichen may form on larger and older trees but this does not generally greatly debilitate the plant.

and will grow to 20 cm in height.

Hippeastrums are popular indoor and outdoor flowers. Preferring frost-free, semi-tropical gardens, they need temperatures of between 15°C and 20°C to flourish. These members of the amaryllis family like to be planted with their necks exposed. In pots, the top third of the bulb should be exposed after planting. These plants require good drainage and a well-fed soil to succeed. Hippeastrums flower better if they can remain

Eucomis comosa

FLOWERS TO PLANT NOW

SOW THESE SEEDS	PLANT THESE SEEDLINGS		PLANT THESE BULBS, RHIZOMES AND TUBERS	
Ageratum*	Ageratum*			
Alyssum	Alyssum	Statice	Allium	Ornithogalum
Anemone	Anemone	Stock	Anemone	Ranunculus
Antirrhinum	Antirrhinum	Sweet pea	Camassia	Romulea
Aquilegia	Aquilegia	Viola	Crocus	Sparaxis
Calendula	Calendula		(spring flowering)	Trillium
Candytuft	Candytuft		Clivia*	Tritonia
Canterbury bells	Canterbury bells		Dutch iris	Tulip
Carnation	Carnation		Galtonia	
Cineraria*	Cineraria*		*Gladiolus cardinalis*,	
Clarkia	Clarkia		G. *carinatus*, G. *alatus*	
Cyclamen	Cyclamen		(winter growing types)	
Forget-me-not	Forget-me-not		Habranthus	
Helichrysum	Helichrysum		Hyacinth	
Hollyhock	Hollyhock		Hyacinthoides (scilla,	
Lobelia	Larkspur		bluebell, endymion)	
Mignonette	Lobelia		Ipheion	
Pansy	Mignonette		Ixia	
Polyanthus	Pansy		Lachenalia	
Russell lupin	Polyanthus		Moraea	
Snapdragon	Russell lupin		Muscari	
Statice	Snapdragon		Narcissus	
Stock				
Sweet pea			*Only practicable in warm areas	
Viola				

dry in the winter. Turning the pots on their side after the foliage has died down is a good way to ensure that the bulbs dry out over the winter. Hyacinths can also be planted into pots for winter and spring flowering.

Liliums can be planted during March and April. They generally prefer cool but frost-free gardens. However, some will cope with frosty areas and some species such as *Lilium regale*, *L. martagon* and *L. formosanum* will grow well and proliferate rapidly. Liliums require perfect drainage to thrive and multiply; plant them in sand if your soil is heavy. Hybrids such as *Lilium* 'Casablanca', *L.* 'Golden Clarion' and *L.* 'Copper King' are highly decorative garden plants.

Eucomis or pineapple lily prefers a frost-free climate but will tolerate cold snaps of −10°C. Plant in the autumn or winter with the neck above the ground in a well-drained, fertile soil in full sun or a little shade.

Prepare tulip bulbs now for planting by chilling them for at least a month in the vegetable bin of the refrigerator. Place the bulbs in a net bag, as plastic or paper bags will cause the bulbs to go mouldy and rot.

Hedges

Quite a few New Zealand native shrubs are highly suitable as hedging plants and many will withstand extreme or exposed conditions. *Olearia forsterii* has a small, gentle, yellow-green, slightly crinkled leaf, and makes an elegant, tough, dense hedge. *Pittosporum crassifolium* and the superior *P. c.* 'Variegatum' make excellent hedging plants and require little trimming.

sowing of new lawns early in the season but very soon morning dew will help to give newly seeded lawns much-needed extra moisture. In heavy soils that have become compacted, a good forking will aerate the lawn and improve drainage. Repair any hollows or bumps in the lawn by cutting the turf with a sharp spade, peeling a strip back and either filling the hollow or removing the soil. Bald patches can be loosened with a fork, moistened and sown with seed.

Feeding the lawn in autumn will help to get it into tiptop form before the winter. Areas suffering from fungal problems such as fusarium can be sprayed using a systemic fungicide. Avoid watering the lawn in the evening at this time of year, when days are often warm and humid, with night temperatures sharply declining, as grass that remains wet overnight is more susceptible to fungal attack. Using a fertiliser such as sulphate of ammonia will give the lawn a greater resistance to fungal diseases. Several handfuls of lime per square metre, well-watered in, will achieve the same end.

The early autumn lawn may respond to the extra moisture from dew or rain, and therefore need more frequent mowing. However, before long the season will cool so the grass will grow more slowly and need less frequent cutting. The cutting height of the blades can be raised a little as the temperature begins to drop. Lawns should not be mown if they are wet or frosty; this only causes damage to individual grass blades. Keep lawns free of fallen leaves. Leaves left lying can cause considerable harm to fine grasses.

The edible garden

Perpetual beet is a very useful crop for colder districts. In warmer districts sow lettuce as usual. In southern areas choose cold-hardy varieties such as Mini Cos and Rouge d'Hiver or plant endive and chicory.

Sowing

In northern districts a wide range of vegetables can still be sown including beetroot, broccoli, carrots, cauliflower, celery, lettuce, radishes, silver beet, spinach and turnip. Spinach is a useful crop for colder regions as well. White turnips and silver beet will be ready to

Among non-natives, the escallonia group also make fine hedges in colder areas; many of this family bear scented flowers. Escallonia also makes a good hedge in colder areas where extreme frost and snow are experienced, as do ligustrum or privet and holly.

Lawns

March is a good time for sowing a new lawn or patching bald spots. Dry soil in many areas will prevent the

VEGETABLES TO PLANT NOW

SOW THESE SEEDS	PLANT THESE SEEDLINGS
Beetroot*	Beetroot
Broccoli*	Broad bean
Cabbage	Broccoli
Carrot	Brussels sprout
Cauliflower*	Cabbage
Celery	Carrot
Cress	Cauliflower
Leek	Leek
Lettuce, winter	Lettuce, winter
Parsnip*	Parsnip
Peas*	Pea
Radish	Silver beet
Silver beet*	Spinach
Spinach	Spring onion
Spring onion	Swede
Swede*	
Turnip	*Only practicable in warm areas

LEFT ABOVE AND BELOW: Bald patches in a lawn can be loosened and spot sown with grass seed.
BELOW: Leeks, *Allium porrum*
RIGHT: Spinach leaves, *Spinacia oleracea*

harvest later in the autumn, whereas turnips and swedes sown now will be ready for use in late winter. Summer lettuce will grow all year round in warmer districts but in cold areas a hardy variety such as cos should be chosen. Salad crops can still be sown in warmer regions.

Potato and kumara tubers should be lifted and stored in a cool, dry, airy place.

Perennial herbs can be sown now in colder areas.

Planting

Seedlings of beetroot, broccoli, Brussels sprouts, cabbage and carrots can be planted in the warmer regions. Leeks, parsnip, spinach, spring onion, swedes, turnip and winter lettuce will race ahead and gain strength to survive the winter. In southern districts broad beans can be planted along with cabbage and spinach. Remember to protect young plants from slugs and snails.

In colder areas division of perennial herbs can be completed. Balm, hyssop, horehound, lovage, sorrel and winter savory can be divided up, cut back and placed in new areas of the garden to become established before the cold of winter begins.

Harvesting

The autumn vegetable garden continues to provide an abundance of produce. Nothing is quite like picking your own fresh vegetables straight from the garden. Sweet corn picked fully ripe, taken straight to the kitchen and cooked has to be tasted to be believed. The sugar content is still high and any starchiness has not yet developed. Zucchini taken directly from the garden glow with life and are sweet enough to eat raw, either sliced or grated into a salad. If they are left for several days they become bitter and are only suitable for cooking. Tomatoes are best picked as soon as they show colour, or sudden rains will cause them first to crack and then rot. Beetroot planted in late November will now be ready for harvest and can be either bottled or pickled.

Fruit

Many stone and pip fruit trees will have shed their summer crops and be preparing to drop their leaves. Spray late peaches with Saprol if brown rot appears. Other remaining stone fruit may also require spraying to check the spread of caterpillars and pear slugs. Spraying with a copper-based spray in the autumn and winter will limit the extent of the damage in the following summer.

Fig trees will be either finishing their crop or in the full flush of fruiting by the end of this month. Hang nets and shiny tin lids in the trees to limit bird damage to this soft crop. Varieties such as 'Brown Turkey' and 'White Adriatic' are common throughout New Zealand and many other choice but less common varieties are now available. As autumn progresses persimmon trees will become a blaze of colour before the leaves fall, revealing an early winter crop of orange or vermilion coloured fruit.

Citrus trees should receive a light dressing of manure to encourage the development of the crops that have set. Any signs of scale should be checked immediately with an oil-based spray. Watering trees on the trunk and under the leaves can effectively wash away tiny newly hatched scale before they develop their resilient protective shells.

Remove the old fruiting canes of currants and late raspberries once they have finished their cropping to encourage new growth.

Grape vines will be in full production. Lightweight paper bags tied around bunches will protect grapes from wasps and birds. Tubes made from old stockings or pantyhose can also be used, but material that is too dense will slow ripening and encourage fungal diseases.

March features

Ribbonwood

Hoheria sexstylosa (ribbonwood) will grow to at least 6 metres. It has a strong, erect trunk and main branches, with graceful pendent branches that carry sweetly scented, pure white flowers in late summer and early autumn. The leaves have sharply toothed margins, particularly when they are young. This hoheria is moderately frost-hardy and will grow in many temperate parts of both the North and South Islands. It will flourish in sun or semi-shade, as long as the soil is fertile and well-drained.

All members of the hoheria genus, including the beautiful *H. lyallii* and the houhere or lacebark, *H. populnea*, respond well to light pruning when they are young but can be badly affected if the bark is torn or damaged. You can propagate them from seed sown in the autumn or from tip cuttings taken in the summer.

LEFT: Ribbonwood, *Hoheria sexstylosa*
BELOW FROM LEFT: *Chrysanthemum* syn. *Dendranthema × grandiflorum* Florist hybrid (potted mum); *Rosa rugosa* 'Anne Endt'; *Aster* 'Barr's Pink'

Chrysanthemum

Chrysanthemums are generally frost-hardy and grow best in a sunny position in well-drained soil that has been enriched with plenty of compost or well-rotted manure. They dislike waterlogged soil. Chrysanthemums are surface rooting plants and so respond quickly to a produce truly opulent hips. *Rosa rugosa* 'Scabrosa', introduced by the English firm of Harkness in 1960, grows to over 2 metres high and wide, with vigorous branches covered in broad, luxuriant, crinkled leaves. The deep cerise-pink, single flowers are very fragrant. They are produced throughout the summer and are followed by large clusters of tomato-shaped hips. *Rosa rugosa* 'Anne Endt', named by the rose grower Ken Nobbs after the well-known Auckland gardener and rose enthusiast, produces masses of red hips in the autumn. The remarkable hips of *Rosa moyesii* 'Geranium' are worth growing for their beauty alone.

surface dressing with a mix of top soil, wood ashes and bone dust. Blood and bone is also a suitable fertiliser but should be used sparingly. Liquid fertiliser applied when the buds are forming will also produce good results. Don't give lots of nitrogenous fertiliser, or you will have leaves at the expense of flowers.

Rose hips

The species rugosa roses such as 'Rugosa Rubra', 'Rugosa' and 'Rugosa Typica' are native to Japan and parts of western Asia. Like most of their offspring, they

Aster

Aster novae-angliae or Michaelmas daisy is a perennial autumn-flowering beauty. Introduced into Europe in the eighteenth century, these plants will grow up to 1.5 metres and produce stout stems that can be stored and used for useful spring stakes. *A. n.* 'Barrs Pink' and 'Harrington's Pink' are both fine garden varieties. The broad heads of pale mauve-pink and pink, yellow-centred flowers start flowering in late February and last for several months. At the first signs of mildew, it is good sense to spray with a fungicide.

April

Temperature and climate

Differences in regional temperatures become very clear in the second month of autumn and in some places night temperatures will start to drop noticeably: –5°C at night may not seem much, but it will slow growth and damage tropical and subtropical plants. Southern areas will have already experienced light frosts whereas many northern cities and towns will be enjoying an Indian summer that in some areas of the 'winterless' north may extend into early June. Sudden squally showers can sweep across the country bringing rapid drops in temperature, breaking down unstaked chrysanthemums

LEFT: *Viola* 'Sky Clear Purple'
BELOW FROM LEFT: Citrus ready for planting in well drained soil; *Viola tricolor*; using rolls of newspaper to trap earwigs.

Food and water

Autumn rain will reduce the need for regular watering. In cold areas where the soil is still dry but also becoming colder, early morning watering is preferable, as it pre-

trenches filled with scoria will help drain excess water away and protect trees and shrubs from rot.

Pests and diseases

Pest and disease control in the garden during April should concentrate on the destruction of any diseased vegetation and leaves that have fallen, as these are potential sources of infection in the coming season. Many pests overwinter in such conditions, to return refreshed and eager in the spring. Burning or burying is the best way to remove diseased material. Brown rot on apples, pears and plums can be prevented by practising

vents plants from sitting overnight in wet, soggy, cold conditions. Watering in the evening can cause many plants to suffer shock and become susceptible to disease.

Drainage must be considered when you are planting new trees. A lemon tree planted in a heavy clay soil will become waterlogged and drown during the rainy winter months. Careful preparation of planting holes is required and it is often better to dig the hole deeper than at first seems necessary. Breaking through the top layer of the soil to the subsoil is a good way to ensure better drainage. In some places the laying of slit drains or

these habits of good garden hygiene systematically.

Dahlia flowers are subject to earwig damage. These pests are most active at night and they can be removed by hand, or trapped in paper tubes or small boxes filled with straw. Red spider mite and whitefly can damage ornamentals and crops alike, and should be sprayed with a general insecticide. Ornamentals and cabbage crops attacked by aphids and caterpillars need spraying with an insecticide; caterpillars can be removed by hand. Codling moths are beginning the next stage of their life cycle, dropping to the soil where they

ABOVE LEFT: Infestation of whitefly.
ABOVE CENTRE: White butterfly damage on cabbage.
ABOVE RIGHT: Sowing seed under cover in planter boxes.
BELOW RIGHT: Planting polyanthus.

will pupate to return the following spring. Now is the best time to collect and destroy or spray them.

Stone fruits should be sprayed against leaf curl. An application of a copper-based spray to all fruit trees and roses at leaf fall is good gardening practice. Citrus trees should also be treated with a copper spray. Indoor and patio plants are particularly vulnerable to insect damage at this time. At the first sign of their presence either remove them by hand or spray the plant.

Protect late crops and fruiting plants from slugs and bird damage. Grape crops and young lettuce plants can be protected with wire netting or fine plastic mesh. Watch for grey mould and botrytis in areas where there is high humidity. Spraying with a general fungicide will prevent this disease from destroying plants. Don't give up with weeds — late-seeding weeds such as nightshade should be removed before they have time to ripen.

The flower garden

Autumn planting is the best for evergreens. Now is a good time to plant trees and shrubs and it is also a good time to prepare rose beds for planting in the coming months. Once the beds have been thoroughly dug over, composted and fertilised they can be left to settle for several weeks before planting.

Sowing

Many seeds are best sown under cover in planter boxes where they can be protected from pests and carefully tended until they are ready for planting out into the garden. Seeds of a wide range of flowering annuals and perennials can be sown (see list on page 108). Calendula (English pot marigold) is happier during the colder months and less susceptible to mildew than in summer. Alyssum, cornflower, dianthus, lobelia, lupin, stock, sweet peas, viola and the *Viola tricolor* (heartsease pansy) will quickly establish themselves before the coldest of the winter weather if sown now. Snapdragons and stocks sown in April or May will be ready for flowering in the early spring garden.

TASKS FOR APRIL
- Plant spring-flowering bulbs as soon as possible. Many bulbs planted in the previous season will be advanced in leaf growth.
- Chrysanthemum plants should be fed and debudded to get the best flowers.
- Dahlias that are still in flower should be continually dead-headed to encourage ongoing flowering.
- Start another compost heap; make the most of the extra suitable material at this time of year. Do not use diseased material in your compost heap.
- Plant new fruit trees.
- Start a new strawberry bed by preparing the ground.
- Collect any remaining vegetable crops and store for winter use.

Propagation and division

Many herbaceous plants such as phlox, heleniums, helianthus and Michaelmas daisies are best lifted and divided now. Fresh, healthy, vigorous parts of the plant should be replanted in soil that has been enriched with compost and fertiliser. The old exhausted part of the plant should be discarded.

Planting

Cyclamen, pansies and polyanthus are particularly good for pots. If they are placed in a sheltered, warm part of the garden and fed regularly they will flower through the winter and into spring. Seedlings of many ornamentals such as anemone, hollyhock, Iceland poppies, larkspur, pansies, polyanthus and snapdragon should all be planted now. (See the list on page 108.)

Bulbs, corms and tubers

April is a good month in which to plant bulbs. As the weather begins to cool many of the cold climate bulbs should now be planted, including alliums, chionodoxa (glory-of-the-snow), crocosmia (montbretia), hyacinths and tulips. Tulips and hyacinths should only be planted when the soil has cooled down considerably; in warmer districts it is better to wait until the colder month of May. Most tulips are hardy, adaptable plants. They do, however, require good drainage, so add grit and peat to heavy soils. They also require a sheltered position in full

FOUR WAYS TO PROPAGATE BULBS, CORMS AND TUBERS

Propagating your own bulbs, corms and tubers is very satisfying, as well as economical. Within a short space of time you can increase your stock at least tenfold. There are four easy methods of propagation: twin scaling; scooping or scoring; bulb scaling; and cultivating bulbils. These methods are easy if you follow a few simple rules.

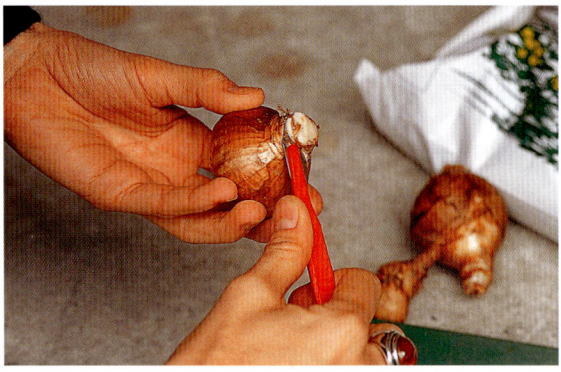

CLEAN THE BULB AND TRIM THE TOP.

- Have what you need at hand: a sharp knife; plastic bags (supermarket bags are good); damp sawdust or vermiculite; fungicide or powdered flowers of sulphur; sand.
- Always use healthy, pest-free parent stock to propagate from.
- Pay strict attention to hygiene. Keep all implements sterile and wear gloves so that fungal and other diseases are not transmitted to your fledgling bulbs.
- Control moisture levels carefully at all stages of development.

TWIN SCALING

This method of propagation is best suited to plants such as daffodils and begonias. With twin scaling, 10 daffodil bulbs can multiply to 300 flowering-sized bulbs in three or four years. Similarly, three bedding begonias can be increased to 30 or more, depending on the size of the tuber.

Using a sharp knife, cut the bulb or corm into segments from top to bottom, retaining a piece of the base plate where the roots spring from in each segment. Dip the cut surfaces in a liquid fungicide or powdered flowers of sulphur. Plant upside down, and leave until they are growing strongly. As long as each segment retains part of the central growing eye or crown, the pieces will quickly grow to form new plants.

SCOOPING OR SCORING

Scooping or scoring works well with hyacinths and gladioli. Wait until the end of the plant's growing season in April. It will take one full year to produce new bulbs or corms with this method of propagation. In three years it is possible to get over 60 corms from only four gladiolus corms.

CUT BULBS WITH SCALPEL INTO TWIN SCALES.

Using a teaspoon with sharp edges, scoop out the growing point (basal plate) of the bulb or corm where the roots spring from. Dip the cut surface of the bulb or corm in a fungicide to prevent rotting. Place in a tray of dry sand with the cut end facing up and store in an airing cupboard. Dampen the sand every three or four days to prevent the bulb from drying out. When tiny bulblets appear on the cut surfaces (after about three months) plant the whole bulb upside down, with the cut end containing the bulblets facing up, in seedling or bulb mix, with the bulblets just below the surface. At the end of the growing season (March), lift the parent bulb and separate the tiny bulblets. Plant them at once in a moist, loose mix of soil.

BULB SCALING

Bulb scaling is a simple procedure. It is an excellent method of increasing stock of such bulbs as fritillaria, lilium and nomocharis, which are comprised of scales. Most average-size bulbs could have four or five scales removed without harming the parent plant. It will take one full year to produce new bulbs with this method of propagation.

LILIUM SCALES IN MOIST VERMICULITE.

Remove individual leaf scales from these naturally segmented bulbs. Place them in a plastic bag and cover with a fungicide. Dust with fungicide and then place in a plastic bag with four times their volume of damp peat, sawdust or vermiculite. Blow into the bag to fill it with air and tie it at the top. Store in an airing cupboard for several months until the scales produce bulblets. Plant each scale leaf in a pot so that its tip is just visible above the soil. Place in a warm, light area until the bulblets develop (about a year). At the end of the growing season (March and April) once the leaves have died down remove the bulblets from the parent scale and replant to grow on.

CULTIVATING BULBILS

Cultivating bulbils is another way of increasing lilium stock. These tiny bulbs form in the leaf axils of stems of certain species of lily such as *Lilium lancifolium* (tiger lily), *L. bulbiferum* and *L. candidum*.

Simply collect the bulbils and place them in a pot or in the garden in a fine, moist compost. Some bulbs may flower in their first year of growth but it is more usual for flowers to appear in the third year.

LILY BULBS READY FOR PLANTING.

RIGHT: Raking out thatch in a lawn.

sun to develop their best form and colour. The blooms will last longer in partial shade, but the stems will become leggy and weak if left in such a position for too long. Bulbs should be planted 10 cm deep and about 15 cm apart, according to size.

Lawns

April is the time to repair any lawn damage. Turf or Ready-Lawn is ideal for worn or thin areas. Ready-grown lawns are useful if you already have this type in your garden, but sowing a general-purpose seed may blend more naturally into the average garden lawn. As an alternative, cut a piece of turf from an area where it is no longer required; use a sharp spade and cut sections to a depth of 10 cm. Thatch (where a layer of fibrous material builds up between the green leaves and the soil) can be a problem at this time. The roots become choked and are unable to get moisture, and the grass turns brown.

FLOWERS TO PLANT NOW

SOW THESE SEEDS	PLANT THESE SEEDLINGS	PLANT THESE BULBS, RHIZOMES AND TUBERS	
Alyssum	Anemone		
Calendula	Hollyhock	Allium	Hyacinthoides
Cornflower	Iceland poppy	Anemone	(bluebell, endymion,
Dianthus	Larkspur	Camassia	scilla)
Lobelia	Pansy	Chionodoxa	Ranunculus
Lupin	Polyanthus	Crocosmia	Romulea
Snapdragon	Primrose	Freesia	Sparaxis
Stock	Ranunculus	Galtonia	Trillium
Sweet pea	Snapdragon	Gladiolus	Tritonia
Viola		Hyacinth	Tulip

The common response is to water the lawn heavily, but this can do more harm than good as the water gets under the thatch, saturating the roots and making them susceptible to fungal diseases. The solution is simply to rake the lawn firmly at regular intervals, and top dress with sand to help aerate the grass roots.

The edible garden

Very few sowings can be made if the soil is cold and wet; however, in warmer districts a few peas, cabbages, cauliflowers, and lettuces can be planted. In sheltered frost-free positions of the garden it is still possible to plant a few potatoes.

Sowing

As the weather in the south becomes colder the variety of crops that can be sown becomes smaller. Broad beans and spinach are still suitable for planting in areas where the first frosts are beginning to be felt.

In central and northern areas of New Zealand a wider range of vegetables can still be sown. Broccoli, cabbage, carrots, cauliflower, leeks and onions can be sown in the open where frosts are not heavy. Celery, winter lettuce and potatoes can be sown in frost-free areas.

The autumn sowing of many herbs, such as chervil, coriander, parsley, rosemary, sage and thyme, will ensure seedlings for spring planting.

Planting

Transplanting of broccoli, Brussels sprouts, cabbage, cauliflower, celery, leeks, lettuce and silver beet can be continued in northern and central parts of the country. A little diluted liquid fertiliser applied to the root area before planting will help young seedlings to become established. If you live in the southern part of the country, choose varieties that are bred to withstand slightly colder temperatures and put in a few extra plants in case some fail to thrive.

Herbs such as endive and chicory can be blanched by covering with a lightproof cover. These are useful winter salad crops.

Harvesting

Harvesting will continue in most areas although in the south of the country the last tomatoes will be ripening before the first frosts. Pick tomatoes as soon as they show any signs of colour and ripen indoors or use for making green tomato chutney, green fried tomatoes or green curried tomatoes. Butternut, kumi kumi, pumpkins and squash can be picked now and stored in a cool airy place for use throughout the winter. A vine bearing semi-ripened fruit will continue to ripen if placed in a warm room in a jar of water containing a little sugar. If you can't be bothered with the fuss, a tomato plant with semi-ripe fruit will also continue to ripen if pulled and hung in the shed.

Pick the last of the pears and apples and store in a cool dark place, or cook and freeze. Passionfruit vines

> **VEGETABLES TO PLANT NOW**
>
> | SOW THESE SEEDS | PLANT THESE SEEDLINGS |
> |---|---|
> | Beetroot* | |
> | Broad beans | Broccoli* |
> | Broccoli* | Brussels sprout |
> | Cabbage | Cabbage |
> | Carrot* | Cauliflower* |
> | Cauliflower* | Celery |
> | Celery* | Leek |
> | Leek | Lettuce |
> | Lettuce (winter)* | Silver beet* |
> | Onion | Spinach* |
> | Potato* | |
> | Spinach | |
> | Turnip | *Only practicable in warm areas |

ABOVE: *Lathyrus nervosus*

will still be bearing in some areas and fruit can be picked as soon as it begins to turn purple. Kiwifruit can be picked as soon as they soften and taken inside to ripen fully; the riper they are picked the sweeter the fruit.

Fruit

Most fruit trees will have lost their leaves, although some will still be holding onto the last of the season's crop. General spraying at this time will check diseases and pests. Copper should be sprayed on all fruit and blossom trees and on citrus plants. Trees badly affected with leaf curl or black spot will greatly benefit from a spraying of copper oxychloride and a fortnightly spraying of Captan thereafter for at least a month. The huge amounts of garden waste at this time of year can be mulched and used for composting, but any diseased material should be burnt or buried.

April features

Sweet peas

April is a good month in which to sow sweet peas. Seeds from last year's plants can be sown directly. Peas planted now will achieve considerable growth before winter. Come the spring they will burst into growth from the root stock that they managed to make in autumn.

Sweet pea is an annual climber, comes in a wide range of colours and is an excellent cut flower.

To ensure a succession of blooms when they are flowering, it is necessary to pick the flowers continuously. If you let the plants go to seed they will stop flowering. Good drainage is essential if you are to grow sweet peas well. Feeding with dried blood in small quantities or a mixture (two to one) of superphosphate and bone dust will produce the best flowers. Overfeeding with too much nitrogenous fertiliser will produce lank growth at the expense of flowers.

In mild northern climates sowing of seed can begin in midsummer, while in colder areas autumn and spring sowings are best. Sweet peas enjoy water during the dry weather months. If they are neglected they may develop fungal diseases, particularly if the soil they are planted in is badly drained or if they are allowed to dry out. Both these extreme conditions weaken the plant's resistance and make it susceptible to disease. Spraying with a copper-based spray will keep most plants free of

BELOW FROM LEFT: *Camellia sasanqua* 'Plantation Pink'; *Camellia japonica* 'Rudolph'; *Camellia saluensis*; *Cotoneaster horizontalis*; *Iris foetidissima*

fungal diseases, but prevention is better than cure and this is achieved by ensuring perfect drainage and adequate levels of moisture during dry weather.

Camellias

Camellia sasanqua is in full flower in April, making quite a feature in the autumn garden. Sasanquas will tolerate types over the larger-flowered japonica and reticulate forms is that the spent flowers are more easily disposed of. Dead-heading of some larger-flowered forms may be necessary to keep the plants looking at their best.

Camellias are remarkably disease-free, but plants showing symptoms of stress may need attention. Bright yellow or blotched leaves may signal a virus infection. Little can be done to combat this and, although unsightly, it will not affect other plants or weaken the host greatly. Bud-drop may affect plants in the middle of their flowering season; this may have been caused by the plants drying out in the late summer and early autumn.

wind and exposure to full sun, unlike many others of their family. The blooms are sweetly scented and they make fine hedges. The shiny, small, sometimes curled leaves clip easily and will soon form a dense hedge. Many varieties of sasanqua are available in a wide range of colours. The hardy and yet delicate *Camellia sasanqua* 'Plantation Pink' forms an ideal hedge but it also makes a beautiful specimen plant. Once established these camellias need little care. Depending on type and local conditions they will grow anywhere from 4 metres to 9 metres. An advantage of the smaller-flowered sasanqua

Infestations of scale insects and aphids should be treated with an insecticide.

Reticulatas are large flowering camellias that produce their blooms in the late spring. Most are hardy to –10°C, require a lime-free soil and a little shelter to flourish. Two forms of reticulate, *Camellia reticulata* 'Buddha' and *C. r.* 'Tataochung', were introduced to the United States in 1948 from the province of Kunming in China and later introduced into Britain. A New Zealand form of reticulata, *C. r.* 'Balderdash', has been popular in Kiwi gardens since the late sixties.

Japonicas produce sports (side-shoots) that often differ from the parent plant, and it is from these sports that many hundreds of new varieties have been developed. Japonicas need warmth if they are to flower well. There is a large colour range and a great variety of leaf forms and sizes. Most leaves are dark green and they blend well into the garden scheme. Japonicas grow quickly and will soon form large trees. Frost, melted by morning sun, will damage flowers in the early spring and it is best to place these plants under eaves, in the shelter of a pergola, or on the south side of the house where they will not be burnt by the sun's rays.

poor soil and will produce a mass of autumn colour, even in northern gardens.

Cotoneaster horizontalis is similarly hardy, growing in full sun or light shade and indifferent to poor soil. It can also be trained on a wall, down a bank or used as ground cover. Birds will steal the berries, given half a chance, but not usually until late winter. *Cotoneaster frigidus* is one of the best berry plants for length of display. One form, *C. f.* 'Pendula', is a most suitable subject for training as a specimen tree.

Some berry trees and plants are also beautiful flowering plants at other times of the year. Crataegus

Berries

Berries are a feature of many autumn gardens, especially in the colder regions of the country. When choosing berry shrubs or trees it is necessary to consider just what you want from them. Some look splendid for only a short time but may be worth consideration for the display alone. Others are beautiful plants even without the berries, some flower as well as berry and yet others are useful for making jam and jelly. The pyracanthas, skimmias and viburnums keep their berries for a long time. Pyracanthas are easy to train against a wall, do not mind

(hawthorn, may) and prunus cultivars such as *Prunus* 'Golden Hornet', *P.* 'Jack Humm' and *P.* 'Red Jade' give a good display of blossom and have large, colourful and useful fruits. Some roses produce both flowers and fruit.

The *Rosa moyesii* roses such as *R. m.* 'Geranium', *R. m.* 'Sealing Wax' and *R. m.* 'Eddie's Crimson' have highly ornamental hips. Others such as *R. m.* 'Mme Grégoire Staechelin' (Spanish Beauty), *R. webbiana*, *R. pendulina*, *R. glauca*, *R. moschata* 'Nepalensis' and also *R. woodsii* 'Fendleri' have splendid hips and should not be pruned until late winter.

May

Temperature and climate

This is the last month of autumn and although temperatures are still warm in the far north, they will be falling to 10°C or lower in the south and central high regions. Cold and often dismal weather soon sees the garden stripped bare of the last of its autumn cover and exposed to the icy blasts of winter. The coming months will put the garden's design and structure and last season's planning and planting to the test. In most regions it is time to stop planting and start planning for the coming spring season. Some gardeners talk of putting their gardens to sleep for the winter. This may be quite

LEFT: Savoy cabbage, *Brassica oleracea* 'Ludessa'
BELOW FROM LEFT: Apply a liquid fertiliser at planting; alyssum, *Lobularia maritima* syn. *Alyssum maritima*

sensible in the furthest reaches of the South Island, but in most of the country much of interest can still be seen in gardens reduced to their bare elements.

Food and water

Food and water are not major preoccupations for the gardener at this time as growth is slowing down. The occasional liquid fertiliser sprayed or watered on to the leaves of small plants will help them to make that final, extra growth they cannot quite accomplish by themselves. Liquid fertilisers are most effective for indoor plants and pot plants in general.

Pests and diseases

Slugs and snails must be deterred at this time of the year otherwise late vegetables will be devoured. Caterpillars and whitefly that have been present since summer still need to be kept under control and spraying with a commercial insecticide is the most effective means of achieving this. Removing rank weeds and spent crops from the ground now will ensure that pests are not overwintering in them.

The flower garden

Late flowering plants such as chrysanthemums will be more successful if they have some shelter from the weather. Potted types can be moved under the house eaves, onto a verandah or into the greenhouse.

Sowing

In warmer parts of the country it is still possible to plant seeds into the open garden. Alyssum (*Lobularia maritima* syn. *Alyssum maritima*), calendula, clarkia and cornflower are contenders for the winter and spring gardens.

Propagation and division

Perennials such as chrysanthemums, helenium, hostas, penstemons, perennial asters, phlox and rudbeckia are some of the many plants that benefit from being split up and replanted. Delphiniums should be

ABOVE: Sweet William, *Dianthus barbatus*

> **TASKS FOR MAY**
> - Watering needs of many plants will have lessened. Water sparingly in the winter.
> - Prepare soil for the spring garden.
> - Control fungal diseases on roses and vegetables.
> - Prepare the soil for roses and spring planting.
> - Add lime to the soil, but watch out for plants that resent lime.
> - Pay attention to the continual problem of slugs and snails.
> - Spray fruit trees and ornamentals to control scale and other pests.
> - Plant strawberry runners in warm regions.

> **TIPS FOR BUYING BULBS**
> - Look out for medium- to large-sized bulbs.
> - Bulbs should be plump and firm.
> - They should feel heavy, and not be shrivelled.
> - There should be no signs of growth.
> - There should be no signs of crushing or damage.
> - There should be no spots of mould.

cut to the ground, split up and replanted in new positions.

Planting

Only in northern gardens is it still warm enough to plant out seedlings. Once they are established, a little care and liquid feeding will help to generate new growth. At this time of the year all growth is slow and special attention must be paid to drainage as well as to slugs and snails. Pansies and violas should be planted out without delay.

Carnation and sweet William (*Dianthus barbatus*) plants can be also planted out.

Bulbs, corms and tubers

Dahlia tubers should be lifted and stored in a cool dry place until the next season. In cold areas lift tender bulbs such as babiana, gladioli and eucomis. Potted bulbs such as lachenalia can be brought into the shelter of a porch, hedge or wall. All spring-flowering bulbs, including tulips, liliums and eucomis, can be planted now.

Lawns

In the late autumn keep lawns constantly clear of falling leaves, as a build-up of leaves will soon kill large areas of lawn, leaving them bare and desolate until mid-spring. Where lawns are wet, worn or muddy, you could pave or lay a line of simple stepping stones cut into the lawn and set below the grass level. A fortnightly mowing may be all that is required once lawn growth slows down.

Moss and hydrocottle can be real problems in shady or very wet lawns, or where the lawn has been mown too close. Removing moss is difficult. It can be treated in the late autumn with a moss killer by mixing one part sulphate of iron with three parts sulphate of ammonia and thirty parts sand. A good handful per square metre is a suitable application rate. Alternatively rake the lawn heavily to remove as much moss as possible and allow light and air in. A light dressing of a nitrogen-based fertiliser will then help fine grasses to re-establish themselves.

FLOWERS TO PLANT NOW

SOW THESE SEEDS
Alyssum*
Calendula*
Carnation
Clarkia*
Cornflower*
Larkspur*
Lupin*
Stock*
Sweet pea*
Sweet William*
  (*Dianthus barbatus*)
Wallflower*

PLANT THESE SEEDLINGS
Clarkia
Delphinium
Geum
Helianthus +
Helenium +
Lupin
Michaelmas daisies +
Pansies
Phlox +
Violas

PLANT THESE BULBS, CORMS AND TUBERS
Alliums
Eucomis
Liliums
Tulips

*In very cold areas sowing seed must be done in a heated seed-raiser or you must wait until warmer spring weather

+These should be cut back, lifted and divided

PROTECTING PLANTS FROM FROST

If you own a glasshouse overwintering tender plants is not problematic. However, careful attention should be paid to ventilation and overwatering. Insufficient ventilation will allow fungal diseases such as botrytis (grey mould) to attack plants; picking off any diseased growth as soon as it is seen is essential. Overwatering can cause plants to wilt. Plants need less water in their dormant or slow-growing period. If potted plants become inadvertently saturated, turn them on their side for several weeks, or lift the affected plant out of its pot and stand it on a bench for several days to dry out, before replacing it in the pot. Bulbs and corms will also rot if they are kept in moist or unventilated places. Dipping them in a fungicide as soon as they are lifted is necessary if they are to survive winter storage.

Without a glasshouse winter protection is more difficult. However, frost and crop-protection cloths, which are light and versatile, are now available. You can use these cloths to cover the ground to warm the soil and then plant through them. Simple cloches can be made by suspending frost cloth over a series of wire hoops and pegging it to the ground. Polycarbonate cloches now available are double-walled and provide good protection from winter cold. Lettuce, parsley and other crops will grow well under the protection of a cloche.

Fuchsias and geraniums can be overwintered on a windowsill. If this is not practicable, cut them back and store them in cardboard boxes in the garage. In spring they can be brought out into the light, pruned of any sickly winter growth and replanted for the coming season.

Agapanthus cope well even with snowy conditions; cover with frost cloth during the coldest days to prevent severe burning. Other more tender bulbs such as amaryllis and galtonia should be heavily mulched with sawdust before the soil gets too wet to protect them from frost. Where conditions are very wet and cold, plants can be protected with a cover of straw or you can resort to homemade covers for the most precious of your garden plants.

The edible garden

When the weather conditions are favourable and the soil remains workable, digging can be continued. A few winter crops will benefit from being lightly cultivated. Young seedlings will benefit greatly from a little liquid fertiliser sprayed on the leaves.

Sowing

Except for the far north of the country, very little can be sown. North of Auckland broad beans, broccoli, savoy cabbage, cauliflower, peas, radish, silver beet and spinach can still be sown. Sweet cicely (*Myrrhis odorata*), a perennial herb, can also be grown from seed, but it takes almost nine months to germinate. In central regions broad beans can still be planted along with carrots and spinach. In the southern parts of the country this is not the season for sowing and planting. Best to wait for the coming spring, unless you have a heated seed-raising bed or a warm, sheltered microclimate.

Planting

Developing winter crops can be lightly cultivated and given a liquid manure either as a foliar spray, if the soil is wet, or watered in, if dry. Garlic can be planted in well-drained sunny places, though it is traditionally planted in mid-winter. Seedlings of winter lettuce, mizuna and parsley can still be planted for salads. Other herbs for planting include angelica, chervil, cress, lavender, mint, rosemary, savory and thyme. This is also a good time to prepare a new asparagus bed, or replenish an old one.

Rhubarb crowns can be planted out now. In milder parts of the country strawberries can be planted from division of runners from last year's plants.

BELOW: Silver beet can be sown or planted out in mild areas.
ABOVE RIGHT: Plant out strawberry runners in mild areas.

VEGETABLES TO PLANT NOW

SOW THESE SEEDS	PLANT THESE SEEDLINGS
Broad bean*	
Broccoli*	Cabbage
Cabbage*	Cauliflower
Carrot*	Lettuce
Cauliflower*	Parsley
Lettuce*	Radish
Onion*	Spinach
Parsley*	
Pea*	
Radish*	
Spinach*	
Silver beet*	*Northern districts only

PLANTING AN ASPARAGUS BED

Asparagus is a perennial vegetable and can last for many years. Select healthy two-year-old crowns such as the new vigorous variety 'Purple Gourmet'; if planted now they will begin to crop reliably after two seasons. Thirty crowns would be needed to feed four or five people. Make a long, narrow bed for the asparagus crowns so that both sides may be easily reached for picking. The soil should ideally be manured and well-drained. Dig out the bed at least 60 cm deep and place a layer of bones or bone dust on the bottom. Mix the top soil with as much rich compost as possible and layer with sand.

The crowns can be planted either now or in July when the bed will have consolidated. Plant in rows 40 cm apart, spreading the roots out, and water in well. Cover with compost or well-rotted manure.

Manure, mulch and water are the secrets to growing fine asparagus. Feed the plants with blood and bone every two or three weeks and sprinkle the surface of the bed with salt and potash from time to time. Mulch the bed in order to keep it moist and to blanch the emerging stems, making them more tender and less bitter.

Asparagus 'Purple Gourmet'

Harvesting

Storing vegetables from the autumn harvest is easy and there are several ways of doing this. In some areas where the soil is dry and cold, root vegetables can be left in the ground, or they can be hung in nets or pantyhose, or stored in paper bags or boxes of sand. You can also freeze or dry your vegetables.

Freezing destroys some minerals and vitamins in the vegetables, but it is a quick and easy method of storage, if you have a large enough freezer. If you intend to freeze vegetables over a long period, it is best to blanch them first to destroy bacteria and enzymes that might affect the final taste and flavour of the crop; this is especially important for sweet corn, carrots, broccoli, cauliflower and Brussels sprouts. Vegetables frozen for shorter periods can be placed directly into the freezer. Where winters are very cold, it makes good sense to use the large deep-freeze provided by nature. Root vegetables such as beets, carrots, swedes and turnips can be left in the ground. In very cold areas before snow falls, mark the rows out with stakes and string, then cover with a mulch such as straw, spent crops or sheet polythene to prevent the crops being frozen into the soil.

Boxes of dry sand are ideal for storing many root vegetables. Kumara can be stored in this way and as long as your vegetable quality is the best and the sand perfectly dry, the crop will last a considerable period. Store potatoes in paper bags, which allows them to breathe and prevents them from rotting. They must remain dry and cool (not cold) and all light must be excluded. Nets or old pantyhose are ideal for storing marrows, onions, pumpkins and savoy cabbages. Air flow is excellent and if they are hung in a cool, dry place they will last well into winter. Garlic and onions can also be plaited into decorative strings.

To dry root vegetables, first slice them thin and then steam until they are just soft. They can then be dried in a slow oven or in a food dryer. Peas and beans can be left on the vine until dry and then collected and stored until they are needed. Chilli peppers can be strung on a thread and hung in muslin bags in a cool, sheltered, airy place. Capsicum should be blanched in boiling water for one minute, then halved and the seeds removed. They can then be slowly dried in the oven or a vegetable dryer.

Fruit

Now is the time to spray and continue with the last of the great clean-ups before winter strikes. Trees that were subject to disease during the growing season should be sprayed now. Leaf diseases such as black spot and blight can be halted by spraying with any of the copper-based sprays on the market. Diseased spores should not be allowed to winter over; they will only reappear, more firmly established, in the spring garden. After spraying, leaves can be safely added to the compost heap or burnt for valuable ash that can either be added directly to the garden or to the compost heap.

If you have had trouble with scale insects, lime sulphur is an ideal clean-up spray.

Lichen on trees can be removed by spraying with a full-strength copper fungicide, or alternatively lime sulphur at winter strength may be used. These sprays are highly incompatible and must not be used together.

Only a few apples and pears remain on the trees. Select perfect fruit, pack in clear, pierced polythene bags and store in a cool dry place. Feijoas, guavas, kiwifruit and tamarillos can be harvested in northern districts. Guavas can be collected by spreading a fine net under the tree and shaking the fruit loose. If you are planning to make guava jelly, this is an ideal way to collect them. Straw spread under feijoa trees will save fruit that drops from being soiled and unusable. Walnuts can be protected from soil-borne bugs by spreading a tarpaulin under the tree to catch the nuts as they fall. Nuts collected in this way will dry quickly and be ready for eating in the winter.

Autumn-fruiting raspberries will continue until the first frosts. Harvest these fruits a few at a time as soon as they ripen and store them in the refrigerator for up to a week until you gather enough for a meal. However, this calls for considerable constraint.

May features

Autumn colour

May is a good time to take note of the colours around you and to decide just how many and which of the autumn leaf-colour trees you wish to have in your garden. In milder northern parts of New Zealand with more rainfall and less contrast between day and night temperatures, autumn foliage can be disappointing. Generally, though, warm, dry autumn days with cold nights will produce the best autumn colour, acid soil will produce richer, more glowing colours than alkaline soil, and the drier the weather, the more intense the colour.

Some trees, such as *Euonymus alatus* (spindle tree), will colour well in autumn, regardless of soil conditions and even does well in shade. More common in the south of both islands, it will grow rapidly to 3 metres in height and about the same in spread. Brilliant pink and red leaves with purple fruit and red seeds make this a spectacular garden plant.

Viburnums are another example of small trees that will colour well regardless of soil conditions.

Amelanchier canadensis and *A. lamarckii* are small trees that do best where winters are cool. They grow to 5 metres in height, spreading to 6 metres when fully grown. These are fine, elegant trees with soft, grey-brown branches and trunks and they bear white flowers in the spring. They produce orange, scarlet and russet-toned leaves in autumn.

Other small trees that colour well in the autumn

and have features during other seasons include the tupelo *Nyssa sylvatica*, which grows slowly into a spreading tree (10 metres by 6 metres) with fine branches. Tupelo has autumn leaves of yellow and scarlet and will grow best in a wet, acid soil.

Betula albo-sinensis has yellow autumn leaves and pinkish copper-coloured bark all year, and *Acer japonicum* 'Vitifolium' bears red and green flowers in the spring and produces a spectacular autumn display of crimson and gold veined leaves. *Parrotia persica* suits the large garden, growing 8 metres by 7 metres. This slow-growing plant has grey bark and beautifully tiered, horizontal branches. In autumn parrotia turns a glowing yellow crimson.

If you are looking for a large shrub for autumn colour rather than a tree, one of the following may appeal: *Acer japonicum* 'Aconitifolium' (3 metres square, with red flowers in spring and crimson leaves in autumn); *Cotinus coggygria* (also known as the smoke bush, grows to 4 metres square and has pink flowers that turn smoky grey, with scarlet leaves in the autumn); or the winter hazel (corylopsis), which grows to 5 metres by 4 metres and has pale yellow spring flowers and pale yellow autumn leaves. *Corylopsis veitchiana* has the added

FAR LEFT: Kiwifruit ripening on the vine
ABOVE: *Acer japonicum* 'Aconitifolium'
BELOW: *Cotinus coggygria*

advantage of having scented flowers and an upward growing habit. *Rhus typhina* or sumach (4 metres by 3 metres) is another spectacular autumn colouring small tree. It will grow well in poor, hungry soil, is inclined to sucker and has astonishing horn-like red and green flowers in spring. In autumn the rhus family are all spectacular trees. *Rhus typhina* colours flame red and orange with touches of green. Note that many rhus are toxic.

Among the smaller shrubs, *Acer palmatum* 'Dissectum' grows to little more than 2 metres square. The leaves of this elegant tree colour orange and pink in autumn. *Hydrangea quercifolia* (the oak-leafed hydrangea) grows to just under 2 metres by 2.5 metres and produces white flowers in late summer and brilliant purple-crimson leaves now. The leaves of many species of rose colour well. The rugosa family of roses such as scabrosa turn orange and red and bear glowing red hips. *Rosa virginiana plena* or St Marks Rose bears pink flowers scrolled at the edges, is lightly scented, copes with poor soil and shade, and grows upright to 2 metres. If this were not enough, the rose displays brilliant leaf colours in autumn.

Trees and shrubs for winter

With a little thought and planning gardens can be alive with colour and interest throughout the winter, and autumn is the ideal time to do this. Evergreens always look good in a garden where most leaves have fallen. Their strong greens and sculptural forms can impart to the garden the very structure that it may otherwise lack at this time of the year.

Without a green background winter colours are either lost in space or hover without a point of reference. Conifers are excellent as a foil for winter flowers. Lawson cypress (*Chamaecyparis lawsoniana*) can give a dark area of the garden a glowing light, and blue forms associate happily with many plants and can also be used in hedging and delineating the garden structure. *Cupressus arizonica* is another good blue conifer that grows quickly and has the advantage of being able to stand considerable drought. It can look superb as a backdrop to a perennial border.

Consider planting trees and shrubs for their different features. The bark of some trees is particularly attractive in the winter garden. The paper-bark maple has unusual brown, curling bark of great interest. The birches also have a pale and golden bark that catches the autumn light, bestowing yet another quality to the shade and texture of the garden. *Acer capillipes* has a silver-grey striped bark, and looks splendid in the autumn garden, ablaze with colour. *Acer griseum* also has striking chocolate-brown, peeling bark throughout the year and a fine colour in the autumn and early winter.

Liliums

Liliums are most desirable garden plants as they flower generously, scent the garden and are also excellent for picking. Multi-crowned bulbs will produce inferior shoots and blooms. From a hundred lily species there have been developed thousands of hybrids in a myriad of colours. These rewarding plants include such straightforward types as *Lilium tigrinum* (the orange tiger lily), *L. henryi*, which is also orange, *L. regale* and the beautiful *L. candidum* (Madonna lily), all of which are easy for aspiring lilium-fanciers to grow.

FAR LEFT: Bark of *Acer griseum*
LEFT: Madonna lily, *Lilium candidum*
BELOW FROM LEFT: Tiger lily, *Lilium lancifolium*; *Delphinium* 'Sir Galahad'; *Delphinium* 'Emily Hawkins'

Delphiniums

Delphiniums require lots of nutrients to thrive, and although they demand extra effort, they are a rewarding addition to the garden. Many splendid forms are available, with the best known white being the stocky free-flowering *Delphinium* 'Sir Galahad', a Pacific hybrid. *D.* 'Emily Hawkins' is a fine blue variety for the garden. Delphiniums come in a wide range of colours including deep purple, lilac, sky blue, cream and white and vary from just under a metre to well over 2 metres in height.

When planting liliums you should have a rich soil, but, most importantly, it must be free-draining. They like to have their roots in the shade and their heads in the sun. They prefer an acid soil, but will usually tolerate moderately alkaline conditions. Many are heavy feeders and a little dried blood or bone dust will produce large and showy blooms. All lilies are shown to best advantage when planted in groups within the mass of the garden border. They look odd standing alone on their long legs. They enjoy dappled light rather than full sun with the exception of the Madonna lily, which prefers full sun. Grown in the border in well-drained conditions they will improve year by year. If your soil is heavy, dig in peat, sand, or anything that will aid drainage. Where they may have to compete for food and water, flowers and plants alike will begin to show signs of decline. It is then time to dig them up and replant in new soil.

The best way to maximise the flowering season of delphiniums is to trim them back after they have flowered. Cut back the flowering stems to the ground immediately after the first blooms have finished and they will respond with fresh flowering spikes and side shoots of colour throughout the autumn months and into winter. For this reason they are highly valued garden perennials, and are especially useful in a border where height and colour are needed.

Delphiniums also make excellent cut flowers. Not only do they look spectacular in large decorations, but they also last well in water. Crush the cut stems before placing in the vase.

WINTER

June marks the beginning of winter throughout the country, with the shortest day of the year on 21 June. For a period of several weeks the hours of daylight remain almost static and then begin their gradual increase. All in the garden seems to have slowed down and except in the most northern parts of the country there is little to do but plan for the spring and wait.

However, there is still much to enjoy in the winter garden despite its general harshness and bleakness. The stark tracery of trees against the evening sun, the refreshing scent of the first narcissus and the early blooms of wintersweet (*Chimonanthus praecox*) are powerful elements of this season.

Perfumed early-flowering shrubs and flowers fill the garden with their scent. Daphne and wintersweet are the most spectacular of these, but also of incredible beauty are the first of the winter-flowering rhododendrons. Bulbs such as galanthus (snowdrops), the miniature daffodils *Narcissus juncifolius* and many of the early flowerers herald the excitement of this season and the promise of the one to come. A pot of *Narcissus bulbicodium*, *Narcissus cantabricus* or one of the cyclamineus types can make a wonderful present for friends or a point of interest inside the house.

Winter can be the most unpredictable season of the year, with icy squalls one day and mild weather the next, and in some areas, rain and more rain. Feeding birds regularly through the winter (and spring in colder areas) will help them survive the cold, blustery weather. Only the keenest gardener will venture out in such unpleasant conditions, yet some time will need to be spent in the garden over the coming months, for winter is one of the most important seasons of the year for preparation.

As winter passes into August the return of spring is a wonderful thing. The dark, bleak days really do seem to be passing, even though frequently this turns out to be illusory. Suddenly we become aware of the reawakening of plants, many already flowering and making it quite clear that, as far as the seasons are concerned, life goes on. In what is officially the last month of winter, August heralds the return to longer daylight hours, balmy evenings in some warmer northern areas and the first real sign of spring — the smell of freshly mown grass.

LEFT: *Chimonanthus praecox*
BELOW: *Narcissus cantabricus* var. *petuioides*

June

Temperature and climate

The temperatures throughout the country will have dropped considerably by the time June arrives and most growth will have come to a halt, except in the most northern parts of the country. Rain across the country will begin to saturate gardens and in the central and southern regions wintry hail and frost will be making themselves felt.

Not much can generally be done outside in the garden during June. Digging flower and vegetable beds may still be achievable in many areas before the winter rains make the soil too difficult to work. In the far north

124   • WINTER

LEFT: Shallots, *Allium cepa* Aggregatum Group
BELOW FROM LEFT: Applying dolomite lime to soil; slatted compost bins allow for several stages of composting; building up sills with compost material.

of the country some sowing and planting is still possible, but in the central and southern regions the process of winter pruning should begin. Once the spraying programmes are complete and the soil is dug, limed and composted, little remains to be done but turn all the prunings and garden debris into compost. June is an ideal time to plan for the following seasons.

and one part bone dust and scatter generously over the bed (a good two handfuls per square metre) to produce a bumper crop. A thick layer of mulch or compost put on the bed now or earlier in autumn will greatly improve the quality of the spring crop.

June is a good month to improve soil fertility in preparation for spring. The vegetable garden will benefit from a good dressing of dolomite lime now. Lime is great for leaf crops and produces fine broccoli, cabbages, rhubarb and silver beet. Building up soils with compost will prepare them for the crops to be planted in August and September. Use a push-hoe wherever possible to

Food and water

The need for food and water diminishes as growth begins to slow down. However, plants that are battling against the elements will appreciate a little foliar feed. At a time when soil temperatures are low and the ground almost unremittingly wet, foliar feeding helps to encourage growth and strengthen struggling roots.

Lightly cultivate asparagus beds once the fern is cut down. Asparagus gain most of the food and water that they need for spring growth at this time of year. Mix two parts dolomite to one part superphosphate

allow air to reach plant roots; this encourages them to grow and also helps to improve drainage.

Too much water is often the problem in many areas at this time of the year. Consider constructing raised beds to solve this problem. These can be an attractive garden feature and winter is a good time to do this. Alternatively, you could install slit drains to improve drainage. Slit drains are easily positioned and are made by cutting a slit in the soil with a sharp spade and inserting the tube-like drain. They are now available at many retail outlets and are reasonably cheap.

Pests and diseases

Slugs and snails are still very active in many gardens and, if left to rampage and multiply unhindered, they will continue to cause irreparable damage to both ornamentals and crops. Winter spraying is very important to control the populations of the many bugs and diseases that attack the garden in the growing season. All deciduous trees, vines and winter vegetables should be sprayed with a copper-based spray to rid them of fungal diseases. On many trees, oil-based sprays are necessary to control scale, woolly aphids and mites that are sitting waiting for the spring.

Lime sulphur is an excellent general fungicide and is best used in the winter when fruit trees and roses are without their leaves. This spray will also kill the destructive red spider and any sucking insects overwintering in your garden. Full-strength winter applications of this multi-purpose spray will, in addition, rid the garden of scale, as well as moss and lichen growths on trees. (A winter mix for all deciduous trees, roses and other deciduous ornamentals is 100 ml lime sulphur in 1.5 litres of water.)

ABOVE: White stock, *Matthiola incana*

The flower garden

The June flower garden requires careful attention as many bulbs and tubers such as dahlias and liliums will rot if they are left in cold, wet ground. Both plants flourish in warm, well-drained soils where they can access plenty of moisture during the summer.

Sowing

It is possible to sow and plant flowers in many areas but regional differences will determine just what will succeed and what will not. Some seeds, such as lobelia, sweet peas and stocks, require winter cold to germinate. Lobelia and sweet peas sown now in well-drained soils will begin to grow. Stocks either sown or planted out will grow despite the cold conditions as long as the soil is well drained.

Alpine plants such as *Aurinia saxatile* syn. *Alyssum saxatile*, aubretia, celmisia, gentian, lewisia, and the alpine poppies can all be sown now in a fine, well-draining soil.

GROWING ALPINE PLANTS

Rock garden plants or alpines are ideal for growing in tubs, pots, sinks and hypertufa troughs. You can plant a mix of alpine plants that flower or have attractive foliage together to get a variety of texture and colour. Choose plants carefully and avoid any that are rampant growers or they may smother their slower growing neighbours. Most alpine plants need full sun and perfect drainage.

Simple steps are all that is required to grow many alpines.
- Place a thin layer of coarse shingle in the bottom of your container.
- Fill the pot with a seed raising mix (preferably lime-free) and firm it lightly.
- Sow the seed and cover with a layer of soil no thicker than the diameter of the seed. (Cover very fine seed with a thin layer of grit rather than seed raising mix.)
- Water by placing the pot to half its depth in water for at least an hour. (Water very fine seed with a mister.)

Propagation and division

Perennial plants can be successfully divided up well into the winter months and planted into their places for the coming season.

Planting

Polyanthus, primrose and primula plants can now be planted out.

Bulbs, corms and tubers

Bulbs will not thrive where shade is dense and the soil is dry and impoverished.

The following bulbs will grow in partial shade with 2–3 hours sun each day if the soil is enriched with plenty of well-rotted compost and bulb food:

Anemone blanda

Colchicum autumnale

Cyclamen coum

Cyclamen hederifolium

Galanthus nivalis (snowdrop)

Leucojum vernum (snowflake)

Muscari armeniacum

Narcissus

Scilla siberica

Plant care

Indoor plants should be watered less during the winter months. When you water always use tepid water. Water which is even a few degrees colder than the pot soil is liable to cause shock to the roots of plants. The soil should be dry to the touch before watering. Many plants, such as tradescantias, cycads, *Beaucarnea recurvata*, anthurium, *Asplenium nidus* and *Paphiopedilum callosum*, respond better to warm water in the winter, although this does not apply to all pot plants. It is best to stop watering plants such as African violets (saintpaulia) and foliage plants such as fittonia, caladium, ficus and maranta, and to water most succulents and cacti sparingly during the winter months, keeping the compost just slightly moist. As long as they received adequate moisture during summer and autumn they will be in the peak of health come spring.

Potted plants can be brought inside from the garden for the coldest of the winter months. Stop or reduce feeding to a low level during winter as unused chemicals

---

> ### TASKS FOR JUNE
> - Do not overwater potted bulbs and ornamentals.
> - Feed young seedlings with a liquid fertiliser sprayed on the leaves.
> - Watch for slugs and snails.
> - Give a general clean-up spray to all ornamental and fruiting deciduous trees, lichen affected trees and roses.
> - Spray indoor plants for scale, woolly aphids and mites.
> - It is sometimes necessary to use an oil-based spray to control scale, woolly aphids and mites on trees, shrubs and ornamentals.

FLOWERS TO PLANT NOW

SOW THESE SEEDS	PLANT THESE SEEDLINGS	PLANT THESE BULBS, CORMS AND TUBERS
Canterbury bells*	Aubretia*	
Delphinium*	Calendula*	Crocosmia
Dianthus	Canterbury bells*	Lilium
Larkspur*	Pansy	Lily of the valley
Lobelia	Polyanthus	Pamianthe (Inca lily)
Lupin	Primrose	Solomon's seal
Stock*	Viola	Tulip
Sweet pea	Wallflower*	Tigridia (jockey cap)

*Only possible in frost-free areas

can build up in the soil and poison the plants if feeding continues at summer strength. Cool, airy conditions suit most pot plants brought indoors; too much heat can delay their flowering, and still, damp air will encourage fungal diseases such as botrytis.

However, humidity suits some pot plants such as palms, ferns, crotons, coffee trees and other leafy tropical and subtropical ornamentals, and a daily misting will benefit them greatly, as will placing the pot on a bed of stones in a tray of water. During winter these plants are often attacked by scale and fluffy mealy bug. A spray with a general insecticide will solve most problems; an old toothbrush or a cotton bud soaked in a little cooking oil or methylated spirits will finish off any scale the spray failed to kill.

Light is important to the ongoing well-being of indoor plants and those brought indoors from the garden. Place them near to north-facing windows, but not where the sun's rays can concentrate and burn them. Some plants, such as ferns, prefer shade and placing them in full sun will damage them. Most indoor plants grown for their foliage prefer filtered light at the very least, if not shade, to look their best.

Lawns

Once the last of the autumn leaves have been cleared, the lawn will not need to be cut very frequently, and then only on dry, sunny days. Overhanging trees and perennial border plants can swamp fine lawn grasses at the edge of the border and leave unsightly bare patches that can persist for several seasons.

Now is the time to thin out tree branches to allow more light to reach the grass and allow it to grow. Lawns struggle to survive if they have to compete for food with large tree roots, so consider planting something other than tall trees near grassy areas, or instead of grass use ground covers which don't mind shade or poor soils, such as the decorative lamiums, the native acaena, or the creeping *Waldsteinia ternata*. (See page 28 for a list of other alternatives to grass lawns.) June is also a good month to carry out any mower repairs and maintenance.

BELOW: African violet, *Saintpaulia* 'Arizona'
BELOW RIGHT: Emerging peas, *Pisum sativum*
BELOW FAR RIGHT: Trimming and dividing rhubarb corms.

The edible garden

Maintain pest control on any pests that might attack growing plants. In the north slugs and snails seldom rest and are always on the lookout for tasty shoots and buds. Even in the south they will occasionally venture out to wreak havoc on tender lettuces.

Sowing

Early varieties of some vegetables can still be sown. Broad beans, onions, peas and potatoes can be sown either in seed trays, cloches, glasshouses or directly into the garden, though this could be risky, as a wet, cold soil can rot rather than germinate seed.

Planting

It is still possible to plant out many vegetables in warm northern areas of the country. Broad beans can still be planted where the soil is not too wet. Broccoli, cabbages, carrots, garlic, lettuce, peas, rhubarb, shallots and turnips can all be planted now in sheltered and warm climates. Rhubarb clumps should be refreshed by digging them up and cutting them back to vigorous roots. They should then be planted in soil that has been enriched with well-rotted animal manure and compost. In cold climates all planting except of the hardiest winter vegetables should wait until late winter or early spring.

The planting out of strong broccoli, cabbage, and cauliflower plants can be completed in mild northern climates. Potatoes can also be planted, but this must be in frost-free areas. Strawberries can also be set into their beds, where they will begin to crop in the early summer.

Harvesting

The winter harvest is at best a meagre one. Winter lettuces such as the French heirloom variety 'Merveille des Quatre Saisons' are surprisingly hardy. They are one source of greens and many such types can be plucked rather than cut to extend their usefulness at this time of the year. At least they will not bolt to seed as they do when conditions are warmer.

Fruit

Deciduous fruit trees should be pruned in winter only after the fruit buds have formed. A fruit or flowering bud is fat and rounded, whereas leaf buds are thin and pointed.

June is also the best month to plant all fruit trees. When planting trees the hole should be dug deep and wide and generous amounts of manure added. Careful preparation now will ensure healthier and more disease-resistant trees later. At planting time it is important to prune and thereby establish the future shape of your tree.

Apple trees do not need a lot of fussy pruning to bear well. It is better to remove a few large branches every fourth year to prevent the centre of the tree from becoming choked. It is important to keep the centre open to the bees and the sun for good crops. Any dead branches should also be removed at pruning time. Branches that cross or are growing very close together should also be removed. Horizontal or near-horizontal branches should be retained as they form the shape of the tree, as well as carrying better and more reachable crops. Branches that grow strongly vertical should be removed unless you like climbing trees to gather the crop. A balanced shape of moderate height and with plenty of space between all the branches is the most desirable result of a pruning programme.

ABOVE: Winter lettuce, 'Merveille des Quatre Saisons'

> ### ENDIVE — AN ALTERNATIVE TO LETTUCE
> If you have difficulty growing lettuce because of the cold you could try growing endive. A close relative of chicory, this plant is now available in many colours and forms, such as 'Ruffec Green Curled' and 'Très Fine Maraichère'. The green curled-leaf, divided-leaf and red-leafed forms are excellent for winter salads but need to be blanched to be really palatable and remove any bitterness. Blanching is easy to do. Choose two or three healthy well-grown plants and place a box or pot over the top of the plant excluding all light but leaving a small gap at the bottom to allow ventilation. In two to three weeks your endive will be ready for using. The leaves will be pale, tender and sweeter than if they had been left untreated. Endive can also be blanched by covering it with a layer of straw or by tying a string around the top of the plant so that the centre is tightly enclosed for at least two weeks. Alternatively, soak endive in warm water before eating to remove any bitterness.

When pruning any branches take care where you cut. Large stumps left after cutting branches look ugly and can cause rot and disease to enter the tree. Cut close to the parent stem when pruning. If the branch is large make the first cut well away from the desired point and remove the bulk of the branch; you can then make the final cut without the weight of the branch falling heavily and tearing the bark. Pruning paste and pruning paint can be used even if they serve no other purpose than to disguise the wound.

Pear trees can be treated in a similar way to apples. They tend to grow more vigorously and may require more regular radical surgery. Old pear trees become very large and clogged with fine growth if they are neglected. Fruiting becomes minimal and the size of the fruit minute. There is only one solution: to remove the central branches of the tree and shorten back all others, maintaining an overall round shape. Fine growths can also be reduced to just a few per branch. This will ensure better fruiting in the coming seasons.

VEGETABLES TO PLANT NOW	
SOW THESE SEEDS	PLANT THESE SEEDLINGS
Broad bean	
Broccoli*	Broccoli*
Cabbage*	Cabbage*
Carrot*	Carrot*
Endive	Endive
Lettuce*	Garlic
Onion	Lettuce*
Pea*	Pea
Potato	Potato*
Spinach*	Rhubarb (crowns)
Turnip*	Shallot
	*Only possible in frost-free areas

Peach and nectarine trees carry fruit only on the new wood that grew in the previous season. Heavy pruning and removal of new wood will guarantee a poor crop. Be gentle with at least half of the new wood, reducing it by no more than a third (this will provide the fruiting spurs of the coming season). The rest of the new wood can be cut back harder, by at least two thirds, providing growth for the fruit spurs in the season after next.

Apricots, cherries, damsons and plums will often crop well without any pruning, but before long their robust natures will quickly produce a tangled mass with fruit forming well out of your reach. Over-vigorous branches and excess upright branches should be removed. Dead branches and twiggy growth should also be cut away. Fruit is carried on old wood in most varieties, but the pruning of worn-out or spindly wood is the only way to regenerate healthy fruiting spurs. The result will be quality fruit in several years' time. To avoid missing a season's crop, carry out this pruning in stages over several seasons.

Vines must be pruned correctly to fruit well. As soon as all the leaves have fallen choose one or two of the healthiest long shoots growing from the main stem and prune away everything else. Remove all side-growths from these shoots, and tie along wires, or fix them to a fence with soft ties. These main stems will develop many new shoots in the spring and the fruit will form on these in the late spring. As the growing season progresses these new shoots will lengthen considerably. Don't let them all grow because overabundant leaf growth will shade the forming grapes and drain food from the desired crop. Pinch most of these shoots back close to where the grapes have formed, leaving one or two to develop into next year's long shoots.

Blackcurrants should be pruned after three or four years of growth, by which time the bushes will have become overcrowded and will not be bearing as well. Remove one in every three stems at the base. Strong new shoots will then appear. The cut butts will also produce new shoots and these should all be retained as they will carry the coming season's crop.

Gooseberries and red and white currants are all densely growing bushes. They quickly become tangled with a resulting drop in the quality and quantity of fruit. All old, tangled wood and any thin, weak shoots should be removed. Old wood and the mature wood from the previous season will carry the crops, so be selective when pruning. Removing all old wood will result in no crop. Keeping the bushes open to the sun and air movement will ensure better produce.

Raspberries are perhaps the easiest of all fruits to prune. Summer-fruiting varieties should have all the old canes removed to make room for the fresh new shoots. Autumn-fruiting varieties can be pruned by reducing all stems to ground level in the winter.

Blackberries, keriberries, loganberries and other hybrids can be treated in a similar way to summer-fruiting raspberries. Cut all canes that have fruited to ground level. In addition, remove thin, weak new shoots. Only new shoots should be left to produce the coming season's crop.

June features

Palms

In recent years there has been a revival in growing palms indoors. Their leaves grow outward from a single stem often in the shape of a fan or feathered into many leaflets. Palms must be kept moist at all times if they are to look their best. Lack of water will cause the tips of the leaves to turn brown, which can only be remedied by removing the leaves.

LEFT: Kentia palm, *Howea forsteriana*
BELOW FROM LEFT: Cowslip, *Primula veris*; white anomalous primrose; *Primula* 'Gold Lace'

Howea forsteriana or the kentia palm is perhaps the most popular plant and one of the best palms for growing indoors. As a young plant its leaves stand erect but as it grows they bow with age, creating a highly decorative habit. It prefers low light, with summer temperatures of 13°C to 18°C and a winter temperature of 13°C. It needs frequent watering in summer as the

growers have many fine plants in this range. (See appendix, page 167.) *Primula veris* (cowslip), *Primula elatior* (oxslip) and the Barnhaven Cowichan polyanthus (primula, polyanthus group) are all highly desirable garden plants. The old double-green primrose is a beautiful and rare plant for the garden and a great talking point for visitors. Anomalous primroses (*Primula veris × vulgaris* or Jack-in-the-greens) were popular in the sixteenth century and can still be obtained if you are determined and persistent in your hunt. The usually single flowers have a ruff of small green leaves behind the bloom. Yellow (*P. × polyantha* 'Eldorado'), crimson (*P. × p.* 'Salamander')

new leaves appear and in winter just enough water to keep the compost moist. Kentias should be repotted every second spring, but only if they are growing well. Hard water will cause the leaves to brown. This can be prevented by adding a small pinch of Epsom salts to the water, or by boiling the water and allowing it to cool before watering.

Primulas

Many of the primulas are exquisite plants but at present it is not easy to find them. Old gardens and specialist

and mauve purple (*P. × p.* 'Tipperary Purple') forms of these plants still survive. They will all grow easily from division during the cooler months of the year.

Primulas and their many cultivars all make ideal plants for the winter and early spring garden. Most withstand the cold weather and frost well and provide welcome splashes of colour at a time of the year when the garden is generally looking bare. They prefer cool temperatures, partial shade and a soil rich in humus. They also appreciate full sun in the spring, but must have semi shade as the temperatures warm and summer approaches. In northern areas where the summers are hot and dry they prefer a south-facing position that is both moist and shaded. In the south they can be planted in full sun but also need constant moisture and shelter from the hottest of the summer sun if they are to survive year after year. They are tolerant of being transplanted and this can be accomplished even when they are in full bloom, especially if conditions are moist and cool.

Winter roses

Hellebores (winter roses) will flower from June until November, brightening up the winter garden. They look splendid at the edge of a path, or planted en masse in the flower bed, or under deciduous trees. Hellebores have healthy leaves that will survive the season and provide a constant backdrop to other flowering plants once their own flowers have faded. They are woodland plants and prefer dappled light rather than full sun and dislike conditions that are hot, dry or too wet. However, *Helleborus argutifolius* syn. *corsicus* is able to cope well both in sun and in dry conditions. It bears pale creamy green flowers from late winter and is not fussy about

BELOW: *Helleborus niger* 'White Magic'
RIGHT: *Helleborus argutifolius*
FAR RIGHT: Persimmon, *Diospyros kaki*

soil, but will benefit from a little compost and peat. *Helleborus niger* and *H. orientalis* are the more commonly grown winter roses, but many others are also very attractive garden plants. *Helleborus odorus* has a green flower and a tangy, currant-like scent, while *H. guttatus* bears white flowers spotted inside with red, and the tender *H. lividus* has green flowers marked with purple and dark green leaves with creamy veins.

Growing hellebores from seed is easy, although only the species will come true. Hybrids will produce a wide range of colours that are great fun to use in the garden. Collect the seed as soon as it ripens in late spring and early summer. Sow it in pots or trays immediately in a mix of compost and fine grit or sharp sand. Frost will help with germination and the seeds should not be allowed to dry out. Germination will occur in the early spring and flowering plants can be had from seed within two years.

Division is another way to propagate hellebores. Divide the individual crowns into separate plants with a sharp knife, or chop a clump in half with a sharp spade and replant both pieces. As little damage as possible will ensure that the divisions grow rapidly.

Persimmon

The persimmon (diospyros) is a most delicious fruit that will grow in a large variety of temperature ranges. Some forms are hardier than others and you will need to discover just what type best suits your climate. In very cold areas subject to hard winter frosts persimmons would not be viable, but will usually grow where lemons can grow. Generally these are small trees; some types will reach 5 metres in 30 years, whereas others will grow quickly to 3 metres at the most. A persimmon will flourish in a well-drained position in full sun.

As an ornamental tree, the persimmon is splendid at all times of the year. With brilliant autumn colour, delicious, highly decorative winter fruit, handsome new foliage in the spring, as well as a fine, grey bark and an elegant, idiosyncratic growth habit, it deserves a place in almost every garden.

New forms of non-astringent persimmons are available and can be eaten when they are still firm. Most astringent persimmons may only be eaten when they are very soft and ripe. The better known 'Fuyu' is eaten when still firm. It is not astringent, and to some palates not as delicious.

July

Temperature and climate

In many parts of the country July has the coldest and worst weather of the year. The air and soil temperatures are regularly at their lowest. Frost strikes many gardens, burning and even killing tender plants; in many districts, rain saturates the soil. This combination of factors conspires against most productive gardening. For some July is seen as the dead heart of winter, for others it marks the beginning of a gardener's year. A few warm days may tempt us to venture outside to plant and sow. With the extremes in the weather at this time of the year, it is usually wiser to wait at least until the soil starts to

LEFT: Good quality secateurs are an essential tool for the gardener.
BELOW FROM LEFT: *Lathyrus odoratus* 'Lord Nelson'; hyacinth, *Hyacinthoides* 'Blue Ensign'; cymbidium orchid

warm up and all danger of severe frosts has passed. In northern parts, this may occur in August; however, further south, frosts may strike as late as mid-September. However, no matter how bleak conditions are, daylight hours are on the increase and spring is not far off. All that remains is to enjoy the inexorable return of germination and growth.

ones. Watering is best done in the morning, so that as the soil warms during the day, the plants can more easily use it. Frost damage can be minimised by watering frostbitten plants in the morning before the sun burns them. In sheltered gardens cymbidium orchids will be coming into flower; a regular liquid feed will greatly improve the general well-being, flower colour and quality of the plants.

Vegetable beds that didn't receive a dressing of lime in June can be given it now and compost can slowly be added to the garden, gradually bringing it into top condition for spring planting.

Food and water

Water pot plants sparingly during these cold winter months. Most of them should be allowed to dry out between waterings so that the top of the soil is dry to the touch. Those plants that are still growing strongly should, however, be fed and watered as usual. Once pots of bulbs begin to show flower buds, bring them inside and feed weekly with a liquid fertiliser. Continue this feeding until the end of the flowering period.

In the outdoor garden it is easy to neglect watering. Cold winds can dry gardens almost as quickly as hot

Pests and diseases

Pests don't give up on the winter garden easily. Destroy mass dormitories of snails and slugs before the first of the sun's warming rays reaches them and they awake on the hunt for anything green and succulent. Indoor plants will need checking for any pests such as scale or woolly aphids that may have developed in the warm, indoor conditions of winter.

A programme of spraying is most useful at this time of the year. Tree diseases such as curly leaf need to be sprayed against now. Any deciduous trees that showed signs of disease last season should be sprayed now if this has not already been done. Lime sulphur can be used as long as bud burst hasn't yet occurred. When you spray, spray the ground as well, because it is here that many pests and fungal diseases rest during winter.

Scale is a problem in many warm gardens. Lime sulphur will kill scale, but it cannot be used at full strength on plants in leaf or in flower, as the sulphur will burn the plant and cause considerable damage. Copper-based sprays are most useful in the ongoing job of keeping the garden free of fungal diseases.

The flower garden

July is a good time to start planting roses, trees, shrubs, climbers and herbaceous plants. Of course much depends on the weather and the state of the soil. Trying to dig or for that matter even walking on very wet soil can do more harm than good.

Sowing

As the hours of daylight lengthen and the soil begins to warm it is again time to decide what flowers you want to have in the garden this coming spring and summer. Raising your own from seed is fun and much cheaper if you choose your plants carefully. If you can persuade a friend or two to collaborate, you will be able to double or triple your collection by exchanging seedlings later.

Seeds will quickly germinate to provide plants for the summer garden in a glasshouse or in a warm and sheltered part of the garden under a sheet of glass. In areas where frosts don't occur, direct sowing of many ornamentals can take place, including the beautiful *Aquilegia longissima*, calendula, carnation, cornflower, mignonette, pansy, stocks and sweet peas. These seeds need to be sown thinly in planter trays.

Propagation and division

Now is a good time to take root cuttings from many perennial plants such as anchusa, dicentra, eryngium, nepeta, and Oriental poppies. Dig plants from the ground and sever the roots with a knife. Once the roots are cut into 10 to 15 cm lengths, toss them in a

BELOW LEFT: *Calendula officinalis*
BELOW: *Aquilegia longissima*

> **TASKS FOR JULY**
> - Prepare flower beds with compost and a general fertiliser.
> - Use liquid fertiliser to boost growth of young seedlings.
> - Prune hydrangeas, fuchsias and roses.
> - Regularly trim conifer hedges from this month on.
> - Spray fruit trees with a copper spray if they were affected by curly leaf.
> - Plant new rhubarb crowns.
> - Use lime sulphur as a general clean-up spray on deciduous trees.
> - Give garden soil a dressing of lime. (Avoid acid-loving plants such as azaleas.)
> - Build up the vegetable beds with compost.

TOP: Sever perennial roots with a knife.
ABOVE: Severed roots cut into lengths.
FAR RIGHT: Root cuttings tossed in a bag with fungicide.

plastic bag with a powdered fungicide and then plant them into seed trays until they are growing strongly. Always take cuttings from healthy plants and ensure they have no signs of disease. Use three parts sand to one part potting mix and make sure your seed trays are sterilised.

Planting

If weather conditions are favourable, this could be the right month to plant a hedge. When deciding what type of hedge to plant, consider what size you want it to be. A 1.8 metre hedge does not require ladders and trestles to enable it to be cut. But where privacy is an issue, a taller hedge may be called for.

Before planting a hedge remove any weeds and feed the soil a little. When planting a hedge in a straight line draw a string between two sticks and mark the exact position for each tree. If planting a hedge in a curve, use

ABOVE: Gladiolus corms and cormlets.

> **PLANTING BULBS**
> - When planting bulbs such as tulips in pots for display, fill the container with enough potting mix (and a little bulb food or bone dust) so that the tops of the bulbs are just below the rim when planted.
> - Place the bulbs close together but don't let them touch the sides of the pot or each other. This gives them room to grow and also enables water and food to reach the roots.
> - Sprinkle potting mix over the bulbs and firm gently.
> - Stand the pot in water up to one third of its depth for several hours. Water will percolate up to the bulbs and their root zone.

a garden hose to mark out the curve beforehand and mark the exact position of the trees with spray paint. Dig a trench to the required depth and drop in a little slow-release fertiliser. It is then a relatively simple task to position and plant your hedge.

Generally speaking, in order to achieve a thick, bushy hedge it is advisable to distance the plants about half the width of the plant apart. For example, if the plant were 1 m wide, the spacing would be approximately 50 cm apart. For a smaller hedge such as the colourful decorative coprosmas or the slower, smaller growing *Buxus sempervirens* 'Suffruticosa' it would be advisable to plant half as close again. Make sure to plant the trees perfectly upright as straight trunks are important to the final look of your hedge. Finally, water the young trees in.

A light prune after planting will help to establish the line of the new hedge. I like to let the hedge grow for at least one full season before trimming it back by about a third. This seemingly drastic action will not only prevent the hedge from becoming hollow at the base but will also keep it dense, compact and looking good.

Erect a wind cloth if necessary in the first year or two of a hedge's development to shelter the trees while they become established. This will not only speed the hedge's establishment, but it will also give a little privacy at the same time.

Trim the hedge at least three times a year while it is young; old, neglected hedges also respond well to this treatment. Feeding young and old hedges will greatly improve their health and vigour. (See page 142 for suitable plants for hedges.)

Bulbs, corms and tubers

Tulips can continue to be planted well into the month of July. Gladiolus corms can also be planted in warmer gardens. Corms planted now will be flowering before Christmas. *Iris sibirica* flowers best where the winter climate is cold. Plant the rhizomes in autumn or winter in a rich, moist but well-drained soil. Once the plants are growing strongly they are able to tolerate very wet soils. In a glasshouse begonia tubers can be placed into trays with a little soil and gently coaxed into growth. Once they are vigorously sprouting they can be planted up into pots and hanging baskets or out into the garden, if conditions are sheltered and frost free. Shift potted hyacinths that have sprouted into a sunny corner of the garden and feed with liquid fertiliser as soon as the buds begin to show colour. Once they are flowering freely they can be brought inside every three or four days to enjoy. Hyacinths that are planted in the garden will also

PRUNING ROSES

WELL PRUNED ICEBERG ROSE

Major rose pruning is usually done in July. There are no hard and fast rules about the timing, but if your area is subject to late frosts, it makes good sense to postpone pruning until all danger of frost has passed. New buds hit by heavy frost will be destroyed and a lot of work will be wasted if you prune too early. Well-pruned roses should be symmetrical and with the branches open to the sun. They should not be congested and full of crossing branches. Roses need to be pruned differently according to the type of rose. (See pages 44–47 to identify different types.) For any pruning you will need a good pair of secateurs and some stout gloves.

GENERAL TIPS

- When making a cut, prune to an outward-facing bud to keep the centre of the rose open and prevent it from becoming congested and subject to disease.
- Make a clean, sloping cut, running away from the bud to ensure quick healing and rapid growth. The cut should not be too close to the chosen bud.
- Reduce long branches that overbalance the plant and could easily be broken in strong winds.
- Remove all dead flowers and hips back to a strong leaf bud and remove soft 'water' growth that may be growing away from the base.
- Remove any congested or spindly growth.

PRUNE TO OUTWARD-FACING BUD

HYBRID TEA AND FLORIBUNDA ROSES

- Remove any old, tired wood that has not produced flowers.
- Shorten all remaining stems by one third.
- Cut any weak stems back hard.

MINIATURE ROSES

- Remove any non-flowering wood.
- Remove weak shoots and clear the centre so that air can move freely throughout the plant.

REMOVE CONGESTED, SPINDLY GROWTH

SHRUB OR OLD-FASHIONED ROSES

These are very individual in their pruning needs. By working with them you will, over a period of time, discover their individual requirements. However, a few general rules can be applied:

- Cut out all old, tired and poorly flowering wood. (You may need a pruning saw to do this.)
- Cut back by half any new shoots growing from the base and shorten all the small side-shoots to a few buds. These buds are the flowering shoots for the coming season.
- Instead of pruning, peg the roses down with string or forked sticks to force new, vigorous growth from all the buds growing along a shoot.

FLOWERS TO PLANT NOW

SOW THESE SEEDS		PLANT THESE SEEDLINGS	PLANT THESE BULBS, CORMS AND TUBERS
Alyssum	Linaria	Aquilegia	Crocosmia
Aquilegia	Mignonette	Calendula	Eucomis
Calendula	Nasturtium*	Canterbury bells	Freesia
Carnation	Pansy	Cornflower	Gladiolus
Cornflower	Snapdragon	Foxglove	Hyacinth
Forget-me-not	Stock	Godetia	Lilium
Godetia	Sweet pea	Hollyhock	Moraea
Larkspur		Larkspur	
		Pansy	
		Polyanthus	
		Rudbeckia	
		Russell lupin	
*Only practicable in warm areas		Stock	

benefit from regular doses of liquid fertiliser once the flower spikes have developed.

Plant care

July is the best month to trim macrocarpa, *Chamaecyparis lawsoniana* and other conifer hedges. A regular light pruning is better than a heavy occasional cut. Never cut back beyond the foliage line or permanent damage can occur. This is also the month to prune roses. (See page 141.) By late winter most of the garden's maintenance should have been completed. Compost will have been made and most of the garden prepared for the coming season.

Hedges

A well-cared-for hedge provides many benefits for the home garden. Perhaps the most useful feature of a large hedge such as escallonia, or the attractive native *Olearia paniculata*, is that they are ideal where a quick-growing shelter is required. They will also reduce wind strength better than a solid barrier. Hedges also filter the air and are particularly suitable in city areas where it is necessary to absorb dust and noise. Many hedge plants are also able to provide an effective visual screen, giving privacy, and by using some of the prickly types, such as holly, berberis, *Osmanthus heterophyllus* or the hardy rugosa roses, you can also add security to your property.

Deciduous flowering hedges such as chaenomeles (flowering quince) provide seasonal beauty and are ideal to use where winter light is at a premium. Evergreen types such as the shiny-leafed autumn-flowering *Camellia sasanqua* suit areas where winter light isn't a problem. They can be used to provide all year round background texture and colour while at the same time complementing other plants in the garden.

Conifers make good hedges. They are evergreen, grow densely, respond well to shaping and trimming, withstand extremes of climate, are not fussy about soil, are long-lived and many are quick-growing. Kawaka, larix, taxus, totara and tsuga are all suitable as hedges.

All types need trimming at least once a year and others such as the tough, resilient escallonia, lonicera and box at least two or three times. Slow-growing types are less trouble in the long term as they need less trimming. Regular light pruning is better for the hedge. Not only does regular trimming build a better structure

LEFT: Trimmed hedges of box, *Buxus sempervirens*, in a knot garden.
ABOVE: A well-cared-for hedge of hornbeam, *Carpinus betulus*.

it is also easier to carry out. Infrequent trimming creates a huge task when it comes to disposing of the waste.

Lawns

Mid-winter lawns differ in the sort of treatment that they need, depending on the type of lawn used and the climate. Summer-growing lawns such as kikuyu and couch grass slow down their growth in autumn and virtually stop growing altogether in the winter. They need little care and almost no mowing. In gardens where cool-season grasses such as Kentucky bluegrass have been planted, they will continue to grow, needing only gentle feeding and the occasional mow. Avoid walking on lawns that have been frosted as every step leaves a mark that will be visible until the lawn begins to grow again.

ABOVE: Planting one head of garlic produces many bulbs.
ABOVE RIGHT: Avoid pushing garlic bulbs down hard when planting.
BELOW RIGHT: Pruning old plum wood.

The edible garden

Green manure crops (such as blue lupin) planted in the autumn will almost be ready for digging in. Dig them in before they become tough and woody. Don't bury them deeply, but rather turn them under shallowly where they can rot down.

Sowing

In northern and milder areas sowing of many crops can begin. When deciding what to plant it is best to make a list of what you like to eat and avoid growing huge amounts of any one crop. Small, regular sowings are better than one large sowing, most of which will be wasted.

Silver beet can be sown in well-drained soil in the second half of the month. Broccoli, cabbage, carrots, cauliflower and onions can be sown now for thinning and planting out later. Peas can be tried but will probably not flourish in soggy, poorly drained soil. Potatoes can be planted and earthed up until spring when all danger of frost has passed. They can also be raised in a half barrel, a tyre or in a large black plastic bag, but it is best to wait until mid-August in southern regions. A potato such as Ilam Hardy will grow in the cold weather and is ideal as an early potato. Red King does well in the south, while Tahi and Rua do best in northern parts of the country. Lettuces and endive can be sown in protected spots or preferably in seed trays for planting out later when the soil has warmed.

VEGETABLES TO PLANT NOW

SOW THESE SEEDS	PLANT THESE SEEDLINGS
Broad bean	
Broccoli	Artichoke (globe)
Cabbage	Broccoli
Carrot	Cabbage
Cauliflower	Carrot
Lettuce	Cauliflower
Onion	Celery
Potato	Cress
Radish	Garlic
Silver beet	Herbs
Spinach	Leek
Turnip	Lettuce
	Onion
	Shallot
	Silver beet

Planting

Planting out the seedlings that you have raised in trays and pots can begin now, but in colder parts planting out even well-established plants will be more successful in a few weeks' time. Seedling vegetables — and in fact all plants — will greatly benefit from side-dressings of fertiliser and also from liquid fertiliser sprinkled on their leaves. Broad beans, celery, potatoes and strawberries will all benefit from spraying with a fungicide spray.

Now is an ideal time to plant garlic. Garlic enjoys growing where there has been a previous root vegetable crop. A free-draining, friable, fertile soil and full sun suits it best and planting can begin any time from May until August. A light sprinkle of lime and a little general-purpose fertiliser can be added to most soils. Separate liming and fertilising by several weeks, then allow the soil to settle for a week or so before planting.

Garlic bulbs start to develop as the daylight hours gradually increase, coming into full maturity around mid-summer. Most types are winter hardy, but if your conditions are very cold they can be planted in trays, under a cloche, or in pots for planting out into the garden when the soil is warmer. A single head of garlic will produce many cloves. Separate them carefully and discard any that are not plump and well formed. Push the selected cloves into the soil very gently, as pushing them hard down will delay and sometimes inhibit the development of strong, healthy roots. Plant the individual cloves 10 to 12 cm apart, in rows, and cover with 2.5 cm of fine soil. Keep the beds well watered and weeded.

Fruit

The planting of fruit trees can continue this month. When the soil dries (if only for only a matter of hours), dig holes to provide drainage for your newly planted trees. Pruning and spraying should be almost completed and the ground cleared of any rotten or diseased fruit that might still remain. All pip fruit trees should be pruned by the end of this month, including any crab apples. Prunus varieties may be better pruned in late August as the sap begins to rise. This prevents diseases like silver leaf from entering the tree and debilitating it. Any diseased wood not yet removed should be cut and burnt. Dumping diseased wood can easily pass diseases on to other unsuspecting gardeners.

All grape and kiwifruit vines must be pruned soon before the sap begins to rise. A vine pruned after the sap has risen will continue to bleed for some time.

July features

Daphne

Some plants only flower in the winter and the scent of *Daphne odora rubra* has to be one of the best. This plant is a highly scented form of daphne. *Daphne odora leucanthe* is a strong-growing plant and soon forms a large bush from which it is possible to pick bunches of flowers to perfume the rooms indoors. Plant them near a doorway or in an area where the perfume can be trapped for fuller enjoyment to get the most out of these divinely scented plants.

When buying a new daphne plant, a few things should be looked for. The leaves should be healthy and shiny, neither wrinkled nor dehydrated, and of a good rich, green colour. A well-branched, evenly balanced plant should be chosen. It should be planted in soil that is well drained, lime-free and cool. The quality of the soil can be improved by adding a little peat, sand and leaf mould. Daphne prefer shade or early morning sun but they will also grow in full sun. A little blood and bone, tea leaves, or even a little Epsom salts scattered around the root zone will help this plant to grow and add perfume to your winter garden.

LEFT: *Daphne odora leucanthe*
BELOW FROM LEFT: *Cyclamen persicum* hybrid; *Iris ensata* syn. *kaempferi*; cymbidium orchid

Cyclamen

Cyclamen are very varied, there being almost 20 species known throughout the world. Perhaps the best known among the hardy cyclamens is *Cyclamen hederifolium* syn. *neapolitanum*, some strains of which are scented. The best known semi-hardy cyclamen is the immensely popular *C. persicum*, which comes in many hybrid

beautiful plants are most suitable for planting at the edge of a pond and do require frequent watering to flourish. Louisiana irises are somewhat frost-tender. They come in the most subtle range of colours and are also very desirable plants for the home garden.

Cymbidium orchids

Cymbidiums are orchids that will grow without a glasshouse in frost free parts of the country. The cymbidium is the easiest of all orchids to grow. It is also readily available commercially and reasonably cheap to buy. It is a generous and forgiving plant, tolerating neg-

forms and is frequently grown in pots. It flowers profusely throughout winter and is ideal for brightening up sheltered frost-free gardens or a cool room.

Siberian irises

Irises of the Sibirica type have intensely coloured flowers and will grow in the widest variety of soils, including extremely wet (even growing in water) and extremely dry (even dry and dusty) conditions. The Japanese ensata or kaempferi irises as they are also known are also able to grow in a wide variety of soil conditions. These

lect yet is still prepared to give a good flowering. This begins in mid-winter, with some hybrids flowering well on into early summer. A fully grown plant can, under reasonable conditions, produce 10 to 30 flower spikes in a single season. Each flower spike can carry more than 10 individual blooms, all lasting for a month or more. Orchids come in a wide variety of colour combinations, including dark red or brown, pink, green, yellow and white. Fully grown plants may stand a metre high, while miniatures are smaller in leaf length and smaller in flower.

August

Temperature and climate

August weather can be the most unpredictable of the year, with icy squalls one day and mild weather the next and, in some areas, rain and more rain. Gardeners need to take advantage of even small breaks in bad weather, for this is one of the most important planting seasons of the year. In the northern and central districts the first welcome signs of spring mean that many seeds and seedlings can either be sown or planted. In the south snow can fall as late as the end of August and hard frosts are often felt until early September. It is wiser either to sow in trays or wait until the coldest weather has passed.

LEFT: *Gladiolus clarkei*

BELOW FROM LEFT: Applying a side dressing of general-purpose fertiliser; *Prunus mume*; *Galanthus caucasicus*

Food and water

Preparation of the vegetable garden should by now be well in hand. Any compost, peat or seaweed added to the garden now will ensure better crops in the spring and early summer garden. A side dressing of a general-purpose manure would be of benefit to the entire garden. Blood and bone added to the strawberry bed

Pests and diseases

All stone fruit trees must be sprayed with a copper spray now if a lime sulphur spray wasn't used before bud burst. The early flowering *Prunus mume*, or flowering apricot, blossoms at the end of winter and should at this time be sprayed with a mild copper spray. An overstrong solution will ruin both the pink form and the pure white form of this tree. Although it doesn't fruit, this tree produces wonderful spring flowers and brilliant foliage colours in the autumn. Spraying it now will ensure that the foliage is healthy and vigorous. Spray roses with a copper spray to prevent black spot.

will bring growth on quickly and establish the first of the crop. For small seedlings a dressing of dried blood will bring quick results without burning the plants.

Most parts of New Zealand have wet winters as is evidenced by the lush green of the countryside. The overabundance of water can often be a problem. Seeds and seedlings cannot cope when they have to sit in pools of cold water for weeks on end. Their roots rot and they slowly die. Citrus trees are very susceptible to cold, wet weather. At the first signs of yellowing leaves, check your drainage; it may save the tree.

The flower garden

As soon as all danger of frost has passed some of the more tender annuals and perennials can be planted out. By the middle of the month many hardy annuals such as mignonette, scabious, cornflower, Virginian stock and Shirley poppies can be sown in the open ground. Gladioli can be planted in parts of the north and carnations, penstemons and antirrhinums (snapdragons) planted out. In the south it pays to wait another month before planting gladioli.

MAKING YOUR OWN LIQUID MANURE

An effective liquid manure can be made from nettle and comfrey leaves. These plants contain nitrogen, phosphorus and potassium, all of great benefit to growing plants.

- Prepare the liquid manure well away from the house, as the aroma can get a little high.
- In a large plastic bucket or drum place at least two kilograms of cut leaves and stalks.
- Cover with 30 litres of water and leave to ferment for several weeks.
- Dilute at a rate of one part of water to one part of concentrate.
- Spray or water onto crops.

Simple liquid manures can also be made from bird, cow, horse and pig manures, or from seaweed, grass clippings or just nettles.

- Soak several large shovelfuls of manure, or a large bag of seaweed or clippings or other material in a 200-litre (44-gallon) drum of water. (This soaking process can be repeated several times with the same base before it is depleted of nutrients.)
- Cover with 30 litres of water and leave to ferment for several weeks.
- Dilute one part concentrate to three parts of water.
- Spray onto leaves or water onto roots to produce quick growing plants.

Sowing

The sowing of many desirable annuals can begin just as soon as the soil has warmed. *Lobularia maritima* (syn. *Alyssum maritimum*) can be easily raised from seed, either in seed trays or sown directly into the soil. Aquilegia will, in southern areas, have been subjected to several frostings and even snow. This process of scarifying will ensure better germination. Hollyhock (*Alcea rosea*) seeds sown into peat pots can easily be planted into the garden just as soon as the temperatures have risen. Pansy and viola seeds are easy to grow and also seem to like a chilling to improve their germination rate. As soon as they have developed their second set of leaves they can be put in the garden, either in pots or directly into the soil. Pansies and violas are desirable garden plants as they flower at all times of the year. An early autumn sowing will see the garden through to the early months of spring, while a spring sowing will ensure a supply of pansies and violas well into the summer.

Propagation and division

Chrysanthemum and any other cuttings, such as salvias, phlox and rudbeckia, that were taken at the end of autumn can now be placed in the garden or left to mature for another month before planting out.

Planting

In the north, planting of many annuals and perennials can begin in earnest. In warm parts of the country sow or plant ageratum, alyssum, aster, bedding begonia, boronia, California poppy, carnation, cosmos, gaillardia, geranium, gerbera, nasturtium, salvia, sunflower, verbena, viscaria and zinnia. In cold areas plant bedding begonias in seed trays and get them sprouted before planting out. Marigold, polyanthus, salvia, scabious, snapdragon and statice can be sown in trays or planted out.

As soon as all danger of frost has passed some of the more tender annuals and perennials such as cineraria, bouvardia and *Euphorbia pulcherrima* (poinsettia) can also be planted into the garden.

LEFT: Hollyhock, *Alcea rosea*
BELOW: Canna lily, *Canna × generalis* 'Alberich'

> **TASKS FOR AUGUST**
> - Divide perennials up and plant out in the garden border.
> - Prune roses in frost-free areas.
> - Plant liliums in sharp sand and peat to ensure perfect drainage.
> - Plant tuberous begonias in seed trays until they have sprouted.
> - Spray vegetables with a copper spray as soon as fungal diseases appear.
> - Watch for slugs and snails.
> - Apply a liquid fertiliser to vegetables and ornamentals to encourage seedling growth.

Bulbs, corms and tubers

In the warm northern parts of the country it is possible to make plantings of gladioli in the open ground and dahlias either in the open ground or in boxes of moist sand.

Agapanthus, canna lilies, dahlias and liliums can be planted in all but the coldest regions. Gladioli are best planted in October in places subject to late frosts. Liliums not planted earlier can be planted now, paying careful attention to drainage.

Lawns

Weed control programmes can begin as soon as there is any sign of spring growth. When a lawn is healthy most weeds simply cannot compete. Regular mowing is one way to keep weeds down, but if they do get out of control, or you simply decide that you must have a bowling green finish, there is a wide variety of selective weed-killers on the market that will help you solve the problem. When handling weedkillers it is important to remember just how lethal they are to children, animals and gardeners alike. Spraying carried out on a windy day can do considerable damage both to your garden and that of your neighbours. An animal or a child can be easily poisoned simply by touching or walking on a lawn that has been sprayed with a weedkiller. When spraying, choose a still day and a time when animals and children are inside. Wear gloves, a mask and always wash your hands and all equipment immediately after use. Store weedkillers in a locked cupboard or well out of the reach of small hands.

FLOWERS TO PLANT NOW

SOW THESE SEEDS

Ageratum*	Mignonette	
Alyssum*	Nasturtium*	
Aquilegia	Pansy	
Aster*	Phlox	
Boronia*	Rudbeckia	
Carnation	Salvia*	
Celosia	Scabious	
Cornflower	Shirley poppy	
Cosmos	Sunflower*	
Gaillardia*	Verbena*	
Geranium*	Viola	
Gerbera*	Virginian stock	
Hollyhock	Viscaria*	
Larkspur	Zinnia*	
Marigold		

PLANT THESE SEEDLINGS

Alyssum	Sweet William
Antirrhinum	Verbena
Candytuft	
Carnation	
Delphinium	
Larkspur	
Lobelia	
Penstemon	
Polyanthus	
Primula	
Salvia	
Scabious	
Statice	
Stock	

PLANT THESE BULBS, CORMS AND TUBERS

Agapanthus
Begonia, tuberous
Dahlia
Gladiolus
Lilium

*Only practicable in warm areas

The edible garden

As the days grow longer and the soils warmer the vegetable garden is becoming increasingly abundant. Now is also a good time to apply a copper spray to combat peach leaf curl that may have afflicted the trees last summer. Apply the spray before the flower buds burst.

Sowing

Important seed-raising is carried out during the last weeks of August. In most areas this must be done under glass in as warm an area as possible, with careful attention to moisture levels (moist soil being better than wet). A great deal is possible in warm northern areas but still, in most of the south, sowing and planting is better left for the spring proper. As the soil begins to warm in northern regions many vegetables can begin to be sown. Cabbage, carrot and silver beet seed can be sown where the soil is well drained and friable. Silver beet can be slow to germinate, as can New Zealand spinach. Soaking these seeds overnight will remove any of the growth inhibitor and ensure even germination. Beetroot and cabbage seed can be sown in warm northern areas as can celery, swede and turnip.

Tender plants such as aubergine, capsicum, marrow and squash can either be sown under glass or left until mid-spring. Aubergine requires five months of warm weather in order to crop, so it is important to start

BELOW: Apple chilli, *Capsicum frutescens*

TIPS FOR RAISING YOUR OWN SEEDLINGS

All seeds need warmth and moisture to germinate. The time they take to germinate depends on the type of seed and its particular requirements. Some seeds have inbuilt inhibitors to germination and may need to be burnt, soaked in hot water, or chilled for a period before they will germinate. Kowhai seeds have an oily tough coat which prevents germination. By sanding away part of the seed cover germination occurs more easily.

FLOWER SEEDS THAT NEED DARKNESS TO GERMINATE

- *Calendula officinalis*
- *Centaurea cyanus* (bachelor's buttons)
- *Cynoglossum amabile* (Chinese forget-me-not)
- Delphinium
- Forget-me-not (*Myosotis* spp.)
- *Gazania rigens*
- Larkspur
- Pansy
- Phlox
- Poppies (excluding oriental, papaver species)
- *Salpiglossis sinuata*
- Sweet pea
- Verbena
- Vervain
- *Vinca* (syn. *Catharanthus*) *roseus* (periwinkle)
- Viola
- Violet

VEGETABLE AND HERB SEEDS THAT NEED DARKNESS TO GERMINATE

- Borage (*Borago officinalis*)
- Coriander (*Coriandrum sativum*)
- Fennel (*Foeniculum* spp.)

Seeds of cyclamen germinate in temperatures that have distinct night and day fluctuations.

When sown in a seed tray, most vegetables will germinate if the temperature fluctuates between 18°C and 25°C. These temperatures will suit most of the commonly used vegetable crops.

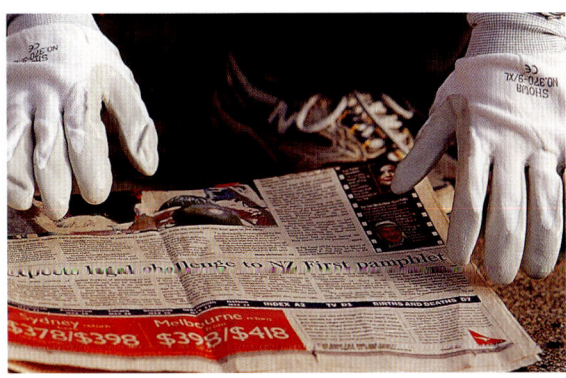

- Water the soil before sowing.
- Carefully sprinkle a small quantity of seed on the surface, sowing as thinly and evenly as possible.
- If you don't have a glasshouse, cover the seed with a sheet of newspaper and a sheet of glass.
- Water every week with care, preferably using a mister, otherwise fine seeds will be washed away and lost.

- Remove the newspaper as soon as germination occurs.
- Prick out seedlings as soon as possible, using a flattened stick. (A chopstick carved away to form a thin, flat spatula is ideal.)
- Always lift the transplanted seedlings by their first leaves (seed leaves) to ensure damage is kept to a minimum.
- After planting, a light spraying with a general fungicide will help prevent diseases such as damping off.

early. *Capsicum annum* (pepper) and *C. frutescens* (chilli pepper) are also slow-maturing crops and are best sown now. Oak compost or any fine compost will germinate peppers very well. Seeds soaked overnight in warm water seem to germinate more rapidly. Plant the seed by spacing it carefully over the surface of the soil and water with a fine mister. Cover the seed with a thin layer of compost, place a sheet of newspaper on top, then a sheet of glass and place the whole box in a warm place. A constant temperature of 20°C will ensure good germination and seedlings will generally germinate quickly. As soon as the capsicum plants are 10 cm high plant them into individual pots or punnets in groups of six or more. Seedlings also require heat to grow well. Planted into a pot they can be lifted in and out of doors depending on the weather. Aubergine can be grown in the same way and, like capsicum, enjoys good compost, liquid feeding and a little extra potash.

Planting

Cauliflower and leeks will begin to grow rapidly in a well-prepared bed. Soil must be well-drained and enriched with well-rotted compost or animal manure. Leeks will not grow in a heavy, wet soil. As a companion plant they are said to repel carrot rust fly and generally keep pests and diseases out of the vegetable garden. Plants can still be bought in bundles and planted out either into individual holes or along a trench. Top and tail the seedlings before planting to consolidate the plant's strength at this early stage.

Kumara require warmth and moisture to grow. In warm northern areas they can be planted now and set out in rows. Like aubergines, they require at least five months' warm weather to produce a good crop. In colder southern areas November may be the only month in which they can be planted. Kumara plants can be bought at the end of August. The vines should be lifted off the ground from time to time so that the growing tendrils do not form roots and take food away from the growing tuber. Frost is a killer of these subtropical plants, so check the local conditions before planting this crop.

Herbs can be sown under glass or old, congested plants such as mint can be divided and replanted in fresh soil or potted up for planting out in the garden as the soil warms.

VEGETABLES TO PLANT NOW

SOW THESE SEEDS	PLANT THESE SEEDLINGS
Beetroot*	
Broccoli	Asparagus
Cabbage	Broccoli
Carrot*	Cabbage
Celery*	Endive
Endive	Lettuce
Lettuce	Rhubarb
Silver beet	Silver beet
Swede*	
Turnip	*Only practicable in warm areas

Harvesting

In early vegetable gardens the first asparagus will be appearing. The first spears are the most delicious and should be cut with a sharp knife in order to avoid damage to the parent plant. Brussels sprouts planted back in April will still be bearing a crop of this useful vegetable. Spinach planted in autumn will also by now

LEFT: Mint grown in a pot will not invade the herb garden.
ABOVE: Brussels sprouts, *Brassica oleracea* Gemmifera Group

be ready to cut, as will silver beet. Broad beans will by now be cropping well, as will early beetroot, broccoli and cabbage. Tamarillo that have hung on the trees almost all winter in more northerly areas can now be picked and eaten raw or stewed.

Fruit

All stone fruit trees must be sprayed with a copper spray now if a lime sulphur spray wasn't used before bud burst. Lime sulphur applied before bud burst will be beneficial in ensuring a healthy year's crop. This applies especially to peach and nectarine trees affected by curly leaf. Apples (including ornamental crabs) must be sprayed for black spot with a fungicide or copper-based spray, otherwise the fruit will be disfigured and the tree generally debilitated for an entire season. This disease also attacks citrus trees, pears and quinces. This is the last month in which to spray fruit trees for moss and lichen.

August is also the final month in which you can plant deciduous fruit trees. Any later plantings will hinder the tree in becoming well established before the dry months of summer.

Lemon trees need feeding now. They are heavy and constant bearers in many parts of the country and must be well fed if they are to continue producing. Trees over ten years old need at least two kilos of a balanced citrus fertiliser per year. Three applications a year would not be too much; one in August, another in November and again in February. Pruning, like feeding, keeps the tree healthy. Excess water at the base of the tree can cause collar rot and before long the bark at ground level dies and chokes the life from the tree. Good drainage combined with regular sprayings of a copper-based spray will help keep infections like this under control.

August features

Gladioli

Gladioli are members of the iris family and are native to southern Africa. They also grow in the Middle East and some in parts of Mediterranean Europe. They cope well with cool, wet winters followed by hot, dry summers. Gladioli prefer a climate that is frost-free or as frost-free as possible. They can be grown all year round as there are both summer and winter-flowering types. They enjoy any free, well-draining soil in the full heat of the sun. Some members of this family will grow to 1.5 metres, while others may only reach 30 cm.

Gladioli enjoy a very long flowering season. Plants will usually flower a hundred days after planting. This makes them suitable for staggered planting to achieve an ongoing succession of flowers. The species *Gladiolus priorii*, *G. carinatus* and *G. alatus* are delicate and elegant flowers for the serious collector. Once the plants have died down, it is important to lift and clean them for the coming season. This is essential in very cold areas, as freezing conditions can damage the corms.

Tuberous begonias

By the end of August tuberous begonias should be available in most garden centres. They are showy plants and when planted in pots they are invaluable to bring light

BELOW FROM LEFT: *Gladiolus alatus*;
Begonia Tuberhybrida, Antonelli strain; *Begonia* 'Pink Lights';
grape hyacinths, *Muscari armeniacum* 'Blue Spike';
Rhododendron yakushimanum;
Paeonia 'Coral Sunset'

to the dark corners of the garden. The pendulous forms are highly decorative in hanging baskets and some, such as *Begonia semperflorens*, make excellent indoor plants. Planting the tubers now will ensure these clear, brightly coloured plants will be flowering for Christmas.

tuber should be encouraged to form roots over its entire surface by placing it in a soil mix of peat and sand with its top just below the surface. Given temperatures of 15°C, it will quickly form shoots. Once the shoots are formed, transfer them into their flowering pots in a good quality potting compost. Plant 3 cm deep and leave in a shady place to develop, as bright sunlight can cause the young leaves to burn. They can gradually be brought out into more brightly lit positions as they develop.

At the end of the growing season (March) the stems can be cut to within 15 cm of ground level. Soon these will also drop and the tubers can be collected,

When selecting tubers, do not allow yourself to be beguiled by the largest ones, as the tuber size often has little to do with the flower quality and vigour of the plant. Quality tubers should feel like new potatoes, be even-skinned and have a mass of short fibrous hairs on the bottom of the tuber. Make sure that the tubers are free of any fungal disease and are firm to the touch. Discard any that are hard, desiccated or rubbery.

Starting begonias growing can sometimes be difficult. The trick is to keep them warm and moist enough to get them growing without rotting. A healthy

cleaned of matted and surplus root and stored in a cool, dry, frost-free place for the next season. Growing new stock can be done by either cutting large tubers into sections (ensuring that each portion has part of the growing crown) or by removing shoots with a piece of the growing crown attached. (See page 106 on propagation.) Cuttings should be dipped in a general fungicide and planted into a peat and sand mixture. Begonias may also be grown from seed, which is very fine. Seedlings can then be picked out individually and planted on to become flowering plants in their first season.

Grape hyacinths

Muscari or grape hyacinths are basically hardy, no-care spring bulbs — so much so that many, such as the well known *Muscari armeniacum* and *M. latifolium*, grow naturally in south-east Europe, Yugoslavia to Turkey and the Caucasus mountains up to 2000 m above sea level. Here they are subject to snow and freezing winter conditions but thrive in the sunny, free-draining conditions on mountain slopes and push their way into flower as spring arrives.

The name muscari comes from the Turkish (musk) and describes the sweet scent of many muscari flowers.

green, shiny leaves with soft, cinnamon-brown backs. Hardy to –25°C, it is easy to grow, is the parent of many dwarf hybrids, and only reaches 2.5 metres in height if planted in a sheltered, semi-shaded part of the garden. The flowers, up to 4 cm long, are borne in tight, medium-sized clusters and are pale pink in the bud, opening and aging to white.

Paeonies

Paeonies are a magnificent plant for areas where the winters are cold and the summers hot. All paeonies prefer cooler parts of the country although the new

There are about 40 to 60 different species of muscari that have tufts of linear, often channelled fleshy leaves, and erect, leafless stems topped by racemes of rounded, bell or urn-shaped flowers, with six small lobes that open as the days begin to warm in the spring. In some species such as *Muscari tubergenianum* the uppermost flowers of each raceme are sterile, smaller and paler.

A winter rhododendron

Rhododendron yakushimanum comes from the Japanese Island of Yakushima and has gloriously dark intersectionals and some of the Saunders-Daphnis hybrids will grow further north. In the main, paeonies dislike humidity and grow best where the spring is also long and cool. All paeonies like an open, sunny, well-drained position. Spring frosts can deform young paeony buds and ruin the flowers, so it pays to plant the early flowering ones where there is a little shelter or cover them when frosts threaten. Heavy rainfall at flowering time will also ruin a fine bloom. Multi-petal forms such as *Paeonia* 'Coral Sunset' will soak up water like blotting paper when they are fully open.

Glossary

Annual A plant that lives for one year or less.
Aphids Green, yellow, black or brown, small, soft insects that suck sap from tender plant growth. Aphids also attack roots.
Biodynamic gardening A garden method that uses crop rotation, companion planting, the juxtaposition of deep-rooted plants with shallow-rooted plants and the extensive use of aromatic herbs and summer-flowering shrubs. Regular use of compost is an important part of the biodynamic method.
Bone dust Fertiliser made from crushed or ground bone.
Botrytis A fungal disease that can attack flowers, fruit and foliage.
Bulb A swollen underground bud that stores food, enabling it to survive winter and drought. This bulb is the centre of the coming season's leaf growth and flowers. The daffodil is a common plant that produces bulbs.
Bulbil A small bulb which forms above the ground on the stems of plants such as liliums. These bulbils can be potted up and grown on.
Cloche A cold frame constructed of glass or plastic to protect crops from the winter frosts.
Collar rot Also known as stem rot, this is a fungal disease often caused by overwatering, which results in the centre and stem of the plant becoming mushy.
Companion planting Plants with different physical demands are well suited to one another. Deep-rooting plants that need a lot of water get along well with shallow-rooting plants that need less moisture. Crops that are heavy feeders should be followed by plants that are light feeders. Marigolds planted in the flower or vegetable bed keep the soil free of nematodes. The odour of marigold leaves is said to keep the garden free of many insects.
Compost The medium in which plants are grown, composed of loam, peat, sand, chalk and fertilisers in varying proportions. Soil-free composts may be made of peat or sand with or without fertilisers.
Corm The base or stem of a plant, such as a crocus, which becomes fleshy and stores food.
Crown The point at which the stem and the root of the plant meet.
Cultivar A plant variety that has arisen in a garden or nursery.
Cutting A piece of plant used to grow a new one. Depending on the plant, tip, stem, leaf and root cuttings can be taken.
Damping off A fungal disease carried in the soil where it attacks young seedlings, often with serious loss.
Deciduous A plant which sheds its leaves every year in the autumn.
Derris dust A non-persistent insecticide made from a plant root.
Division A way in which to propagate plants which have several stems.

Dormancy A resting period when plants slow down their growth and need less water, warmth and light.
Evergreen A plant which stays in leaf all year.
Fertiliser A plant food applied to stimulate growth, flowering and fruiting.
Fibrous roots The small, fine lateral roots forming off main roots.
Foliar feed A fertiliser sprayed onto leaves to stimulate growth.
Frost cloth Light cloth placed over crops in the winter to limit frost damage.
Fungicide A chemical that destroys fungi.
Fungus Mushrooms, mould or mildew that feed on dead or living organic matter.
Genus A classification describing plants with common characteristics distinct from all other groups. A genus usually contains a number of species.
Germination The sprouting of a seed or spore.
Green fertiliser A crop such as rye, lupin or mustard, grown during the late autumn and winter period. In the spring this crop is dug in and acts as a fertiliser.
Hardy A plant that remains outdoors through all seasons, withstanding frost.
Heel The base of a softwood cutting that retains some of the old, hard stem from which it was taken.
Herbaceous Plants not forming wood, and dying down every year.
Herb Grass-like plant used for food, medicine, scent or flavour.
Herbicide Spray used to destroy unwanted plants.
Hybrid A plant produced by crossing different varieties and species.
Leaf mould Decayed leaves used as a planting mix.
Mealy bugs White, fluffy bugs that attack stems and leaves. Often seen on indoor plants.
Microclimate Localised climatic conditions that may differ considerably from nearby areas.
Mildew A fungal disease to which many plants are susceptible.
Miticide A chemical that kills mites and their eggs.
Mulch A layer of waste material applied to the soil surface to conserve moisture and keep plant roots cool.
Peat Partly rotted vegetable matter used for potting plants. Peat gives excellent drainage qualities to compost mixes.
Perennial A plant that can live for more than two years.
Potting on Shifting plants into larger pots as soon as they need more growing space.
Pruning Cutting back a plant to make it grow bushier or to encourage better flowering and fruiting.
'Puddle in' Planting in a muddy puddle of a mixture of soil and water.

Pyrethrum A non-persistent organic insecticide made from chrysanthemum flower heads. This is a useful anti-aphid spray.
Red spider mites Sap-sucking insects that flourish in hot, dry conditions. The plant under attack soon develops leaves speckled with yellow spots which then fall. A miticide is essential to remove these destructive pests.
Root pruning The cutting back of roots before planting, usually dormant plants, in order to promote new and more vigorous root growth.
Rough digging Turning of the soil to a spade's depth and leaving it exposed to the winter cold and rain. This weathering process reduces the soil to a fine tilth.
Rust A fungal disease that attacks many plants. Hollyhocks are very susceptible. All diseased foliage should be removed and burnt.
Secateurs Scissor-like tools used for trimming and pruning trees, herbs and ornamentals.
Scale insect A sucking insect with a scale-like shell. This pest often attacks indoor plants and is best removed by hand or with an oil-based spray.
Sharp sand Coarse river sand free from large amounts of silt.
Shrub A plant without a main central stem; instead it has many stems rising from the ground.
Species A member of a genus which, when grown from seed, will always be the same as its parents, i.e. it breeds true. The generic name of a plant comes first then the species name, e.g. *Rosa* (genus) *centifolia* (species).
Systemic insecticide Chemical spray absorbed by roots and leaves. The toxin spreads throughout the plant, killing insect pests. As systemic sprays are long lasting they can build up in the plant and in the soil. They should be used with care at all times, particularly on crops.
Thrips Flying insects that suck sap and generally debilitate plants. A general insecticide will limit damage.
Thuricide A spray containing bacterial spores that will kill caterpillars.
Tip cutting The tip of a plant that is used for propagation. Tip cuttings are usually taken in spring.
Toxin Any poisonous substance. Many sprays and weedkillers are toxic to human and animal life.
Tuber A swollen underground stem or root from which the plant stem and flowers develop.
Turf A slab of soil with grass growing on it, cut from the surface of the soil.
Variegated Leaves or petals with two or more colours.
Vermiculite Free-draining mineral used for thermal and acoustic insulation, as a packing medium, a soil conditioner, or a starting medium for growing seeds.
Whitefly Moths that suck sap and disfigure leaves and flowers. A general insecticide will rid the garden of whitefly.

Rosa chinensis 'Parsons Pink'

Treatment of pests

PEST	SYMPTOM	CHEMICAL SPRAYS	NATURAL REMEDIES
Aphid	Plants lose vigour and collapse.	General insecticide spray, Confidor.	Soapy water or garlic spray. Plant nasturtium nearby. (See recipe page 67.)
Beetles, bronze, green, etc.	Holes eaten in leaves; flowers become tattered	Target, Nature's Way natural derris dust, Confidor.	Encourage plants to grow rapidly with foliar feed or trap and dispose of beetles.
Carrot rust fly	Young plants wilt and die. Older plants show burrowing.	Diazinon granules scattered in the seed drill as planting proceeds.	Companion planting with onions, leeks, rosemary or sage.
Caterpillars, leaf rollers	Holes eaten in leaves; droppings on leaves.	Target, Nature's Way natural derris dust, Orthene.	Remove manually, or apply *Bacillus thuringiensis* in the form of a thuricide organic spray.
Codling moth	Pale orange worms with brown heads that burrow through fruit pushing out dark crumbly brown excreta at the entrances to their tunnels.	Carbaryl.	Pheromone traps or rings or cloth or paper tied around the tree. Caterpillars crawl down the tree to pupate and will happily do so in a ring of cloth. This is easily removed and the pupae fed to hens (if you have any).
Cutworms	Wilting and collapse of many vegetables where roots have been eaten.	Diazinon granules sown with the seed at planting time, soil insect killer.	An oak leaf mulch applied to the plant's root zone.
Mealy bug	This pest has an oval body covered with white waxy threads. Mealy bugs are usually found in clusters on indoor and balcony plants.	A systemic spray such as Orthene.	Wash plant down outside. Keep plants fed and healthy. Use a garlic spray or remove pests by hand.
Mite	Tiny insect that attacks young buds causing them to contort and twist.	Mite Killer, super sulphur, Carbaryl.	Keep plants moist and spray underside of leaves with water. Pick off and burn first signs of this pest.
Narcissus fly	Bulbs fail to shoot strongly in the spring. Bulbs are eaten out in the centre.	Spray with Orthene.	Mulch the soil surface with sawdust. Plant a ground cover of thyme where bulbs are planted.
Red spider mite	Tiny mites usually found on the underside of leaves. They become bright red in the autumn, flourishing in hot dry conditions.	Mite Killer.	Keep plants and surrounding area sprayed with water. Pick off and destroy the first signs of this pest.

PEST	SYMPTOM	CHEMICAL SPRAYS	NATURAL REMEDIES
Scale	Hard and soft scale are rapid breeders, spread and multiply rapidly. Both forms exude a sticky honeydew that attracts ants. This pest will rapidly debilitate a plant.	An insecticide with a little Conqueror Oil at summer strength.	Remove manually or use an old toothbrush dipped in a weak solution of vinegar, oil and water.
Slaters	Minor damage to crops.	Remove sheltering places such as garden rubbish.	Regular cultivation of the soil.
Slugs and snails	Decimated crops and seedlings.	Mesurol or similar bait.	Trap in stale beer placed in dishes, or in upturned pots; crush by hand or foot, or drown in salty water.
Sooty mould	Tiny insects that feed on the secretions of mealy bug, scale and aphid pests. Appear as a dark soot-like mould.	Orthene, Bravo or other general insecticide.	Garlic spray; soapy water.
Thrips	Very small insects, brown or black, that feed on the sap of many plants. Foliage becomes silvery and dehydrated.	Orthene or Mavrik.*	Garlic spray. Keep plants healthy by regular, even feeding. Water regularly. Pick off and destroy infected leaves as soon as pest is seen.

* Mavrik is an insecticide that has low toxicity for bees. It can kill them, but used carefully is less lethal than other insecticides.

PEST	SYMPTOM	CHEMICAL SPRAYS	NATURAL REMEDIES
Whitefly	Tiny, white and moth-like. Unsightly and destructive sap-sucking pest.	Orthene.	Garlic spray and regular sprayings with soapy water.

Treatment of fungal diseases

DISEASE	SYMPTOM	CHEMICAL SPRAYS	NATURAL REMEDIES
Black spot	This fungal disease weakens plants by killing their leaves. Black or brown spots form on the foliage of apples, citrus, pip fruit and roses.	Spray with a fungicide such as Super Copper, Bravo, Fungus Fighter or Super Shield.	Pick off and burn the first signs of this disease. Clear any diseased leaves that may have fallen on the ground. Mulch with sawdust or seaweed compost. Feed plants and ensure good air circulation.
Blight	This appears on tomatoes and potatoes in warm, humid weather in the late summer. Leaves become distorted and the plant begins to fail.	Regular spraying with a copper-based spray or similar fungicide.	Garlic spray (see recipe page 67). Remove any diseased leaves and burn. Keep a free flow of air around plants by removing lower foliage in the case of tomatoes. Mulch with seaweed. Rotate crops. Sprinkle a little lime under plants.
Curly leaf	This disease appears on pip fruit trees during mild, humid weather. Leaves pucker, swell and blister, changing in colour to a yellow green and then a glowing pink.	Spray with a copper spray during the tree's dormant period (early spring).	Use a garlic spray early in the season and at times of humid weather.
Damping off	Plants sulk, refuse to grow then wilt and collapse at ground level.	Spray with a copper spray or Bravo.	Avoid overwatering, use sterilised soil, keep good air flow.
Downy mildew	Attacks cucumbers, leeks, lettuces, onions, peas, pumpkins, spinach and swede at times when the weather is erratic.	Spray with a copper spray or Bravo.	Garlic spray. Keep air circulating by removing any unnecessary leaves. Plant without crowding. Destroy any signs of the disease by burning.
Powdery mildew	Attacks when the soil is dry and the air is humid. The leaves and skins of cucumbers, marrows, melons and pumpkins are covered in a white powdery coat.	A fungicide spray such as Bravo, copper oxychloride, Greenguard, Saprol or Fungus Fighter.	Space plants so that air can move freely. Rotate crops. Keep soil moist during dry periods. A spray of weak vinegar solution helps. Flowers of sulphur sprinkled on the leaves is also useful.
Rust	This difficult disease can destroy crops of beetroot, broad beans, garlic and leeks. Carnation, gladiolus and hollyhock rust can kill the plants. Spores form on the infected plants, showing as brown or orange spots.	Copper sprays, or weekly sprayings of lime sulphur or Bravo.	Remove and burn all infected leaves as soon as they appear. Mulch the soil heavily with sawdust or seaweed. Rotate crops to prevent re-infection. Avoid using heavily nitrogenous fertiliser. Use rust-resistant seed.

DISEASE	SYMPTOM	CHEMICAL SPRAYS	NATURAL REMEDIES
Verrucosis	This fungal infection primarily attacks citrus. The skins become rough, blistered and distorted. Fruit is not damaged under the skin.	Spray at monthly intervals from October to June with a spray such as Super Copper.	Garlic spray at regular intervals.

Water needs of vegetables

VEGETABLES THAT NEED LITTLE WATER

VEGETABLE	WHEN TO WATER	WHY
Artichoke, globe	Never	Stems will rot at ground level
Artichoke, Jerusalem	Never	Foliage at expense of tubers
Asparagus	Never	Water stored from winter rain
Beetroot	Just before sowing	Establishes plants
Cabbage, spring, winter	'Puddle in' at planting	Establishes plants
Carrot	Never	Foliage at expense of tubers
Cauliflower	'Puddle in' at planting (if soil dry)	
Parsnip	Never	
Swede	Never	
Turnip	Some water worthwhile if very dry	

VEGETABLES THAT BENEFIT FROM SELECTIVE WATERING

VEGETABLE	WHEN TO WATER	WHY
Beans	Before sowing	Better yield. Water at other times
Broad beans	At flowering and pod swell	Encourages leaf growth
Brussels sprouts	'Puddle in' at planting	Water produces small sprouts
Cabbage, summer	'Puddle in' at planting	Establishes plants
Marrow	When fruit begins to swell	Water produces leaf growth
Onion (bulbs)	Only before planting	Establishes plants
Sweet corn	At planting and cob swell	Aids growth and crop juiciness
Zucchini	When fruit begins to swell	Water produces leaf growth

VEGETABLES THAT REQUIRE A LOT OF WATER

VEGETABLE	WHEN TO WATER	WHY
Beans, runner	Throughout growth	More flowers, better bean size
Cauliflower, summer, autumn	At sowing, and as heads form	Establishes and increases size
Celery	Throughout growth	Likes copious water
Cucumber	Throughout growth	Quicker and juicier growth
Leek	Throughout growth	Bigger stems and leaves
Lettuce	Throughout growth	Bigger size and succulence
Onion, salad	Throughout growth	Shallow-rooted, needs moisture
Peas	At sowing, flower, pod swell	Increases crop, not foliage
Potato, early	Throughout growth	Crop comes earlier
Potato, main crop	When flowers appear	Larger crop
Radish	Throughout growth	Roots more succulent, milder
Spinach	Throughout growth	Encourages foliage and stems
Tomato	Regularly throughout growth	Excess can decrease flavour

Matching plants and propagation methods

PLANTS THAT PROPAGATE WELL FROM DIVISION

HERBACEOUS PLANTS

Achillea
Alchemilla
Alyssum
Aster
Astilbe
Caltha palustris
 (marsh marigold)
Campanula
Chrysanthemum
Doronicum
Erigeron
Gentiana
Geranium
Helenium
Hemerocallis
Hosta
Lupin
Monarda
Polemonium
 (Jacob's ladder)
Rudbeckia
Scabious
Solidago (golden rod)
Tanacetum
Veronica

WOODY HERBACEOUS PLANTS

Cortaderia
Phormium
Yucca

SEMI-WOODY SHRUBS

Aronia
Blackthorn (sloe)
Lilac

ALPINE PLANTS

Aubretia
Campanula
Primula (European)
Thalictrum

PLANTS THAT PROPAGATE WELL FROM ROOT CUTTINGS

HERBACEOUS PLANTS

Anemone hupehensis
 (Japanese anemone)
Acanthus
Eryngium (sea holly)
Papaver
Phlox
Statice
Verbascum

CLIMBERS

Bignonia
Campsis
Passiflora (passionfruit)

ALPINES

Anchusa
Anemone
Erodium
Geranium
Morisia hypogaea
Primula
Pulsatilla
Verbascum

SHRUBS

Aralia
Chaenomeles (flowering quince)
Clerodendrum
Daphne genkwa
Prunus
Rhus
Rubus

TREES

Acacia
Ailanthus
Catalpa
Koelreuteria
Paulownia
Robinia

PLANTS THAT PROPAGATE WELL FROM CUTTINGS

SEMI-RIPE CUTTINGS

Currants, flowering
Deutzia
Diervilla
Dogwood
Forsythia
Philadelphus
Plum
Weigela

GREEN WOODS

Berry fruits
Ceanothus
Chrysanthemum
Delphinium
Forsythia
Geranium
Gooseberry
Philadelphus
Vines (fruiting and ornamental)

EVERGREENS

Abelia
Aucuba
Ceanothus
Cherry laurel
Choisya
Daphne
Elaeagnus
Escallonia
Hebe
Magnolia grandiflora
Pyracantha

HARDWOODS

Blackcurrant
Cotoneaster
Dogwood
Poplar
Roses
Spiraea
Viburnum
Willow

CONIFERS

Chamaecyparis
Cupressus
Juniperus
Podocarpus
Sequoia
Sequoiadendron
Taxus
Thuja

Specialist nurseries and other useful addresses

Bamboo
Bamboo Specialists Nursery
833 West Coast Road
Oratia
Ph: 09 814 9847
Email: bamboogro@xtra.co.nz

Bulbs
Aorangi Bulb Nurseries
Cnr Durie and Campbell Roads
RD 5
Feilding
Ph: 06 323 4516

Daffodil Acre
94 Wairoa Road
RD 1
Tauranga
Ph: 07 552 5383
Carries a wide range of bulbs, including some of the more obscure muscari species in February and March.

Chrysanthemum
Coulters Nursery
183 Weston Road
Christchurch
Ph: 03 355 4656 or 027 2211590
Also supplies tuberous begonias, fuchsias and bedding plants. Catalogues are available for both the chrysanthemums and fuchsias.

Exotics
Nestlebrae Exotics
www.helensville.co.nz/nestlebrae
Supplies exotics including fruit, palms and ornamentals, mostly warm climate subtropicals.

Fruit trees
Landsendt Exotic Plants and Fruit Trees
108 Parker Road
Oratia
Ph: 09 818 6914

Te Hana Nurseries
RD 4
Wellsford
Ph: 09 423 8595

Waimea Nurseries
Golden Hills Road
Richmond
Nelson
Ph: 03 544 2700

Hydrangeas
Blue Mountain Nursery
99 Bushy Hill Street
Tapanui
Ph: 03 204 8250

Harbour Hydrangeas
4973 State Highway 75
Little River
Ph: 03 325 1334
Website: www.hydrangeas.co.nz

Iris
Joy Plants
78 Jericho Road Road
Pukekohe
Ph: 09 2389129
Website: www.joyplants.co.nz
Supplies higo, japonica, Siberica and Louisiana irises, and also a huge range of perennials and natives.

Rossmore Gardens
17 Pethig Place
Christchurch
Ph: 03 322 7776

Paeonies
Marsal Paeonies
Old South Road
Dunsandal
RD 2
Leeston
Canterbury
Ph: 03 325 4003
Fax: 03 325 4222

Situated 45 kilometres from Christchurch; take the Hororata Road at Dunsandel, then the Old South Road and look for the cemetery sign.

Omeo Paeonies
61 Hawley Road
RD 1
Alexandra
Ph: 03 449 2097

Simmons Paeonies
16 Rountree Street
Ilam
Ph: 03 348 0777

Primula, cottage garden plants and perennials
Ashton Glen Perennials
284 Estate Road
Wairuna
RD Clinton
Otago
Ph: 03 415 7687
Also supplies bulbs, perennials, trees and shrubs.

Ayn Dara Nurseries
State Highway 30
RD 1
Taupo
Ph: 07 333 2258
Also supplies a huge range of bulbs, perennials, trees and shrubs.

Cottage Plants Ltd
RD 2
Akaroa
Ph: 03 304 5882
Mail order only. Will send a catalogue for 4 x 45-cent stamps.

Garden Treasures
59 Chancellor Street
Christchurch
Ph: 03 385 8456
Email: gtreasures@clear.net.nz

Website:
www.gardentreasures.8k.com
Has many varieties of primroses, bulbs and other garden plants. Mail order catalogue available.

Mara Nurseries
Allen Road
RD 12
Hawera
Ph: 06 272 2806
Carries a wide range of plants, including primula.

Millstream Gardens
Pukehou
Private Bag
Napier
Ph: 06 878 1511
Also supplies pond plants and herbs.

Parva Plants
P O Box 2503
Tauranga
Ph: 07 552 4902
Website: parvaplants.co.nz
Mail order nursery specialising in rare and unusual plants.

Southwell Plants
Hillend
No 2 Road
Balclutha
Ph: 03 418 2465
Offers a range of plants.
Mail order catalogue available.

Wanaka Garden and Seeds
32 Warren Street
Wanaka
Ph: 03 443 8866
Will courier plants.

Rhododendron
Many species are hard to find but from time to time the following nurseries will have some of the mentioned varieties and other species types available for sale.

Blue Mountain Nurseries
99 Bushy Hill Street
Tapanui
Ph: 03 204 8250

Caves Tree Nursery
RD 3
Hamilton
Ph: 07 827 6601

Old Stables Nurseries
363 Hasketts Road
RD 5
Christchurch

Riverwood Rhododendrons
Main Road
Little River
Christchurch
Ph: 03 325 1040

If you are interested in growing rhododendrons, why not join The New Zealand Rhododendron Association. By meeting enthusiasts in your local area you will sometimes be able to obtain cuttings, layered plants and share experiences of growing species and other rhododendrons.

Norma Goodman (secretary)
The New Zealand Rhododendron Association
21 Horopito Road
Waikanae

Roses
Littlerose Garden and Nursery
1771 Highway 72
Ph and fax: 03 312 5704
Situated at Cust on the main road from Rangiora to Oxford, 40 kilometres from Christchurch.

Roseneath
918 State Highway 17
Albany
Ph: 09 415 9204
Email: shore@xtra.co.nz

Tasman Bay Roses
45 Chamberlain Street
Moteuka
Ph: 03 528 7449

Trevor Griffiths Roses
304 Pages Road
Timaru
Ph: 03 686 1060

Trinity Farm
Box 50
Otaki Railway
202 Waitohu Valley Road
Otaki
Ph: 0800 955555
Specialises in old-fashioned roses.

Sarracenia
Carnivorous Plant Nursery
9a Avoca Valley Road
Christchurch
Ph: 03 384 2606
Email: cpnurseries@hotmail.com
Mail order all over New Zealand.

Seed suppliers
Kings Seeds
P O Box 283
Katikati
Ph: 07 549 3409
Email: kings.seeds@xtra.co.nz
For vegetable, flower and some old plant seed varieties. Kings also have an organic seed selection available.

Nestlebrae Exotics
Website:
www.helensville.co.nz/nestlebrae
Supplies a wide range of perennial and tree crop seeds.

Succulents
Architectural Plants
508 Buchanans Road
Yaldhurst
R D 6
Ph: 03 342 3732

Texture Plants
P O Box 11186
Sockburn
Christchurch
Ph: 03 349 7296
Stocks a huge variety of interesting plants and will post anywhere in country.

Zenith Succulents
RD 1
Kohukohu
Ph: 09 405 5701
A mail order catalogue is available on request for $4.

Trees, shrubs and ornamentals
Blue Mountain Nurseries
99 Bushy Hill Street
Tapanui
West Otago
Ph: 03 204 8250

Caves Tree Nursery
Pukeroro
RD 3
Hamilton
Ph: 07 827 6601

Tikitere Rhododendron Park
104 State Highway 30
Te Ngae Junction
Ph: 07 345 5036
Supplies rhododendrons, maples, hostas and Siberica iris.

Trotts Nursery
371 Racecourse Road
RD 6
Ashburton
Ph: 03 308 9530

Waterplants
Wai Mara
Streamlands Swamps Road
Kaipara Flats
P O Box 374
Warkworth
Ph: 09 425 9262
Specialist water garden trees and shrubs.

Waihi Water Lily Gardens
414 Pukekauri Road
RD 2
Waihi
Ph: 07 863 8267

Wrights Water Gardens
RD 31
128 Mauku Road
Pukekohe
Ph: 09 236 3642

Bergamot (top) with pelargoniums and nasturtium

Sunflower *Helianthus* 'Moulin Rouge'

Feature tips

September
How fertilisers work 12
Tips for planting roses 14
Growing potatoes 17

October
Dealing with slugs and snails 24
Making a topiary 28
Alternatives to a lawn 28

November
The benefits of mulching 36

December
Drought-resistant plants 52
Dead-heading and cutting back after flowering 56

January
Tips for watering 66
Making your own garden sprays 67
Companion planting 71

February
Saving seed 80
Making the most of your herbs 81

March
Making the most of clay soil 90
Methods of propagation 93
Planting and caring for rhododendrons 94

April
Four ways to propagate bulbs, corms and tubers 106

May
Tips for buying bulbs 114
Protecting plants from frost 115
Planting an asparagus bed 117

June
Growing alpine plants 126
Endive — an alternative to lettuce 130

July
Planting bulbs 140
Pruning roses 141

August
Making your own liquid manure 150
Tips for raising your own seedlings 153

Index

Page numbers in **bold** indicate illustrations

abutilon, 78, 87
Acaena, 128
   A. purpurea, 28
acanthus, 90, 166
Acer campestre, 87
   A. capillipes, 120
   A. griseum, 120, **120**
   A. japonicum 'Aconitifolium', **86**, 87, 119, **119**
      A. j. 'Vitifolium', 119
   A. palmatum 'Dissectum', 119
Achillea millefolium, 64, 166
achimenes, 38, 55
aconite, 8, 56, 69, 79
African violet, **128**
agapanthus, 26, 38, 68, 69, 79, 115, 151, 152
ageratum, 15, 24, 26, 37, 38, 54, 55, 56, 69, 79, 97, 151, 152
Agrostemma, 26
Alcea rosea, 15, 26, 54, 79, 97, 105, 108, 142, 150, **150**, 152
allium, 38, 67, 97, 104, 108
alpines, 76, 126, 166
Alstroemeria, 26, 67, 69
   A. pulchella, 61, **61**
Alyssum, 15, 26, 37, 38, 55, 56, 69, 77, 79, 92, 97, 104, 108, 113, 115, 142, 151, 152, 166
   A. maritimum syn. *Lobularia maritima*, 113, **113**, 150
   A. saxatile, 126
amaranthus, 26, 38, 54, 55
amaryllis, 26, 38, 54, 55, 68, 69, 115
Amelanchier canadensis, 118
   A. lamarckii, 118
anchusa, 138, 166
Anemone, 55, 79, 94, 97, 105, 108, 166
   A. blanda, 127
      A. b. 'Atrocaerulea', 94, **94**
   A. coronaria, 94
   A. hupehensis, 87, 166
   A. nemorosa, 94
annuals, 24, 37, 51, 70, 75, 92, 104, 149, 150, 151
anomatheca, 54, 55
Anthemis nobilis, 28
antirrhinum, 15, 26, 55, 79, 97, 105, 108, 142, 149, 152
aphids, 23, 24, 36, 66, 71, 76, 91, 103, 126, 160
Aponogeton distachyos
apples, 18, 31, 36, 41, 58, 83, 103, 108, 118, 130, 155
apricot, 58, **58**, 82, 131
April, 102–11
aquilegia, 26, 38, 55, 77, 79, 97, 138, **138**, 142, 152
Arctotis hybrid cultivar, **49**
argenome, 56
Arisaema, 14, 15, 67
   A. candidissimum, 14

artemesia, 69
artichoke, globe, 16, 18, 32, 57, **62**, 164
artichoke, Jerusalem, 164
asparagus, 16, 18, 58, 71, 116, 117, 125, 154, 164
Aster, 15, 24, 26, 37, 38, 54, 55, 69, 76, 79, 92, 101, 113, 151, 152, 166
   A. novae-angliae 'Barr's Pink', 101, **101**
astilbe, 26, 90, 166
aubergine, 18, 32, 40, 57, 72, 152, 154
aubretia, 126, 127, 166
August, 148–57
Aurinia saxatile – see *Alyssum saxatile*
Autumn, 86–121
azaleas, 25, 35, 75, 78

babiana, 79, 114
balsam, 54, 55
bamboo, 64, 90
basil, 30, 31, 32, **63**, 65
Bassia scoparia syn. *Kochia scoparia*, 15
bay, 70
beans, 31, 40, 70, 82, 119
   broad, 16, **16**, 18, 57, 79, 90, 109, 116, 129, 131, 144, 145, 155, 164
   dwarf, 32, 57, 71, 81
   French, 28, 32, 72
   runner, 32, 57, 71, 72, 165
beauty bush, 21, **21**
bees, 53, 71
beet – see red beet; silver beet
beetles, 160
beetroot, 16, 18, 57, 70, 72, 79, 81, 98, 99, 100, 109, 117, 152, 154, 155, 164
begonia, bedding, 151
   begonia, tuberous, 15, 26, 38, 106, 140, 152, 155–6, 156
   Begonia, Tuberhybrida, Antonelli strain **156**
   B. 'Pink Lights' **156**
   B. semperflorens, 156
belladonna lilies, 26, 38, 54, 55, 68, 69, 115
Bellis perennis, 55
bells of Ireland, 26, 38
Berberis, 90, 140
   B. atropurpurea, 21
   B. darwinii, 21
   B. thunbergii, 21, **78**
bergamot, 85, 85, 169
bergenia, 90
berry fruit, 18, 58, 166 – see also specific berries
berry shrubs and trees, 111, **111**
Betula albo-sinensis, 119
birds, 12, 24, 41, 100, 104
black-eyed Susan, 13, 15
black spot, 54, 67, 75, 109, 118,

155, 162
blackberries, 131
blackcurrants, 90, 131, 166
bladder plum, 58
blight, 118, 162
blood and bone, 75, 89, 121, 149
blossom trees, **20**, 21, 22, **23**, 87, 111, 143, 144, 149, 155, 166
bluebell, 90
blueberries, 58
borage, 71, 153
boronia, 151, 152
botrytis, 59, 104, 115, 128
bottlebrush, 52
bouvardia, 151
box, 27, **27**
boysenberries, 58
Bracteantha bracteata, 38
broccoli, 16, 18, 31, 32, 40, 57, 70, 71, 81, 90, 98, 99, 108, 109, 116, 117, 129, 131, 144, 155
bronze beetle, 23, 36, 160
broom, 26, 52
brown patch, 72
brown rot, 58, 72, 91, 100, 103
Brussels sprouts, 40, 70, 108, 109, 117, 154, **155**, 164
Buddleja, 69
   B. davidii, 11, 15
   B. salvifolia, 15
bulbs, 52, 90
   for autumn planting, 94–7, 105–7, 114
   for spring planting, 11, 14–15, 15–16, 26, 35, 38
   for summer planting, 54, 55, 67–8, 79
   for winter planting, 127, 140, 142, 151
   propagating, 68, 106–7
   selecting, 68, 114
butternut, 108
Buxus sempervirens, 27, **27**, 140, 142, 143

cabbage, 16, 18, **18**, 24, 28, **30**, 31, 32, 40, 57, 70, 71, 81, 89, 90, 91, 98, 99, 103, 108, 109, **113**, 116, 117, 129, 131, 144, 152, 154, 155, 164
cabbage tree, 90
caladium, 54, 55
calendula, 15, 26, 55, 56, 77, **78**, **88**, 92, 97, 104, 108, 113, 115, 127, 138, **138**, 142, 153
callas, 26
callistemon, 52
calostemma, 38
Caltha palustris, 166
camassia, 97, 108
Camellia, 75, 78, 92, 110
   C. japonica, 111
      C. j. 'Rudolph', 110
   C. reticulata, 110
   C. saluenensis, **110**
   C. sasanqua, 92, 110, 143
      C. s. 'Plantation Pink', 110, **110**
Campanula, 79, 166
   C. persicifolia, 56

candytuft, 15, 24, 26, 37, 38, 79, 97
canna, 26, 151, **151**
Canterbury bells, 15, 54, 97, 127, 142
capsicum, 16, 32, 40, 57, 72, 82, 117, 152, 154
caraway, 30, 32
carnation, 13, 15, 24, 26, 55, 78, 79, 97, 114, 115, 138, 142, 149, 151, 152
Carpinus betulus, **143**
carrot, 16, 18, 29, 32, 40, 57, 70, 71, 72, 81, 98, 99, 108, 109, 117, 129, 131, 144, 152, 154, 164
carrot rust fly, 71, 154, 160
catananche, 15, 26
caterpillars, 23, 54, 76, 91, 100, 103, 113
cauliflower, 16, 18, 24, 28, 32, 40, 57, 70, 81, 91, 98, 99, 108, 109, 116, 117, 144, 154, 164, 165
ceanothus, 15, 166
celery, 16, 18, 40, 57, 70, 71, 72, 81, 98, 99, 108, 109, 144, 145, 152, 154, 165
celmisia, 126
celosia, 54, 55, 69, 152
centaurea, 56, 153
Chaenomeles, 143, 166
   C. 'Flame', 20
   C. × superba, 21
Chamaecyparis lawsoniana, 120, 142
chamomile, 28, 64
cherries, 58, **58**, 90, 131
chervil, 16, 30, 32, 108, 116
chestnuts, 87
chicory, 40, 81, 108
chilli, 117, 152, 152, 154
Chimonanthus praecox, 122, 123
chionodoxa, 9, 105, 108
chives, 71
chlorosis, 94
Chrysanthemum × grandiflorum, 25, 37, 38, 69, 75–6, 92, 101, 113, 151, 166
   C. 'Chenile', **89**
   C. Forest hybrid, **101**
   C. 'Red Wendy', 75, **76**
cineraria, 54, 55, 69, 79, 97, 151
citrus, 31, 35, 58, 73, 100, **103**, 104, 149, 155
claret ash, 87
clarkia, 15, 37, 38, 97, 113, 115
claytonia, 81
Clematis armandii, 15
   C. cirrhosa, 15
   C. paniculata, 18, **19**
cleome, 15, 26, 54, 55, 69
climate, 10, 22–3, 50, 62, 74, 88–9, 112–13, 124–5
climbers, 52, 166
clivia, 68, 69, 79, 97
cloches, 12, 16, 81, 115, 145
Cobaea scandens, 13
codling moth, 23, 31–2, 36, 58, 103–4, 160

coffee tree, 128
Colchicum, 55, 69
   C. autumnale, 55, 87, 127
coleus, 55
colour, 56, 67, 73, 87, 118–20
companion planting, 71, 160
Compositae, 38
compost, 11, 23, 51, 59, 89, 90, 94, 109, 125, 149, 154
   making, 51, 63–4, 125, **125**
   biodynamic, 64
conifers, 142, 143, 166
coreopsis, 24, 26, 56
coriander, 16, 30, 31, 32, 108, 153
corncockle, 26
cornflower, 15, 24, 26, 37, 38, 55, 69, 79, 104, 108, 113, 115, 138, 142, 149, 152
Cornus, 90, 166
   C. alba, 11, 15
Corylopsis veitchiana, 119
corymbosa, 54, 55
cosmos, 15, 26, 37, 38, 54, 55, 56, 69, 79, 151, 152
   chocolate, 84–5, **84**
Cotinus coggygria, 119, 119
Cotoneaster, 90
   C. frigidus, 111
      C. f. 'Pendula', 111
   C. horizontalis, **110**, 111
Cotula, 28
   C. squalida, 28
couch grass, 143
cowslip, 133, **144**
crab apples, 87, 155
craetagus, 111
cress, 81, 99, 116, 144
crimson flag, 15
Crinum, 15, 68, 69
   C. moorei, 38–9
crocosmia, 105, 108, 127, 142
crocus, 55, 69, 79, 97
crop rotation, 12, 91, 162
crotons, 128
cucumber, 16, 18, 31, 32, 40, 57, 70, 71, 72, 89, 165
cup-and-saucer vine, 13
Cupressus arizonica, 120
curly leaf, 58, 137, 162
currants, 19, **19**, 100, 131, 166
cuttings, 13, 25, 78, 92, 93, **93**, 138–9, **139**, 166
cutworms, 24, 160
Cyclamen, 38, 55, 69, 79, 97, 104, 147, 153
   C. coum, 127
   C. hederifolium, 87, 127, 147
   C. persicum, 147, **147**
cymbidium orchids, 137, **137**, 147, **147**
Cynara cardunculus, 73
Cynoglossum amabile, 153
cytisus, 26

daffodils, 8, 10, 79, 94, 106
Dahlia, 15, 24, 25, 26, 38, 54–5, 56, 67, 69, 91, 103, 114, 151, 152
   D. 'Maltby Shirley', 55, **55**
daisies

   Livingstone, 24, **24**, 26
   Michaelmas, 101, 105, 115
   shasta, 8, 69, 90
dame's rocket, 56
damson plums, 83, **83**, 131
damping off, 162
dandelion, 64
Daphne, 75, 78, 146, 166
   D. genkwa, 166
   D. odora leucanthe, 146, **146**
   D. o. rubra, 146
day lily, 15, 26, 90, 166
dead-heading, 26, 35, 43, 56, 94
December, 50–61
deciduous trees and shrubs, 87, 88, 126, 137–8, 155
Delphinium, 15, 23, 25, 26, 37, 38, 55, 56, 79, 113–4, 121, 127, 153, 166
   D. 'Emily Hawkins', 121, **121**
   D. 'Sir Galahad', 121, **121**
derris dust, 24, 53, 58, 66–7, 68, 76, 91, 160
deutzia, 26, 166
Dianthus, 15, 54, 55, 79, 85, 104, 108, 127 – *see also* carnations; sweet William
   D. 'Royal Velvet', 85, 85
   D. chinensis 'Strawberry Parfait', 56, **56**
dicentra, 138
dierama, 15, 54, 55
dill, 16, 30, 31
dimorphotheca, 79
disease prevention, 12, 18
dividing plants, 13, 25, 54, 78, 92, **93**, 113–4, 135, 138–9, **139**, 151, 166
dogwood, 11, 15, 90, 166
Dorotheanthus bellidiformis, 24, **24**, 26
drainage, 11, 103, 114, 125, 149, 155
   slit drains, 103, 125
drought, 75–6
drought-resistant plants, 52

earwigs, 36, 91, 103
echinacea, 56
Echinops ritro, 26
eggplant, 18, 32, 40, 57, 72, 152, 154
elder, 61, **61**, 52
elephant ears, 54, 55
endive, 81, 100, 130, 131, 144
eranthis, 69, 79
erigeron, 26, 56, 166
eryngium, 26, 138, 166
erythronium, 69, 79
escallonia, 98, 142, 143, 166
eucharis, 15
Eucomis, 114, 115, 142
   E. comosa, **96**, 97
Euonymus alatus, 118
Euphorbia pulcherrima, 151

February, 74–85
feijoa, 31, 52, 118
fennel, 57
ferns, 128
fertilisers, 12, 35, 56, 75, 89,

145 – *see also* compost; manure
crops, 75
   citrus, 59, 100, 155
   green crops, 89, 91
   inorganic, 63, 89
   liquid, 11, 14, 23, 30, 35, 50, 75, 113, 116, 137, 140, 142, 150
   organic, 11, 63, 89, 91
fig, 31, 90, 100
flax, 90, 166
flowering, prolonging, 56, 92
flowers
   picking, 68–9
   planting, 14, 25–6, 38, 54, 67, 78, 92–3, 104, 108, 114, 127, 139–40, 142, 151, 152
   propagation and division, 13, 25, 54, 78, 92, 93, 105, 113–14, 127, 138–9, 151
   sowing, 12–13, 15, 24, 37, 54, 67, 69, 77, 92, **104**, 104, 108, 113, 115, 126, 127, 138, 142, 150, 152
   to plant now, 15, 26, 38, 55, 69, 79, 97, 108, 115, 127, 142, 152
foliar feeding, 23, 35, 75, 113, 116, 125
food, 11–12, 23–4, 35–6, 50–1, 62–4, 75, 89–91, 113, 125, 137, 149
   overfeeding, 12, 35
forget-me-not, 37, 38, 97, 142, 153
foxglove, 54, 55, 56, 79, 142
fragrant plants, 84–5
Fraxinus excelsior 'Aurea', 88, **89**
   F. oxycarpa 'Raywood', 87
freesia, **50**, 55, 69, 108, 142
fritillaria, 55, 69, 79
frost, 8, 23, 102, 136, 137
   protection, 39, 115, 117
fruit trees, 31–2, 35, 36, 40–1, 58–9, 73, 82–3, 100, 118, 129–31, 145
   pruning, 73, 82–3, 129, 130–1, 145, **145**
   spraying, 18, 31–2, 73, 92, 100, 109, 118, 145, 149, 155
   thinning, 41–2
fruit worm, 76
fuchsias, 11, 15, 25, **25**, 65, 78, 87, 115
fungal diseases, 16, 18, 36, 51, 54, 59, 76, 91, 92, 104, 115, 126, 128
   chemical treatment, 18, 32, 36, 59, 92, 104, 126, 145, 162–3
   organic treatment, 59, 162–3
fungicide, systemic, 18, 115, 162
fusarium disease, 98

Gaillardia, 151, 152
   G. grandiflora 'Kobold', **51**

   G. 'Mahogany', 49
Galanthus, 10, 69, 123
   G. nivalis, 55, 90, 123, 127
Galtonia, 14, 15, 67, 97, 108, 115
   G. candicans, 15
garden hygiene, 12, 18, 104, 113
gardenia, 35, 69, 52
garlic, 57–8, 116, 117, 129, 131, 144, **144**, 145
garlic spray, 67, 160, 161, 162, 163
gazania, 69, 153
gentian, 126, 166
geranium, 15, 26, 56, 58, 92, 115, 151, 152, 166
gerbera, 25, 69, 79
geum, 26, 37, 38, 56, 115
gherkins, 72
gifts, plants and produce, 67, 87
Gladiolus, 23, 26, 36, 38, 67, 69, 79, 106, 114, 141, 142, 149, 151, 152, 155
   G. alatus, 97, 155, **156**
   G. cardinalis, 97
   G. carinatus, 97, 155
   G. 'Circe', **95**
   G. 'Lowland Queen', 67, **68**
   G. priorii, 155
glasshouse, 115
gloriosa lily, 14, 15
glory-of-the-snow, 105, 108
gloxinia, 26
godetia, 26, 38, 142
gooseberries, 18, 36, 59, 90, 131, 166
granny's bonnet, 26, 38, 55, 77, 79, 97, 138, **138**, 142, 152
grape hyacinth, 97, 127, 157, **157**
grapes, 32, 59, 104, 131, 145
grey mould, 59, 104, 115, 128
guava, 118
gypsophila, 15, 55, 79

habranthus, 69, 79, 97
haemanthus, 15
hawthorn, 111
Hebe, 78, 90, 166
   H. 'Wiri Spears', 9, **9**
hedge, 27, 64–5, 76, 97–8, 139–40, 142–3, **142**, **143**
   pruning, 56, 140, 142
helenium, 105, 113, 115, 166
Helianthus, 25–6, 37, 38, 69, 75, 105, 115, 151, 152
   H. annuus, 25, **25**
   H. 'Moulin Rouge', 26, **170**
helichrysum, 37, 38, 56, 97
Helipterum 'Paper Cascade', 38
Helleborus, 90, 134–5
   H. argutifolius syn. *corsicus*, 134–5, **135**
   H. guttatus, 135
   H. lividus, 135
   H. niger, 135
      H. n. 'White Magic', **134**
   H. odorus, 135
   H. orientalis, 90, 135
hemerocallis, 15, 26, 90, 166

herbs, 16, 30, 52, 70, 81, 82, 99, 108, 116, 144, 154
  storing, 81
hesperis, 56
Hibiscus, 15, 75
  H. hugelii, 32, **33**
hippeastrum, 67, 79, 95, 97
hoeing, **65**, 66, 70, 125
Hoheria sexstylosa, 100, **100**
  H. lyalli, 100
  H. populnea, 100
holly, 26, 90, 98, 142
hollyhock, 15, 26, 54, 79, 97, 105, 108, 142, 150, **150**, 152
honesty, 15, 55, 69, 79, 142
honeysuckle, 143
hornbeam, **143**
hoses, 51, 53, 64
hosta, 90, 113, 166
Howea forsteriana, 132, **133**
humidity, 104, 128
hyacinth, 79, 94, 95, 97, 105, 108, 106, **137**, 140, 142
Hydrangea, 8, 11, 15, 25, 89
  H. macrophylla 'Madame Emile Mouillere', 69
    H. m. 'Mrs Kumiko', 69
  H. quercifolia, 119
hydrocottle, 114
Hymenocallis littoralis, 15, 67
hypericum, 90

iberis, 56
Ilex aquifolium, 27
impatiens, 15
indoor plants, 11, 23, 36, 65, 69, 76, 92, 104, 127–8, 137, 140
insect pests, 23–4, 31–2, 36, 53–4, 58, 66–7, 76, 91–2, 103–4, 113, 126, 137–8, 160–1
  plants that protect others, 71
insecticide, 32, 36, 54, 58, 76, 91, 92, 103–4, 113, 127, 160–1
ipheion, 69, 97
Iris, 68, 69, 76
  Dutch, 79, 97
  Japanese, 147
  Louisiana, 147
  I. ensata syn. *kaempferi*, 147, **147**
  I. foetidissima, **111**
  I. sibirica, 140, 147,
ivy, 67, 69
ixia, 79, 97

Jack-in-the-pulpit, 14
January, 62–73
Japanese anemone, 87, 166
japonica, 52
jasmine, 69
Jekyll, Gertrude, 73
July, 136–47
June, 124–35

kale, 40
kauri, 90
kawaka, 143
kentia palm, **132**, 133
Kentucky bluegrass, 143
keriberries, 36, 131
kikuyu, 143

kiwifruit, 109, 118, **118**, 145
kniphofia, 69
Kolkwitzia amabilis, 21, **21**, 52
kowhai, 19, **19**, 52, 153
kumara, 16, 18, 29, 32, 40, 57, 99, 117, 154
kumi kumi, 82, 108

lachenalia, 68, 69, 79, 97, 114
lamb's ears, 26
lamium, 128
larix, 143
larkspur, 15, 26, 37, 38, 54, 55, 79, 92, 97, 105, 108, 127, 142, 152, 153
Lathyrus nervosus, **109**
  L. odoratus, 15, 26, 55, 56, 69, 79, **84**, 85, 89, 92, 97, 104, 108, 109–10, 126, 127, **137**, 138, 142, 153
laurel, 27, 52, 90
Lavandula 'Innocence', 54, **55**
  L. stoechas 'Pippa Alba', 51
lavender, 52, 54, 69, 70, 78, 92, 116
lawns
  alternatives, 28
  draining, 27
  feeding, 15, 27, 39, 56, 70, 80, 98, 114, 143
  mowing, 15, 27, 39, 56, 70, 98, 114, 128, 143, 151
  repairing, 79–80, 98, **98**, 107–8, **108**
  scented, 28
Lawson cyprus, 120, 142
leaf curl, 104, 109, 152, 155
leaf rollers, 66, **66**, 160
leek, 16, 18, 32, 40, 57, 70, 71, 81, 98, 99, **99**, 108, 109, 144, 154, 165
lemon, 58, 69, 155
lettuce, 16, 18, 29–30, **29**, 32, 35, 40, 57, 70, 71, 72, 81, 82, 91, 98, 99, 104, 108, 109, 116, 129, **130**, 131, 144, 165
Leucojum, 69, 90, 123
  L. vernum, 90, 127
lewisia, 76, 126
lichen, 94, 118, 155
ligustrum, 98
lilac, 90
Lilium, 67, 68, 97, 114, 115, 120–1, 127, 142, 151, 152
  L. bulbiferum, 107
  L. candidum, 107, 120, **120**
  L. 'Casablanca', 85, 97
  L. 'Copper King', 97
  L. formosanum, 97
  L. 'Golden Clarion', 97
  L. henryi, 120
  L. lancifolium, 107, **121**
  L. martagon, 97
  L. regale, 97, 120
  L. tigrinum, 120
lily of the valley, 127
lime, 12, 64, 89, 125, 137, 145
Limonium, 26
linaria, 15, 55, 69, 79, 142
lobelia, 15, 97, 104, 108, 126, 127
Lobelia maritima – see *Alyssum maritimum*

loganberries, 36, 131
lonicera, 143
lucerne, 91
lupin, 15, 26, 37, 38, 55, 56, 69, 79, 89, 91, 97, 104, 108, 127, 142, 166
lycoris, 55, 69, 79

Madonna lily, 120, 121
Magnolia
  buying, 32–3
  growing, 33
  M. campbelli, 9, 33, **33**
  M. delavayi, 33
  M. grandiflora, 33, 166
  M. 'Heaven Scent', 9, **9**
  M. 'Iolanthe', 9
  M. stellata, 33, **33**
mallow, 52, 75
Malus floribunda, 22, **22**
  M. 'Golden Hornet', 87
  M. ioensis 'Plena', 87
  M. 'Jack Humm', 87
  M. 'Red Jade', 87
  M. tschonoskii, 87
manure, 11, 30, 75, 149, 150, 154 – see also compost; fertilisers
March, 88–101
marigold, 15, 37, 38, 54, 55, 71, 79
  French, 26
  marsh, 166
marjoram, 16, 28, 31, 70
marrow, 32, 57, 65, 70, 76, 117, 152
May, 112–21
mealy bug, 23, 66, **66**, 76, 128, 160
melon, 16, 18, 32, 40, 57, 70, 71, 72, 75, 82
Mentha requenii, 28
Mercury Bay weed, 28
Metrosideros excelsus, 59, **60**, 61
  M. fulgens aurata, 61
  M. umbellata, 61
mignonette, 15, 37, 38, 55, 69, 79, 97, 138, 142, 149, 152
mildew, 54, 59, 67, 75, 76, 89, **91**, 92, 162
miners' lettuce, 81
mint, 28, 71, 116, 154, 154
mites, 53, 71, 126, 160
Moluccella, 26, 38
Monarda didyma, 85, **85**, 166
mondo grass, 28
montbretia, 105, 108
moraea, 97, 142
morning glory, 38
Morus alba, 87
  M. nigra, **72**
moss, 27, 114, 155
mulberry, **72**, 87
mulch, 30, 31, 35, 36, 51, 66, 70, 91
Muscari, 97,
  M. armeniacum, 127, 157,
  M. a. 'Blue Spike', **157**
  M. latifolium, 157
  M. tubergenianum, 157

mustard, 91

naked lady, 26, 38, 54, 55, 68, 69, 115
Narcissus, 69, 79, 90, 97, 127
  N. bulbocodium, 123
  N. cantabricus var. *petuioides*, 123, **123**
  N. juncifolius, 123
narcissus fly, 160
nasturtium, 15, 26, 30, 32, 37, 38, 55, 69, 71, 142, 151, 152, **169**
native plants, 75, 97
nectarine, 40, 73, 132, 155
nemesia, 56
nepeta, 138
Nerine, 26, 55, 68, 69, 79, 92
  N. bowdenii, **92**
Nerium oleander, 52, **68**
nettles, 64
nicotiana, 69
nigella, 26, 79
nitrogen, 12, 30, 56, 114
November, 34–47
Nyssa sylvatica, 119

oats, 91
October, 22–33
oleander, 69, 75
Olearia, 27
  O. forsterii, 97
  O. paniculata, 142
onion, 16, 18, 32, 57, **57**, 58, 71, 108, 109, 117, 129, 131, 144, 165
Onopordum acanthium, 69, **69**
Ophiopogon, 28
  O. planiscapus 'Nigrescens', 28
orange, 69
orchids, 137, **137**, 147, **147**
oregano, 28, 31, **31**
organic gardeners, 63–4
ornamentals, 15, 22, 26, 36, 38, 87, 89, 92, 103, 104, 138
ornithogalum, 97
Osmanthus heterophyllus, 142
oxalis, 55, 69

Paeonia, 14, 19–21, 94
  P. delavayi, 20
  P. 'Coral Sunset', 157, **157**
  P. 'Dutch Gem', 21
  P. lactiflora 'Yachiye Tsubaki', 20, **90**
  P. lutea, 19–20
  P. suffruticosa, 19, 20
  P. 'Timaru', 20
palms, 128, 131–3
pamianthe, 127
pansy, 37, 38, 56, 67, 69, 79, 92, 97, 105, 108, 127, 138, 142, 150, 152, 153
Papaver – see poppies
parsley, 30, 31, 32, 71, 81, 108, 116
parsnip, 18, 32, 40, 57, **64**, 70, 81, 99, 164
passionfruit, 32, 108–9, 166
peach, 18, 31, 40, 58, 73, 82, 132, 152, 155
pear, 18, 31, 36, 40, **83**, 103, 108,

118, 130, 155
pear slug, 58, 100
peas, 16, 18, 32, 40, 57, 71, 99, 116, 117, 129, **129**, 131, 144, 165
pelargoniums, 92, **169**
penstemon, 15, 92, 113, 149, **152**
pepper – *see* capsicum; chilli
perennials, 13, 24, 51, 52, 75, 90, 92, 104, 113, 138–9, 149, 151
persimmon, 31, 100, 135, 135
pests, 12, 23–4, 31–2, 36, 53–4, 58, 66–7, 76, 91–2, 103–4, 126, 137–8
  chemical control, 23–4, 32, 36, 53, 54, 58, 66, 76, 91, 92, 103–4, 113, 126, 138, 160–1
  organic control, 12, 24, 53, 54, 58, 66–7, 76, 91, 92, 160–1
petunia, 15, 26, 54, 55, 69, 75
philadelphus, 26, 166
phlox, 8, 26, 37, 38, 54, 55, 56, 69, 75, 105, 113, 152, 153, 166
phosphate, 12
pineapple lily, **96**, 97
pineapple sage, 84, **84**
pip fruit, 18, 73, 100
Pittosporum, 27
  P. crassifolium, 97
  P. c. 'Variegatum', 97
plum, 31, 40–1, 58, 82, 90, 103, 131, 166
Plumbago auriculata syn. *capensis*, 13, 15
  P. a. syn. *c.* 'Alba', **51**
pohutukawa, 59, **60**, 61
  golden, 61
poinsettia, 151
polyanthus, 15, 54, 55, 67, 79, 92, 97, 105, **105**, 108, 127, 142, 151, 152
polyxena, 54, 55
poppies, 24, 26, 153, 166
  alpine, 126
  Californian, 56, **72**, 151
  Iceland, 54, 55, 69, 79, 105, 108
  opium, 69
  Oriental, 37, 39, **40**, 56, 138
  Shirley, 56, 79, 149, 152
porina caterpillars, 24
  moth, 54
pot plants, 11, 23, 36, 65, 67, 69, 76, 92, 104, 105, **105**, 127–8, 137, 140
potash, 12, 154
potato, 16, 17, 29, 32, 57, **58**, 71, 90, 99, 108, 109, 129, 131, 144, 145, 165
  seed, 16, 17
primrose, 127
  anomalous, 133, **133**
Primula, 69, 79, 92, 127, 133–4, 166
  P. elatior, 133
  P. 'Gold Lace', 133

P. veris, 133, **133**
  P. v. x *vulgaris*, 133
privet, 27, 98
propagation, 13, 25, 54, 78, 92, 93, 113, 151, 166
  bulbs, corms and tubers, 106–7
pruning, 15, 26
Prunus, 145, 166
  P. 'Awanui', 22, **23**
  P. 'Golden Hornet', 111
  P. 'Jack Humm', 111
  P. mume, 149
  P.. 'Red Jade', 111
puawananga, 18, **19**
pulsatilla, 166
pumpkin, 32, 40, 57, 65, 71, 75, 82, **82**, 89, 108, 117
purslane, 81
pyracantha, 90, 166

Queen Emma lily, 67
quince, **20**, 21, 31, 58, 143, 155

radish, 32, 35, 40, 57, 70, 71, 72, 81, 116, 144, 165
rain, 23, 34, 102–3, 124–5, 136, 148
raised beds, 90, 125
Ranunculus, 79, 97
  R. asiaticus, 94
raspberries, 18, 36, 41, 58, 83, **83**, 100, 118, 131
recipes, 67
red beet, **39**, 40, 57
red spider mite, 53, 94, 103, 126, 160
red thread, 54, 70
Rhododendron, 35, 41–3, 75, 78
  planting, 43, 94
  recommended, 41
  R. 'Anna Rose Whitney', 41
  R. 'Barbara Jury', 41
  R. 'Blue Diamond', 41
  R. campylogynum, 41
  R. 'Charisma', 41
  R. 'Charlotte de Rothschild', 41, **42**
  R. 'Dora Amateis', 41
  R. falconeri, **43**
  R. 'Floral Dance', 41
  R. 'Fragrantissimum', 41, **43**
  R. 'Ginny Gee', 41
  R. 'Ptarmigan', 41
  R. 'Pink Drift', 41
  R. 'September Snow', 41
  R. 'Trewithen Orange', **6**, 41
  R. 'Unique', 41
  R. wardii, 41
    R. w. 'Ludlow', 41
    R. w. 'Sheriff', 41
  R. williamsianum, 41
  R. yakushimanum, 41, 157, **157**
rhubarb, 71, 116, 129, **129**, 131
rhubarb spray, 67
Rhus typhina, 52, 119
ribbonwood, 101, **101**
Ribes sanguineum, 19, **19**
romulea, 97, 108
Rosa
  classification, 45–6

planting, 14
pruning, 141, **141**
spraying, 36, 67, 92, 104, 149
watering, 23
R. alba 'Königen von Dänemark', 46
R. 'Archduke Joseph', 46, **47**
R. 'Autumn Delight', **44**
R. centifolia 'Fantin Latour', 46
  R. c. 'Chapeau de Napoléon', 46
  R. c. 'Muscosa', 46
R. 'Charlotte de Rothschild', 46
R. chinensis 'Parson's Pink', 159
R. 'Cornelia', 45
R. 'Fimbriata', 45
R. 'Felicia', 45
R. gallica officinalis, 45
  R. gallica versicolor, **45**
R. glauca, 111
R. 'Ispahan', 46
R. 'Jeanne d'Arc', **46**
R. 'Madame Hardy', 46
R. 'Mme Isaac Pereire', 46
R. moschata 'Nepalensis', 111
R. moyesii, 111
  R. m. 'Geranium', **44**, 45, 101, 111
  R. m. 'Eddie's Crimson', 111
  R. m. 'Mme Grégoire Staechelin', 111
  R. m. 'Sealing Wax', 111
R. 'Mrs Oakley Fisher', **47**
R. 'Parson's Pink', 46
R. pendulina, 111
R. 'Prosperity', 45
R. 'Rosa Mundi', 45
R. 'Rose de Rescht', **45**, 46
R. 'Rubrifolia', 45
R. rugosa, **44**, 45, 101, 142
  R. r. 'Anne Endt', 101, **101**
  R. r. 'Roseraie de l'Haÿ', 45
  R. r. 'Scabrosa', 45, 100
R. 'Shaillers White Moss', **47**
R. 'Souvenir de la Malmaison', **47**
R. virginiana plena, 45, 119–20
R. webbiana, 111
R. 'Wife of Bath', **44**, 45
rosemary, 28, 31, 52, 70, 71, 92, 108, 111, 116
rudbeckia, 54, 55, 69, 90, 113, 142, 152
Russell lupin, 97, 142
rust, 75, 162

sage, 31, 52, **63**, 70, 81, 108
Saintpaulia 'Arizona', **128**
salpiglossis, 55, 69, 153
Salvia, 26, 54, 55, 151, 152
  S. argentea, **64**, 65
  S. elegans, 84, **84**
  S. officinalis, 31, 52, **63**, 70, 81, 108
Sambucus, 61
  S. nigra, 61, 61
sandersonia, 15
savory, 99, 116
scabious, 15, 24, 26, 55, 56, 79, 149, 152, 166

scale, 54, 58–9, 76, 92, 100, 118, 128, 138, 161
scarification, 150
Schizostylis, 15, 54, 55
  S. coccinea, 15
Scilla siberica, 127
Scleranthus biflorus, 28
sea holly, 26
Sedum mexicana, 28
seed
  collecting, 80
  germination, 152, 153, 154
  sowing, 55, 79 – *see also* flowers; vegetables
  storing, 80
seed trays, 13, **37**, 37, 77, **77**, 138, 144, 151, 153
seedlings
  feeding, 23
  planting, 15, 18, 39, 55, 69, 93–4, 97 – *see also* flowers; vegetables
  transplanting, 13
September, 10–21
shallot, **124**, 129, 131, 144
shrubs, 52, 87, 90 – *see also* specific shrubs
  for winter, 120
  spring-flowering, 15, 35
silver beet, 18, 28, 32, 40, 57, 70, 71, 81, 98, 99, 108, 109, 116, **116**, 144, 152, 154
slaters, 161
slugs, 23–4, 54, 76, 77, 92, 104, 113, 114, 126, 137, 161
smoke bush, 119, **119**
snail vine, 13, 15
snails, 23–4, 54, 76, 77, 92, 113, 114, 126, 137, 161
  bait, 12, 24, 161
snapdragon, 15, 26, 55, 97, 105, 108, 142, 149, 152
snowdrop, 55, 90, 123, 127
snowflake, 69, 90, 127
soak-hoses, 51, 64, 65
soil
  clay, 90
  heavy, 89, 90, 94, 98
  limy, 25
  sandy, 89
Solomon's seal, 127
sooty mould, 161
Sophora microphylla, 19
  S. tetraptera, 19, **19**
sorrel, 70, 99
sparaxis, 79, 97
spider lily, 67
spinach, 16, 18, 32, 71, 81, 98, 99, **99**, 108, 109, 116, 144, 165
spindle tree, 118
spittle bugs, 66, **66**
sprekelia, 79
Spring, 8–47
spring onion, 57, 81, 99
sprinklers, 51
squash, 16, 18, 57, 82, 152
stachys, 26
statice, 26, 55, 79, 97, 151, 152, 166
Sternbergia, 55, 68, 69, 79
  S. lutea, 55

stock, 69, 78, 92, 97, 104, 108, 115, 126, 127, 138, 142, 152
stokesia, 26
stone fruit, 58, 73, 100, 104, 149
strawberries, 32, 41, 57, 71, 90, **116**, 129, 145, 149
sumac, 52, 119
Summer, 48–85
Summer hyacinth, 14
sunflowers, 15, 25–6, 37, 38, 69, 75, 105, 115, 151, 152, **170**
dwarf, 25
swede, 57, 70, 81, 99, 117, 152, 154, 164
sweet corn, 28, 30–1, 32, 40, 57, 71, 72, 76, 100, 117, 164
sweet pea, 15, 26, 55, 56, 69, 79, **84**, 85, 89, 92, 97, 104, 108, 109–10, 126, 127, **137**, 138, 142, 153
sweet William, 54, 55, 67, 79, **114**, 115

tamarillo, 118, 155
tarragon, 16, 31
taxus, 143, 166
temperature
  air, 10, 25, 34, 62, 74, 88–9, 102–3, 112–3, 124, 136–7, 148
  soil, 10, 13, 16, 22, 25, 50, 136–7, 148, 150, 152
thalictrum, 166
thatch, 79–80, 107–8, **107**
thistle, Scotch, 69, **69**
thrips, 36, 53, 76, 94, 161

Thunbergia alata, 13, 15
thyme, 16, 28, 31, 81, 116
tiger lily, 107, 120, **121**
Tigridia, 15, 67, 127
T. pavonia, 15, 67, **68**
tomato, 16, 18, 28, 30, 32, 40, 53, 57, 71, 72, 76, 82, 100, 108, 165
  ripening, 82
topiary plants, 28
totara, 90, 143
tree paeonies, 19–21
trees – *see also* specific trees
  deciduous, 87, 88, 126, 137–8
  drought resistant, 52
  for winter, 120
trillium, 97, 108
tritelia, 79
tritonia, 97, 108
tsuga, 143
Tropaeolum peregrinum, 15
  T. tricolorum, 15
  T. tuberosum, 15
Tulipa, 94, 97, 105, 106, 108, 127, 140
turnip, 40, 57, 70, 71, 81, 98, 99, 109, 117, 129, 131, 144, 152, 154, 164

Urtica dioica, 64

valerian, 64
vegetables
  harvesting, 57–8, 72, 82, 100, 108–9, 117, 129, 154–5
  planting, 16, 30–1, 40, 57, 70–1, 81, 99, 108, 109, 116–7, 129, 145, 154
  sowing, 16, 28–30, 40, 57, 70, 81, 98–9, 108, 109, 116, 129, 144, 152, 154
  storing, 117
  to plant now, 18, 32, 40, 57, 70, 81, 99, 109, 116, 131, 145, 154
water needs, 75, 164–5
veltheimia, 79
verbascum, 26, 166
verbena, 15, 26, 56, 70, 79, 92, 151, 152, 153
verrucosis, 163
vervain, 153
viburnum, 26, 78, 90, 118, 166
Vigna caracalla, 13, 15
vinca, 153
vine fruit, 18, 32, 59, 13, 16, 61
Viola, 15, 26, 55, 56, 67, 69, 79, 92, 97, 104, 108, 127, 150, 152, 153
  V. 'Sky Clear Purple', **102**
  V. Touch of Pink series, **9**
  V. tricolor, **103**, 104
violets, 13, 25, 36, 70, 153
viscaria, 69, 151, 152

Waldsteinia ternata, 128
wallflower, 15, 26, 37, 38, 55, 69, 79, 115, 127
walnuts, 87, 118
wasps, 100
water, 11, 23, 35, 51, 75–6, 91, 103, 113, 137 – *see also* drainage
  overwatering, 12, 76, 115, 127, 162
  shortage, 51, 65–6, 75
  stress, 51, 76, 89
  watering, tips, 64–5, 66
  watering systems, automatic, 51, 64
watsonia, 69
weedkiller, 151
weeds, 39, 40, 66, 89, 104, 113, 151
weigela, 26, 90, 166
wheat, 91
white butterfly, 24, 71, 76, **104**
whitefly, 23, 36, 53, 71, 103, **104**, 113, 161
willow, 166
wind, 34
  cloth, 12, 94
Winter, 122–57
  plants for, 120
Winter roses, 134–5, **134**, **135**
wintersweet, **122**, 123
worm casts, 27

yarrow, 64, 70
yew, 27

zephyranthes, 26, 87
zinnia, 15, 26, 37, 38, 54, 55, 69, 75, 151, 152
zucchini, 16, 18, 32, 40, 57, 72, 75, 76, 82, **82**, 100, 164

First published in 2005 by New Holland Publishers (NZ) Ltd
Auckland · Sydney · London · Cape Town

218 Lake Road, Northcote, Auckland, New Zealand
Unit 1, 66 Gibbes Street, Chatswood, NSW 2067, Australia
86–88 Edgware Road, London W2 2EA, United Kingdom
80 McKenzie Street, Cape Town 8001, South Africa

www.newhollandpublishers.co.nz

The text in this book has been adapted from *The New Zealand Gardener's Yearbook*,
first published in 1995 by HarperCollins*Publishers*

Copyright © 2005 in text and photographs: Dennis Greville
Copyright © 2005 New Holland Publishers (NZ) Ltd

ISBN: 978 1 86966 083 3

Publishing manager: Christine Thomson
Project manager: Linda Cassells
Design: Gina Hochstein
Cover design: Justine Mackenzie
Commissioned by Renée Lang

A catalogue record for this book is available from the National Library of New Zealand

7 9 10 8 6

Colour reproduction by Pica Digital Pte Ltd, Singapore
Printed in China through Colorcraft Ltd, Hong Kong

All rights reserved. No part of this publication may be reproduced, stored in a retrieval system, or transmitted in any form or by any means, electronic, mechanical, photocopying, recording or otherwise, without the prior written permission of the publishers and copyright holders.

While every care has been taken to ensure the information contained in this book is accurate, the author and publishers cannot accept responsibility for any loss, injury or inconvenience sustained by any person using the advice contained herein.